BEATING THE DEVIL OUT OF THEM

BEATING THE DEVIL OUT OF THEM

Corporal Punishment in American Families and its Effects on Children

Murray A. Straus
with Denise A. Donnelly

With a new introduction by the author

Transaction Publishers
New Brunswick (U.S.A.) and London (U.K.)

Library of Congress Catalog Number: 00-059930
ISBN: 0-7658-0754-8
Printed in the United States of America

Library of Congress Cataloging-in-Publication Data

Straus, Murray A. (Murray Arnold), 1926-
    Beating the devil out of them : corporal punishment in American families and its effects on children / Murray A. Straus with Denise A. Donnelly ; with a new introduction by the author.—2nd ed.
        p. cm.
    Includes bibliographical references and index.
    ISBN 0-7658-0754-8 (pbk.: alk. paper)
        1. Corporal punishment—United States. 2. Child abuse—United States. 3. Discipline of children—United States. I. Donnelly, Denise A. II. Title.

HQ770.4 .S77 2001
306.874—dc21   00-059930

To Dorothy

Chapter Co-Authors

Denise A. Donnelly, Chapters 3 and 8
Mary M. Moynihan, Chapter 4
Holley S. Gimpel, Chapter 9
Carrie L. Yodanis, Chapter 5

Contents

Introduction to the
Transaction Edition

R esearch on corporal punishment by parents took a dramatic leap forward since the publication of *Beating the Devil Out of Them* in 1994. The most important change was the appearance of five longitudinal studies. These studies provide more conclusive evidence that corporal punishment has long-term harmful side effects than all the cross-sectional research of the previous 45 years. Consequently, it would be misleading to reissue the book without informing readers of the changed state of scientific knowledge about corporal punishment. This edition brings readers up to date by adding a twelfth chapter to summarize that new research.

Another major change is a revision of the first part of the Chapter 11. The old concluding chapter cautioned readers that, on the basis of the evidence then available, "...it is not possible to come to a definitive conclusion about whether corporal punishment caused the behavior problems." Now, the combination of the accumulated evidence and the new prospective studies leave little doubt about the harmful effects of corporal punishment.

The third major difference from the first edition is this new preface. It examines the reaction to the first edition and how those reactions relate to changes in American culture relative to corporal punishment. It also discusses the media reaction to the new research on corporal punishment.

In addition to these major additions and revisions, there are minor wording changes in most of the chapters and a new subtitle. When I planned the first edition, the subtitle I had in mind was "Corporal Punishment And Its Effects On American Children." But I soon realized that the cross-sectional evidence in Part II made "effects on children" an overstatement, and I changed it to "Corporal Punishment In American Families." Now, in the light of the new prospective study evidence, it is time to go back to the subtitle that points to the main issue.

Reception of the Book

The history of *Beating the Devil Out of Them* tells us more than the ups and downs of a particular book. I hope that it will contribute to the sociology of science by providing a case example that illustrates how decisions in the publishing industry affect the dissemination of research; and how cultural norms about the issue being studied affect the response to that research by the public, by the media, and by other scientists. It also provides an example of the emotions aroused when a favored theory is attacked. Colleagues who critiqued a draft of this preface urged me to tone it down, to not criticize those who "are on my side" and to make it less defensive. I did not follow their advice because, as I said, part of my purpose is to contribute a case example to the sociology of science of what is involved in the dissemination of research. Rather than write a preface in the style of the "reconstructed logic" (Kaplan, 1964) that editors would require if it were a journal article, I retained the critique of those who share my never-spank position and the defensiveness in response to those who ignored or criticized the book.

Orphaned By Corporate Mergers

Beating the Devil Out of Them was virtually stillborn. The month it was published, the original publisher, Lexington Books, was sold to Macmillan and the planned advertising and book tour never happened. Given the merger frenzy of the mid-1990's this probably happened to many books. Every book needs an editor who "owns" a book as his or her project. Without that, it risks becoming an orphan. Unless it seems like it will be a "best seller," a book without an editor to advocate for it can get lost in the competition for advertising and other promotional efforts.

The positive side of the merger seemed to be that Macmillan is a long established and respected publisher of social science books. However, when Macmillan did nothing to advertise or promote the book—not even to list it in their catalog, I realized there was a fundamental problem. This was dramatically illustrated by my appearance on the Phil Donahue show, which had an audience of many millions. When an author is on that type of show, publishers usually make sure there are copies in bookstores around the country. Not in this case.

Then Macmillan was sold to Simon and Schuster. Large publishers of academic books and textbooks probably publish about 500 books a year, so *Beating the Devil Out of Them* was even more likely to be lost in the shuffle. Then Simon and Schuster was sold to the TV and media giant Viacom. A year had now passed and the book was still not listed in any publisher's catalog. I was sure things could not get worse. But they did despite what at first seemed like a lucky break. Viacom had also acquired Jossey-Bass, a small social science publisher that markets its books very well. They transferred *Beating the Devil Out of Them* to them. I received a warm letter from the publisher saying they were planning to promote the book and that I would shortly hear from the psychology editor.

To my amazement, months went by and no word was received. I wrote to the psychology editor, and received no answer. I phoned and he said he was working on it. When the next Jossey-Bass catalog came out, it was not displayed. I presented a paper on corporal punishment at the American Psychological Association meeting that year. Jossey-Bass had a large display at the meeting. Even though I called to make sure copies would be on display, none were. And when I looked at the catalog on display at the meeting, there was no sign of *Beating the Devil Out of Them*.

The end of this tale occurred when, in desperation, I contacted the president of Jossey-Bass and asked to have the rights to the book so that I could arrange to have it published elsewhere. His response was to apologize and to say he would work with the psychology editor to list and publicize the book. Again, nothing happened. So, after another year, and after increasingly strident complaints, including a threat of legal action, Jossey-Bass finally returned the copyright to me and made it possible for Transaction Publications to publish a second edition.

Media Reviews

Review copies were distributed to the national press and magazines before Lexington Books was lost in the merger process, and the dust jacket had enthusiastic endorsements from five leading pediatricians and psychologists. Despite this, there were almost no reviews of *Beating the Devil Out of Them* in newspapers and magazines. This raises the uncomfortable possibility that the problem lay in the book itself rather than just the bad luck of being lost in the merger frenzy of the mid-1990s.

One obstacle is that most of the chapters report the results of statistical analyses and there are many graphs (although no tables). However, all the methodological information and statistical details are in appendices and the text was written to be understandable by college educated general readers as well as to social scientists. It is almost totally free of technical jargon. This strategy was successful with a previous book on family violence (Straus, Gelles, and Steinmetz, 1980), which was widely reviewed. That leads me to suspect that there was also a more fundamental problem.

The more fundamental problem might be that it presented evidence which led me to conclude that a child should never, ever, under any circumstances be spanked. Editors and potential reviewers may have perceived those findings as implausible and the conclusion as outrageous. Given the overwhelming number of books to review every week, it is no wonder that they passed up *Beating the Devil Out of Them*. Even more preposterously, it concluded with the suggestion that if spanking were ended, society as whole, not just children, would be likely to change for the better in fundamental ways. These findings and conclusions run smack against the stone wall of a deeply entrenched set of cultural beliefs. In Chapter 10, I called these beliefs cultural myths, whereas most people view these myths as common sense. In Chapter 1, I quoted the Director of Child Protection at one of the America's premier children's hospitals to show that even professionals who are clearly against corporal punishment, believe that spanking may sometimes be necessary. That, however, was more than a decade ago. The situation has changed since then, but not much. For example, in January, 2000, the director of an organization devoted to ending corporal punishment in schools, when asked by a reporter whether parents should be prohibited from spanking, said that a few swats on the rear by loving parents is nothing to worry about.

As these examples illustrate, sensible people "know" that the idea of never spanking a child is unrealistic. What if a child keeps running out into the street? It is possible that ignoring the book was a way of dealing with the contradiction between what editors and book reviewers "know" is true and the evidence in *Beating the Devil Out of Them*.

I suspect, however, that the reasons are more subtle than just disagreeing with the conclusions. If that was the problem, it could be resolved by critical reviews. Why was the book ignored rather than panned? One possibility is that just ignoring it was a way out of a bind. The bind occurs because, as the new postscript chapter shows, there has been a dramatic shift of public opinion. Figure 12–4, in Chapter 12, shows that as recently as 1968, literally everyone (94 percent) believed that spanking was necessary. By 1999, only a bare majority (55 percent) supported spanking. At the same time, as I indicated previously, almost no one thinks it is possible to bring up a well behaved child without ever spanking. In addition, although corporal punishment of older children has decreased substantially, as recently as 1995, 94 percent of parents of toddlers were still spanking (Straus and Stewart, 1999). In the new Chapter 12, I explain why so many parents who no longer "believe in spanking" continue to spank toddlers.

Nevertheless, public approval of spanking has declined, and this makes it uncomfortable for people who think that spanking is necessary to voice their opinion. Many social scientists and pediatricians who believe this have retreated to saying that they do not advocate spanking, but there are situations where it may be necessary, for example, as a back up when other methods do not work (e.g., Larzelere, Sather, Schneider, Larson, and Pike, 1998). They also continue to condone spanking in other ways, for example, by admonishing "being respectful of parents," which in this context means respecting their right to hit children.

Because it is no longer fashionable to be in favor of spanking, book reviewers who might previously have written a review that challenged the outrageous conclusion that children should never be spanked, may not have wanted to appear to be advocates of spanking. As for writing a favorable review, that also poses problems. It puts the reviewer in the position of denying common sense by agreeing with the idea that children should never, ever be spanked. These inconsistent and contradictory positions reflect a culture in transition and may have created a bind for editors that was avoided by not reviewing the book.

Academic Reviews

Reviews in sociological and psychological journals display another pattern, but one that also suggests some of the cultural contradictions and changes in attitude concerning spanking. Although some reviews followed a typical pattern of praising some parts of the book and criticizing other parts, other reviews were highly polarized. They saw it as either a unique and extremely important contribution and expressed no criticism, or they saw it as propaganda without scientific merit. The two extremes, however, had something in common: Internal evidence suggesting that the reviews were written without having read the book, as will be shown in the discussion of the review in *Contemporary Psychology* below.

If that suspicion is correct, it was probably not because of laziness or incompetence. I think it was a reaction to the "no-spanking, ever," position announced in the preface and opening chapter. This tends to arouse deep but opposite value concerns. On the one hand, were reviewers who perceived it as utter nonsense and a threat to children and families. On the other hand were reviewers who may have said as they read the first chapter, "Thank God someone has finally nailed this down." But both were wrong. In numerous places, *Beating the Devil Out of Them* warned readers that, because of methodological problems, the evidence did not nail things down conclusively.

A possible scenario was that reviewers who favor corporal punishment were so outraged by those opening pages that they skimmed over the balance of the book and rushed to their word processor to condemn the book. Similarly, reviewers who were opposed to spanking were so enthralled by the unequivocal no-spanking stand in the introduction that they too skimmed over the rest of the book and rushed to their word processor, but in their haste to praise the book, ignoring the problems. One enthusiastic reviewer even identified "findings" that are not in the book.

The flavor of the polarized reviews and my reaction can be seen in the vituperative review in *Contemporary Psychology*, and my accusatory response to that review. I am embarrassed by the defensive and angry tone of my response, but because part of the objective of this new preface is to contribute a case example to sociology of science, it is important to quote from some of that exchange.

The tone of the review (Holloway, 1996) is indicated by the title "Beating The Devil Out of *the Reader*" (emphasis added) and the closing sentence "Ultimately, reading this book was like getting a verbal spanking." I agree that the book is, as Holloway says, an "impassioned condemnation of hitting children." However, she also describes it as "infuriating." In my response, entitled "Beating up the Bearer of the Bad News About Corporal Punishment (Straus, 1997), I suggested that she found it infuriating because she regards corporal punishment as legitimate if done in moderation by loving parents. She in turn accuses me of "remote-access psychotherapeutic" reasoning, and of smearing her character and quality of her scholarship.

Those are some of the polemics. The other issue is whether Holloway read the book. I doubt that she did because she alleges omissions of major issues that are covered in several chapters and are a main focus of two other chapters. I do not think these errors could have been made had she read the book. Here are some of the examples from my rejoinder:

> Dr. Holloway asserts that I do not "look at how [the effects of corporal punishment] may be conditional on such variables as parental warmth." On the contrary, the models tested for two of the chapters do consider warmth. The chapter on the relation between corporal punishment (CP) and alienation concludes " [the model] also tested the widely held belief that if the hitting is done by loving parents who explain what they are doing, there will be no adverse side effects" (Straus, 1994, p.144). In the chapter on "The Fusion of Sex and Violence, " the graph on p.133 shows that CP is related to masochistic sexual arousal among respondents in the top quintile of parental warmth as well as among those with parents in the bottom quintile of warmth. Although a reviewer might easily miss one of the many graphs in this book, it is difficult to understand how an entire chapter centrally focused on the interaction of CP with warmth could be overlooked.
>
> Dr. Holloway asserts that "in most analyses, use of corporal punishment is the only socialization variable included in the model." On the contrary, in addition to parental warmth, the model for the chapter on masochistic sexual arousal includes monitoring, consistency, and reasoning. Reasoning and nurturance were also in the models tested for the chapter on alienation and income. Moreover, witnessing violence between parents was included in the models for all five of the chapters investigating possible harmful side effects of CP because of the strong empirical evidence that this is a socialization variable that is associated with increased risk for clinical level behavior problems (Jaffe, Suderman, and Reitzel, 1992; Jouriles, Norwood, McDonald, Vincent, and Mahoney, 1996; Straus, 1992).
>
> An adequately specified model must also take into account characteristics of the current environment that could affect the level of dependent

variables such as depression. Consequently, all models included specifications for socioeconomic status and gender of the respondent. The following variables were also controlled in some models: depression (except for the model in which depression is the dependent variable), age of the respondent, heavy drinking, being a victim of violence by the spouse of the respondent, attitudes approving violence, violence between respondent and the other parent, the level of conflict with the other parent, number of minor children at home, and the age of the index child.

Holloway's review provides an example of what I presume to be deeply held value commitments leading to departures from basic scientific principles, including the obligation to read a book before reviewing it. Moreover, I think her final response may also indicate a willingness to fabricate evidence in support of the cherished belief. Holloway attempts to rebut my chiding of social scientists for paying so little attention to an almost universal aspect of the socialization experiences of American children by citing Vonnie McLloyd as an example of someone who has studied corporal punishment. I had not come across McLloyd's research on corporal punishment and, of course, I wanted to find out about it. But when I phoned, McLloyd said she has not done and was not currently doing research on corporal punishment per se.[1]

Although Holloway denies being a defender of corporal punishment, I believe that the last sentence of her Final Response again indicates her defense of corporal punishment. This time it is clothed in the guise of being "respectful of parents." Holloway can urge us to "respect" parents who use corporal punishment, i.e., to avoid urging them to stop, if she believes it is not harmful. I don't think she would find it disrespectful to urge parents to buckle up their children's seatbelts, or to stop psychological attacks on a child. The difference is a matter of what Holloway (and society) defines as wrong. Failing to use seat belts and calling a child "a lazy slob" are defined as wrong, as they should be, whereas hitting children is not defined as wrong, but should be.

To balance things out, I could have also written about a review that praised the book extravagantly. The internal evidence in that review, like the internal evidence in Holloway's review, suggests that the author had not read the book. But, for obvious reasons I refrained from writing a rejoinder to the over enthusiastic review.

The point of discussing the exchange with Holloway is to illustrate the principle that the deeper the value commitments, the greater the risk of departure from sound scientific procedure. The same point is also illustrated by the research of Larzelere and of Roberts discussed below. Both found that corporal punishment does correct misbehavior, but they also found that non-corporal punishment works just as well. Despite this, both recommend spanking. Larzelere went so far as to conclude from a review of what he regarded as the "eight strongest studies" (Larzelere, 1996) that all show the "benefits" of corporal punishment. However, he omitted pointing out that every study comparing corporal and non-corporal punishment found non-corporal punishments to be just as effective.

These examples require a revision of the statement in the preface to the first edition where I disputed the idea that deep value commitments are incompatible with objective science. I still believe that value motivated research can be done as objectively as research having other initial motivations. In fact, I would be in a difficult position if it were not true because my deep value commitment to non-violence is part of what motivates me to do research on corporal punishment. The revision is that I should have said that deep value commitments are not *necessarily* incompatible with objective science. The coexistence of value-based motivations for research and objective research depends on following the rules of science, which does not always happen, just as it does not always happen when other motivations set the research agenda.

Academic Recognition

The W. J. Goode Award. Perhaps the ultimate academic review occurs when prizes are awarded by a scientific society. It was an honor I deeply appreciated when *Beating the Devil Out of Them* was the runner-up for the William J. Goode award of the family section of the American Sociological Association. But why did it get second rather than first place? Probably it was because the first-place book was better. But it could also have been influenced by the fact that almost everyone is concerned with the topic of the winning book—the plight of single parents and their children. A very large number of people want to do something to help them; whereas only a tiny minority of the public, social scientists and pediatricians, are concerned about the plight of children whose parents occasionally use "mild" corporal punishment. This is illustrated by a recent study of 237 clinical child psychologists. It found that a third had, at least on occasion, recommended spanking, and two-thirds thought it was ethical for psychologists to recommend spanking under some circumstances (Schenck, Lyman, and Bodin, 2000, Tables 3 and 4). The study did not investigate how many thought it was important to take steps that will lead to children never being spanked. But my estimate is that at most 10 percent, and perhaps closer to one percent, would regard no-spanking as a high priority issue. This estimate is based on the fact that two-thirds of the psychologists in the study just cited would recommend spanking, on the basis of the content analysis of leading child development text books showing that corporal punishment is ignored (see Chapter 1 and, for an update, Straus and Stewart, 1999), and on the basis of many discussions with colleagues. I have often been told that there are more important issues such as poverty.

Thus, despite 45 years of studies showing the harmful effects of spanking, only a few social scientists or pediatricians think "moderate" spanking by loving parents interferes with a child's development. In general, professionals concerned with the family, although they do not explicitly favor spanking, believe corporal punishment is sometimes necessary (Anderson and Anderson, 1976; McCormick, 1992; Schenck, Lyman, and Bodin, 2000; White, 1993). They do not think about or realize the inconsistency that this implies. There are similar contradictions within the work of social scientists who ignore the evidence from their own research. For example, both Larzelere and Roberts recommend spanking as a back-up when a child repeatedly disobeys or breaks time out. But Larzelere's own studies (Larzelere et al., 1998; Larzelere, Schneider, Larson, and Pike, 1996), show that non-spanking back ups work just as well. The same applies to the experiments by Roberts' and colleagues (Roberts, 1988; Roberts and Powers, 1990). Roberts not only found that non-violent back-ups work just as well, but also the there was less distress on the part of the child. I take this as illustrating the fact that the presumed necessity of sometimes spanking is so ingrained in American culture that it leads social scientists to ignore the research evidence in general, sometimes including even the evidence from their own research. In the postscript chapter, I show how this cultural myth also results in parents misperceiving the effectiveness of different discipline strategies and leads them to erroneously "see with their own eyes" that spanking works when everything else does not.

Although I estimate that, at most 10 percent of professionals concerned with children think that a child should never, ever, be spanked, and think that ending spanking is important for children and the nation, the changes that I noted in the concluding chapter of the first edition (Chapter 11) are continuing. For example, the Institute of Child Development and the Family Social Science Department at the University of Minnesota recently stated their opposition to corporal punishment.

Citation of the Book. Citation of a work in textbooks is another indication of academic recognition, and here the picture is also mixed. If the criterion is sociology textbooks, *Beating the Devil Out of Them* was cited in about half of sociology of the family textbooks published in 1999 and 2000, and also in some introductory sociology and criminology books. But the opposite prevails in developmental psychology textbooks. I have found only one that cites it. The absence of citations of *Beating the Devil Out of Them* in developmental psychology textbooks is part of a more general pattern of ignoring corporal punishment demonstrated by the content analysis of ten leading child development textbooks from the 1980's in Chapter 1. Despite the fact that almost all American children experience corporal punishment as toddlers, these books devoted an average of only three tenths of a page to the topic. A second content analysis for books published in the 1990's found just about identical results (Straus and Stewart, 1999).

An ironic aspect of the difference between sociology and developmental psychology textbooks is that almost all the research on corporal punishment has been done by psychologists rather than sociologists, yet this research is cited in sociology rather than psychology textbooks. Consequently, the virtual absence of corporal punishment, including *Beating the Devil Out of Them*, from child developmental textbooks cannot reflect the usual tendency of psychologists to read only the psychological literature and sociologists to read only the sociological literature (and be hard pressed to keep up with even that). It may also reflect a difference in the intellectual cultures of sociology and psychology. Sociology has a long history of questioning the established social order. Many sociologists, myself included, glory in their muckraking tradition (Berger, 1973). A challenge to something as deeply entrenched in the established social order as the cultural norms and beliefs supporting corporal punishment is therefore likely to be more intriguing to sociologists than to psychologists.

The Mass Media and the Shift Away
from Corporal Punishment

This section uses the recent longitudinal research on corporal punishment described in the postscript chapter to illuminate the interrelation of scientific research, social trends, and social institutions such as scientific societies and the mass media.

Beating the Devil Out of Them may have been virtually ignored by book reviewers, but the same cannot be said for the new longitudinal research that is summarized in the postscript chapter. The first of these groundbreaking longitudinal studies was the research I did with Jean Giles-Sims and David Sugarman on the relation between spanking and subsequent antisocial behavior (Straus, Sugarman, and Giles-Sims, 1997). Although there was some hostile coverage of the new research (for example Lemonick and Park, 1997; Rosellini, 1998), most of the coverage was very favorable. Moreover the number of newspaper and TV reports on the findings was almost beyond belief. For more than a week, my phone rang all day with calls from reporters from the press, radio, and TV. The study was given a prominent place on all the major TV networks in the United States, and at least 100 radio and TV stations worldwide. There were articles in just about all the major newspapers and news magazines in the US.

A Public Need for Reassurance

What could explain the deluge of media coverage? It would be very gratifying if it occurred solely because of the merits of the study. It was a good study, perhaps even a landmark study for the reasons given in Chapter 12. However, the merit of the study was only a part, and perhaps only a small part, of the explanation for the worldwide press coverage. Probably a more fundamental reason is that, even though almost all parents continue to hit toddlers, fewer are hitting older children and teen-agers, and much fewer believe it is a preferred type of discipline. Parents in many countries, including the US, are changing, but they are not sure it is the right thing to do because it goes contrary to ancient teachings and to the way they themselves were brought up. They therefore want to hear that there is scientific support for what they are doing.

Bias Reflects the Decline of Spanking

We are used to hearing about media influences on public opinion, and I believe media influence is very important. However, there is a great deal of evidence that the media also *reflects* public opinion (Huggins and Straus, 1980). Journalists who cover family and children issues usually intend to write about things that they think readers want to read. They use this as one basis for selecting from a huge flow of research. Journalists, like other parents, are themselves shifting away from corporal punishment; and as members of an intellectual class, they are probably further along in this shift than other citizens. At the back of their mind, they understand that much of the public wants reassurance that ending corporal punishment is good for children. In short, despite some negative commentary, journalists tend to be biased in favor of the goals of ending corporal punishment.

One can see this bias at work by comparing the media treatment of two studies of the long term effects of corporal punishment summarized in the new postscript chapter (Gunnoe and Mariner, 1997b, Straus, Sugarman, and Giles-Sims, 1997). They were published in the same issue of the *Archives of Pediatric and Adolescent Medicine*. Why did the press officer of the American Medical Association issue a press release on the Straus et al. article and not the Gunnoe and Mariner article, or both? I suggest that one of the reasons is that the Straus et al. study provided more clear evidence that corporal punishment is harmful. Whatever the reason, the American Medical Association sent out 2,800 press releases to journalists around the world. But journalists are flooded with press releases. So it is possible that the same bias, i.e. wanting to hear that avoiding corporal punishment is really good for children, led to this article being picked up by media around the world.

Future Contribution of the Media

Corporal punishment used to be simply taken-for-granted as something parents sometimes needed to do. It was not controversial. The presumed necessity and effectiveness were so deeply ingrained in American culture and American thinking that, as explained in Chapter 1, few child psychologists investigated it and it was hardly even mentioned in child development textbooks. But as public opinion has become less favorable to corporal punishment, those who continue to believe in it have had to speak out. The recent press attention to corporal punishment stands in contrast to the previous tendency to ignore corporal punishment. It is a sign that what was once taken-for-granted is now debatable. As part of that debate, press coverage in support of corporal punishment has also increased. In the postscript chapter, I argue that this represents the dying gasp of a mode of child rearing that is headed toward extinction. If so, the articles supporting corporal punishment result from the evaporation of support for corporal punishment, not from a backlash.

It seems likely that as the trend away from corporal punishment gains momentum, and as new research continues to appear, there will be even more media attention to corporal punishment. The media attention is important because, although an increasing number of parents are reducing or ending corporal punishment, a still larger number continue even though many are opposed to it in principle. Both groups will be eager readers of newspaper and magazine articles on corporal punishment. Parents who are committed to corporal punishment will be eager readers of articles defending it. Parents who are ending or reducing use of corporal punishment will wonder if it really is best for their children, and will want the confirmation of research that supports what they are doing or thinking of doing. For the reasons given in the postscript chapter, the new media attention to this once taken-for-granted and unmentioned aspect of parenting is likely, on balance, to favor ending corporal punishment. If so, it will help further accelerate the movement away from corporal punishment. It will reassure parents who do not spank that they are doing the right thing. And it will bring us closer to the day when corporal punishment is eradicated as a socially approved and expected mode of child rearing.

Social Science, Social Evolution, and the End of Corporal Punishment

The section of Chapter 11 speculating on "A society without corporal punishment" cautions that the effects of even the most desirable social changes are unpredictable. This perspective reflects the influence on me, even after more than 50 years, of sociological functionalists such as Robert Merton (1949) and instrumentalist social philosophers such as John Dewey (1939) and Abraham

Kaplan (1964). More recently, I belatedly discovered the work of Isaiah Berlin and recognized elements that made me think that his perspective must also be lodging somewhere in my memory.

The aspect of Berlin that made me feel so at home is his insistence that many fundamental values and behavioral principles are incompatible with each other and that things frequently turn out to be what they are not, or not what they are purported to be. Moreover, Berlin rejected the idea that, if basic values conflict, some must be true and others false. Thus, at the behavioral level, we believe that one should not tell lies and also that one should avoid telling people truths that hurt if they cannot be altered. We believe that haste makes waste and also that a stitch in time saves nine. At the fundamental values level, we believe in individual liberty and also in social order, which necessarily restricts individual liberty. We believe in retributive justice and also in mercy, but these are often in conflict. Berlin argues that:

> "Collisions of values are of the essence of ...what we are... The notion of the perfect whole, the ultimate solution, in which all good things coexist, seems to me to be not merely unattainable—that is a truism—but conceptually incoherent. We are doomed to choice, and every choice may entail an irreparable loss" (Berlin, 1998).

Non-violence is a fundamental value for me. Consequently, it would take overwhelming scientific evidence that a policy of never spanking harms children for me to abandon believing that children should never be spanked. Fortunately, I do not have to face a clash between my ethical and my scientific commitments because the evidence is ever more conclusive that CP is counterproductive and has harmful psychological effects.

Let us assume the evidence is absolutely definitive and that a change to a society without CP will produce better behaved children. Even with these assumptions, the choice to end this form of violence, like all choices, to quote Berlin again, "may entail an irreparable loss." New evils may replace old evils. The psychological problems now linked to spanking may be replaced by other unwanted psychological effects. For example, bringing up whole generations non-violently might produce such a strong commitment to non-violence that democratic nations might not be able to defend themselves from a totalitarian threat. It is difficult to think of more realistic examples because the adverse consequences of desirable social changes tend to occur in ways that neither proponents nor opponents of the change can envision (Merton, 1949).

Given this risk, why not leave well enough alone? The answer is that "well enough" is not good enough. Striving to improve society and individual well-being are part of the human condition. The form and direction of the resulting changes are infinitely varied, and sometimes disastrous. Moreover, for the reasons elucidated by Berlin, I do not believe that a perfect society is possible, and perhaps not even desirable. But social evolution, like biological evolution will not cease. Moreover, the historical evidence shows that the effect of social evolution has, on average, been the development of more compassionate, just, and less violent societies. Just listing the ancient evils that no longer exist would take a whole chapter. Of course, there are new evils. Nevertheless, I believe that, on balance, there has been a tremendous net gain for humanity. Sooner or later, and rightly or wrongly, once an existing evil is recognized, fear of what may replace it will not long be sufficient to block steps to change it.

The evidence in this book demonstrates that corporal punishment is an existing evil. Individuals and organizations working to end corporal punishment can speed up the process of ending that evil, but I believe the end of corporal punishment as a socially approved and expected pattern will come as a normal part of social evolution because of the social changes described in Chapter 11, and because, as knowledge of the lesser effectiveness and harmful side effects diffuses to parents, they will vote with their feet to end this ancient evil. Indeed, as shown in Chapters 11 and 12, that aspect of social evolution is already well underway.

Acknowledgements

Denise A. Donnely, Michael J. Donnelly, Peter Newell, and Ronald L. Pitzer read the new preface, the revisions to the first part of Chapter 11, and Chapter 12. It is a pleasure to acknowledge the many valuable suggestions each of them made.

Note

1. My call may have helped change that. Four years later, the week I read the proofs for this preface, McLloyd and Smith presented a paper on corporal punishment at the 2000 annual meeting of the American Sociological Association.

Preface

G ood science tends to be a labor of love. Unfortunately, my love is mostly unrequited. As of this writing, almost no social scientists have embraced my belief, even as a hypothesis, that spanking, that is, hitting children, is a major psychological and social problem. A somewhat larger number considers corporal punishment undesirable for both parents and children, but not truly a major problem. Even among those who disapprove of spanking, it would be hard to find anyone who puts hitting children in the same class as hitting wives.

I am a feminist, but my theory that corporal punishment is one of the causes of wife beating has been denounced by some of my feminist colleagues as a diversionary tactic that takes away attention from the "real" cause—male dominance (Breines and Gordon, 1983; Pagelow, 1984). I am a scientist, but my theory that corporal punishment in and of itself causes serious psychological harm typically is regarded as not even worthy of discussion (see McCord, 1988 for an exception) because it does not deal with the "real" cause—incompetent parenting in general. For these reasons, I want to add a few words about the view that inadequate parenting is the "real" cause of the harmful side effects of corporal punishment. Chapter 1 picks up that theme and attempts to explain why social scientists have ignored corporal punishment of children, except as an incidental part of harsh parenting.

Hitting Children and Hitting Wives are Equivalent

For more than 20 years I argued that slapping a wife is a unique type of family violence. Writing this book caused me to reconsider that and come to what will seem like an outrageous conclusion to most people—that slapping a child deserves equal billing with hitting wives because the problems are equivalent. Consider some of the ways that hitting children and hitting wives are believed to be different, but really are similar.

Hitting children is legal and socially approved, but hitting a spouse is a crime. This is the case now, but hitting a wife was legal until the 1870s, when courts in the United States stopped recognizing the common-law principle that a husband had the right to "physically chastise an errant wife" (Calvert, 1974). It is time to also change the law on hitting children.

Children themselves believe they sometimes need "strong discipline." This is not very different from the fact that many wives think they "deserved it," as did many slaves who were "disciplined" by their masters. The battered-women's movement has worked for years to tell women that no one deserves to be hit and no one should tolerate it. Now it is time to do the same for children. All children misbehave, but no child deserves to be physically assaulted.

Hitting children is thought to be different from hitting wives because it rarely results in physical injury. The low injury rate is correct, but this also applies to hitting wives. There have been only two studies of assaults on wives in the general population. One shows that 97 percent of women who were physically assaulted by their spouses did *not* suffer an injury that required medical attention (Stets and Straus, 1990). The other study showed that 99 percent were not physically injured (Brush, 1990). Staff members of battered-women's shelters do not see this because injury is one of the reasons women go to a shelter.

When done in moderation, corporal punishment is believed to be different from hitting wives because it does not cause the psychological injuries that assaulted wives experience. On the contrary, all the chapters in Part II of this book show that children who have been hit by their parents suffer serious psychological harm, just as wives suffer serious psychological injury as a result of being hit by their husbands.

Minor assaults on wives, such as slapping, are thought to be different from minor assaults on children (corporal punishment) because the minor assaults on wives can escalate into severe assaults, namely, wife beating. Unfortunately, corporal punishment can escalate into physical abuse as well (see Chapter 5, and Kadushin and Martin, 1981). While slapping a child and slapping a wife can escalate, research shows that "minor" violence against wives does *not* typically escalate into severe assaults in the form of wife beating. Usually, minor violence stops there (Fagan, 1988; Feld and Straus, 1989; Suitor, Pillemer, and Straus, 1990). Of course, this is not apparent because women whose partners have stopped hitting them do not seek help from a shelter. Just because violence against wives typically stops at the minor level does not mean that minor violence is acceptable. Minor violence against women must stop, and the violence by parents that goes under the euphemism of physical punishment must also stop. Sweden has taken the lead by making all spanking and other forms of corporal punishment illegal (see Chapter 11).

Spanking or slapping a child is an act of violence, just as slapping a wife is an act of violence. In both cases, the perpetrators can say, as one man told me, "I didn't hurt her." Almost all parents say the same thing about slapping their children.

The campaign to end violence against women and the creation of shelters for battered women are major achievements of the women's movement. Ending corporal punishment of children should be added to the feminist agenda for at least two reasons. First, since hitting children is an act of violence, ending that violence is part of the feminist ideal of a non-violent world. Second, the evidence in Chapter 7 indicates that ordinary spanking is one of the root causes of wife beating. Ending corporal punishment is an important step toward protecting women from such assaults.

The main differences between hitting children and hitting spouses are that hitting children is still legal and that parents do not realize the harmful side effects of corporal punishment because those effects do not show up until later in life. When a parent spanks a child, there is no obvious clue to signal that this is increasing the chance that the child will grow up to beat his wife, physically abuse her children, or suffer from mental illness or other social and psychological ills.

When I say that hitting children and hitting wives is fundamentally the same, I am referring to spanking and other legal forms of corporal punishment, and to the "minor violence" that occurs at least once in perhaps two-thirds of American marriages (Straus,

Gelles, and Steinmetz, 1980: 34-36). This type of minor violence is different from repeated, severe assaults on children called physical abuse, and repeated, severe assaults on female partners called wife beating. There is no question in my mind about the need to give top priority in funding and services to physical abuse of children and wife beating because of the greater harm suffered by victims of these more extreme forms of family violence.

Corporal Punishment is a Major Social Problem

This book also stands in contrast to the view that corporal punishment by itself is not a problem. The prevailing view among social scientists is that the real problem is harsh or incompetent parenting. Hitting children is regarded as only a surface manifestation of that problem. Of course, harsh or incompetent parenting is a serious problem. Nevertheless, the assumption that guided this research is that corporal punishment, by itself, has harmful psychological side effects for children and hurts the society as a whole. Regardless of whether the parents are otherwise good or bad parents, this book shows that corporal punishment is related to an increased probability that a child will suffer from many social and psychological problems. These problems range from attacks on siblings to juvenile delinquency, wife beating, depression, distorted sexual behavior, to lower occupational success and income.

I also assume that corporal punishment predisposes a society to use aggressive and punitive methods for dealing with social problems (see Chapter 7). This includes corporal punishment in schools and capital punishment of murderers, prison terms for drug use, punitively low welfare payments, or bombing raids to punish countries that support terrorists. It would be outlandish to suggest that corporal punishment by itself is responsible for these policies. They have many causes. My view is simply that corporal punishment is *one* of a complex system of economic, political, psychological, religious, and other causes of a society's punitive attitude. Those causes tend to be interrelated, however. So, in addition to the intrinsic merit of ending corporal punishment, doing something about ending corporal punishment exerts pressure for change on the other parts of the social system.

Values and Science

A labor of love is not dispassionate. Therefore, it is appropriate to confront the old false belief that deep value commitments are incompatible with objective science. The members of the British Royal Academy in the seventeenth century were devout Christians. They believed they were doing God's will by conducting research that would reveal the wonders of His nature (Merton, 1938), and, as it turned out, science and commitment to God were a fruitful alliance. Similarly, as a humanist, I see a fruitful alliance between my humanitarian values and my commitment to the scientific method (Straus, 1992a). Non-violence is one of my deepest commitments. That is why, for more than 20 years, I devoted most of my research to intra-family violence.

Corporal punishment has been a continuous, but not central part of my research on family violence all these years. Indeed, the paper that inaugurated the Family Violence Research Program at the University of New Hampshire was on corporal punishment (Straus, 1971b). I followed this in 1972 with a paper in which I argued that the family is the "cradle of violence" (Steinmetz and Straus, 1973) and that a reduction in the largely taken for granted family violence called spanking is one of the most important steps we can make toward achieving a less violent world.

In papers and books since then, I have argued that using corporal punishment as a morally correct way of stopping wrong behavior tends to spill over to other relationships, especially close relationships between siblings, friends, and spouses. The social acceptance of corporal punishment, and the personal experience of having been hit as a child and having used it as a parent spill over to become the principle that under certain circumstances it is acceptable to use physical violence to deal with adults who do something wrong. It spills over to marriage, for example. As long ago as 1980, I showed that the husband or wife who persists in doing something his or her spouse considers wrong (which, on occasion, is probably most husbands and wives), runs a much higher risk of being physically assaulted if the spouse was brought up with frequent corporal punishment (Straus, Gelles, and Steinmetz, 1980). These assaults can range from slapping to murder (Straus, 1986). In those previous publications, the focus was on "real violence" such as wife beating or murder. Corporal punishment was treated as only one of many risk factors for these more extreme forms of violence. The research reported in this book marks a return to a primary focus on corporal punishment.

The research reported in this book supports the idea that ending corporal punishment is one of the most important steps to achieving a less violent world. I am not saying that the evidence is definitive. I believe future research will confirm the conclusion that the violence we so abhor and fear has part of its origins in the actions of loving parents who, by spanking children, unintentionally teach violence along with responsibility, honesty, cleanliness, and Godliness. If that proposition is correct, helping parents to bring up children without *ever* spanking is clearly a high-priority objective for humanity. I do not believe we should wait for definitive evidence. We should act now because corporal punishment is violence. Therefore, regardless of whether it reduces what most people think of as the "real violence," a society that stops hitting children is a less violent and more humane society.

Acknowledgments

F irst I would like to acknowledge the more than 50 scholars who have been members of the Family Violence Research Program of the Family Research Laboratory at the University of New Hampshire since it began in 1971 (see Straus, 1992a for a description of that program). They contributed to my knowledge and understanding of interpersonal violence in countless ways. I am especially grateful to David Finkelhor, Richard J. Gelles, and Kirk R. Williams, whose contributions, although less direct than the following list of, were extremely important.

It is also a pleasure to acknowledge the specific contributions of the following people:

Storme Altmansberger for skilled secretarial assistance that was critical in completing the book.

Nancy Burns, with whom I collaborated on the research in Chapter 7 on corporal punishment attitudes in 10 nations and its relationship to infant homicide rates.

Barbara A. Carson, who has done research on parents who don't spank that I draw on in several places.

Denise A. Donnelly is the co-author of two of the chapters and helped revise and edit the entire book.

Michael J. Donnelly carefully read the concluding chapter and made a number of important suggestions.

Sieglinde Horsch Fizz, the program administrator of the Family Research Laboratory, who does most of the things I am supposed to do as co-director of the Laboratory, freeing my time to work on this book.

Glenda Kaufman Kantor is the co-author of a paper that shows that corporal punishment is also associated with an increased probability of alcohol abuse (Straus and Kaufman Kantor, 1994). She helped me think through many important aspects of the causes and consequences of family violence from a feminist perspective.

Adrienne Ahlgren Haeuser for the improvement in the book based on her meticulous and insightful reading of a draft.

Lawrence C. Hamilton, who introduced me to logistic regression and advised and helped me on many statistical issues.

Roger Libby co-authored a paper entitled "Make Love Not War? Sex, Sexual Meanings, and Violence in a Sample of College Students" (Libby and Straus, 1979) that is the precursor of the chapter on the fusion of sex and violence.

David W. Moore collaborated on two articles (Moore and Straus, 1987; Straus and Moore, 1990) that also contributed to the development of this book.

Mary M. Monynihan worked on much of the early statistical analysis, made many helpful suggestions, and is the co-author of Chapter 4.

David J. Owens assisted in the data analysis in the early stages of the Family Violence Research Program. His M.A. thesis and our article on "The Social Structure of Violence and Approval of Violence as an Adult" (Owens and Straus, 1975) were precursors of this book.

Jean Giles-Sims read a draft of part of the book and contributed many helpful suggestions.

Suzanne K. Steinmetz's doubts about the interpretations in my first paper on corporal punishment (Straus, 1971) and the research she did to test those ideas (Steinmetz, 1971) led to our collaboration on the book *Violence In The Family* (1974) and to crystallizing what would otherwise have been an incidental aspect of my research into what became the Family Violence Research Program.

Carrie L. Yodanis did much of the most complicated statistical work and is the co-author of Chapter 6.

Financial and Organizational Support

An organization such as the Family Research Laboratory cannot exist without strong institutional support. On behalf of all the members of the Laboratory, I would like to acknowledge and thank the following persons and organizations for this vital support:

Roy Erickson, dean of the Graduate School, at the University of New Hampshire. His foresight and financial support enabled the founding of the Family Research Laboratory. In most universities office space is a bitterly contested resource. Keeping this in mind, you can get a sense of the strength of Dean Erickson's support from the fact that he actually gave up some of the Graduate School's limited space to enable the Family Research Laboratory to be established.

Stuart Palmer, dean of the College of Liberal Arts, at the University of New Hampshire, was the key figure in my move to the University of New Hampshire and supported this research in many ways.

A sabbatical leave from the University of New Hampshire enabled me to complete this book.

The National Institute of Mental Health (NIMH), whose grants R01MH40027 and R01MH27557 provided the funds for the two National Family Violence surveys, which are the main sources of the data in this book. NIMH Grant T32MH15161 for Family Violence Research Training provided the pre-doctoral and post-doctoral research fellowships that enabled the creation of a true community of scholars that nurtured the development of the Family Violence Research Program and this book in particular, and also supported the work of Denise Donnelly.

The New Hampshire Committee on Prevention of Child Abuse provided part of the funds for the survey on child abuse and corporal punishment in New Hampshire (Moore and Straus, 1987).

Batya Hyman, whose dissertation on *The Economic Consequences of Child Sexual Abuse in Women* (1993) was the inspiration for Chapter 9.

Part I

Spanking—
The Virtuous Violence

1

The Conspiracy of Silence

"Beating the devil out of him" is now just a hyperbola for spanking. Not long ago it also had a religious meaning based on the ideas of original sin and being possessed by the devil. Even today, the idea of a child being possessed by the devil has probably crossed the mind of parents because all children misbehave. Some misbehave more than others, but all children sometimes fail to do what a parent wants or do things that the parent does not want. Many parents now believe in a modern version of original sin—the willful or stubborn child. Almost all contemporary American parents believe that spanking is sometimes necessary for the child's own good. With this in mind, this book will look at two critically important questions:

- When children misbehave, what leads some parents to routinely spank or slap, others to do it rarely, and a very few to never hit their child?
- What effect does it have on the children, on the parents, and on society?

I assume that, with few exceptions, parents would prefer not to "have to" hit their children. Even so, evidence shows that more than 90 percent of American parents hit toddlers and most continue to hit their children for years. In short, almost all American children have been hit by their parents—usually for many years. For at least one out of five, and probably closer to half of all children, hitting begins when they are infants and does not end until they leave home.

3

One of the ironies of corporal punishment is that, widespread as it is, it is an almost invisible part of American life. It is invisible in part because almost everyone has been spanked or spanks. This makes corporal punishment so unremarkable, so taken for granted, that few people give it much thought. If they do think about it, they tend to believe that when done in moderation, corporal punishment has no consequence besides its immediate disciplinary purpose or the larger purpose of making the child obedient in general. But reality is different. The research in the chapters that follow suggests that corporal punishment is an extremely important part of the experiences and psychological development of almost all American children. Corporal punishment has many consequences; the irony is that most of these consequences are the opposite of what parents think they are achieving.

Most parents use corporal punishment to stop a child from misbehaving and to make him or her well-behaved. While that may be their intention, the evidence in this book indicates that spanking and other legal forms of corporal punishment are more likely to block that goal. The immediate effect of corporal punishment may be to stop the misbehavior, but the long-term effect is to increase the chances of worse behavior and other problems, including impaired learning and delinquency; and later in life, depression, child abuse, wife beating, and other crimes.

Another irony of corporal punishment is that it tends to be ignored in social science research. This chapter documents that avoidance and suggests why it has occurred.

What Is Corporal Punishment?

Without a clear definition of corporal punishment it is almost impossible to do research that will add up to a coherent body of knowledge. The following definition guided this study:

> Corporal punishment is the use of physical force with the intention of causing a child to experience pain, but not injury, for the purpose of correction or control of the child's behavior.

Everyone does not have to agree with the definition but everyone does need to know what was studied and what was not studied. For example, this definition includes the phrase *but not injury* in order to distinguish corporal punishment from physical abuse. It mentions the *intention of causing a child to experience pain* for two reasons. The first reason is to distinguish it from acts that have other purposes but that also may cause pain, such as putting antiseptic on a cut. The second reason is to make clear the fact that causing pain is intentional. This may seem obvious, but our culture leads people to focus on why the child was hit, rather than on the fact that hitting hurts. Consider the parent who says, If you don't stop crying, I'll give you something to cry about; or think about what is likely to happen if a spanked child says, It doesn't hurt.

The most frequent forms of corporal punishment are spanking, slapping, grabbing or shoving a child roughly (with more force than is needed to move the child), and hitting with certain objects such as a hair brush, belt, or paddle.

When it comes to translating this definition into specific acts in order to find out who is using corporal punishment, I excluded hitting with an object such as a hair brush, belt, or paddle even though traditional cultural norms permit it. Hitting of this type was excluded because it poses a significant risk of causing an injury that needs medical treatment and, therefore, falls into the category of physical abuse. Another reason for excluding hitting with objects is because public opinion is moving in that direction. A 1978 survey in Texas found that only a third of the adult population considered hitting a child with a belt or wooden paddle to be physical abuse. When the study was repeated in 1991, almost half saw these acts as physical abuse rather than corporal punishment (Teske and Thurman, 1992, Table 12).

What this means is that corporal punishment as discussed in this book is different from the laws of every state in the U.S. The laws in each state give parents the right to hit a child with an object provided no serious injury results. As recently as 1992, the New Hampshire Supreme court upheld a parent's right to hit a child this way.

Ordinary language is ambiguous. In many poor and minority communities *beating* is a generic term for any corporal punishment. To some, *spanking* means slapping a child on the buttocks (and traditionally, the bare buttocks). But for middle-class Americans, spanking tends to be a generic term for slapping or hitting any part of the child. Probably the most frequent form of corporal punishment is slapping a child's hand for touching something.

Two State Laws

The legal status of corporal punishment can be illustrated by the laws of Texas and New Hampshire. The section on "General Justification" of violence in the Texas Penal Code (9.61, West Publishing Company, 1983), declares:

> (a) The use of force, but not deadly force, against a child younger than 18 years is justified: 1. if the actor is the child's parent or step-parent or is acting in *loco parentis* to the child and; 2. when and to the degree the actor reasonably believes that force is necessary to discipline the child or to safeguard or promote welfare.

The New Hampshire Criminal Code (627.6:I, Equity Publishing, 1985) similarly declares:

> A parent, guardian, or other person responsible for the general care and welfare of a minor is justified in using force against such a minor when and to the extent that he reasonably believes it necessary to prevent or punish such a minor's misconduct.

Neither statute limits the degree of force, except that in Texas, it cannot be "deadly." In both states the statutes also apply to teachers. In New Hampshire, however, the state education department has issued regulations ending corporal punishment in all state-funded schools. The New Hampshire legislature did not object to these regulations, but it rejected bills in 1988 and 1990 to ban corporal punishment in all schools, not just state-funded schools. The Texas legislature defeated a bill in 1992 to forbid corporal punishment by teachers.

Still another irony related to corporal punishment occurred as part of the wave of legislation on child abuse that swept through the United States in the late 1960s. By 1970, every state had passed a child-abuse prevention and treatment act. Well-meaning as it was, however, this legislation further institutionalized one of the fundamental causes of child abuse—corporal punishment (see Chapter 5). Most of these laws protect a parent's right to use corporal punishment; so, legislation intended to reduce violence against children just reinforced the ancient common-law right of parents to hit their children.

To this day, the federal government's National Center on Child Abuse and Neglect gives tacit approval to corporal punishment. A

1992 publication states that, "The injury [from physical abuse] may have resulted from over-discipline or physical punishment that is inappropriate to the child's age" (National Center on Child Abuse and Neglect, 1992, p. 2).

Is Corporal Punishment Violence?

The concept of violence also needs to be defined. The following definition makes clear the conceptual basis for our research:

> Violence is an act carried out with the intention, or perceived intention, of causing physical pain or injury to another person.

This definition and alternative definitions are analyzed in Gelles and Straus (1979) and Straus (1990b).[1]

Violence as we have just defined it is the same thing as *physical aggression*, a term used in social psychology (Bandura, 1973; Berkowitz, 1962). It overlaps, but is not the same as the legal concept of assault. Assault, like violence, refers to an *act*, regardless of whether the act causes injury. Suppose you are chased around a room by a person with a knife. Legally that is the felony-level crime of "aggravated assault," even if you get out the door without being touched. Violence has a broader scope. Not all acts of physical violence are crimes for one thing. The law permits violence for self-defense and for punishing children. Some violent acts—capital punishment, for example—are even required by law.

Corporal punishment of children is permitted in every state of the U.S.; and friends and relatives expect parents to use corporal punishment if a child persistently misbehaves. Carson (1986) studied a sample of parents who did not use corporal punishment and found that the pressure from others was very strong and hard to resist. The non-spanking parents frequently had to defend their child-rearing methods to skeptical neighbors and relatives, often with great difficulty.

Clearly, corporal punishment is both legal and violent. Compare the definitions of corporal punishment and violence and you will see that all but one of the key elements are identical. Both are intentional, and in both cases the intention is to cause pain. The only difference is that violence also covers acts that cause injury. If parents cause an injury, the same act is no longer legal corporal punishment, it is physical abuse.

What to Call It

I use the term *corporal punishment* rather than *physical punishment* because it more specifically indicates what is involved—an attack on the child's body. *Spanking, hitting,* and, occasionally, *physical attack* and *physical assault* will be used as synonyms. One objection to using terms such as *hit* and *physically attacked* is that they have a negative connotation. That is certainly correct, and in fact it is one of the reasons for using those terms. The negative connotation, however, does not make these terms any more biased than *physical punishment*. The only difference is in the direction of the bias. *Physical punishment* and *spanking* refer to the same acts, but they have a positive connotation because they signal the legality of the violent acts.

If survey questions were asked "are you in favor of hitting children," few people would agree; but survey after survey shows that almost everyone is in favor of physical punishment or spanking (see Chapter 2). To put it bluntly the term *physical punishment* reflects that fact that the law transforms an act that would otherwise be a crime (a physical attack on another person) into legal and morally correct behavior. Even if we wanted to use a totally neutral word, no such word exists.

Physical Abuse Versus Corporal Punishment

Keep in mind that this book is about socially acceptable and legal corporal punishment, not *physical abuse* of children as that term is used in the law and by social scientists. As we have said, physical abuse is an attack on a child that results in or is very likely to result in an injury. Parents also can be charged with physical abuse if the hitting is more frequent and severe than that allowed by cultural norms for disciplining children. In fact, that rarely happens. The reasons are that chil-protective services rarely have the resources to focus on such cases and because the norms are not clear.[2]

The line between corporal punishment and physical abuse also depends on whether the child is psychologically damaged. If parents hit a child frequently and the child exhibits psychological problems such as severe lack of self esteem, severe aggression to other children, anxiety, or withdrawal, it is called "abuse." However, the same acts are regarded as permissible corporal punishment if the child shows no sign of psychological problems.

Importance of Corporal Punishment

Corporal punishment has an important effect on the well-being of children, the family, and indeed, the whole society. This book documents many of the reasons why it is so important. First of all, corporal punishment is so widespread that it is part of growing up for most children in most countries of the world.

Corporal punishment can tremendously influence the psychological development of children because it often begins in infancy (before age one), it happens very frequently—probably every day for many toddlers (see Chapter 2), and it continues through the preschool years when the deepest layers of personality are presumably being formed. For at least half of all American children, it continues into the teenage years. As a result, corporal punishment may have lasting effects.

Corporal punishment may serve to *legitimize other* forms of violence. Used by authority figures who tend to be loved or respected as a way to achieve a morally correct end, it carries a powerful message aside from the immediate effect intended. The message is that if someone is doing something outrageous and other methods of getting the person to listen to reason have failed, it is ok to use physical violence. This message tends to carry over to adulthood. The socially approved and legal violence in the parent-child relationship may spill over to other relationships in which hitting is not legal. This is because sooner or later, in almost all interpersonal relationships, someone will persist in doing something wrong and won't listen to reason. Children often are selfish or do mean things to other children, ignore the pleas of the other child, and get hit by that child. Husbands and wives often do things that infuriate their partners, won't listen to reason, and are hit (Straus, Gelles, and Steinmetz, p. 109). The more a person was spanked as a child, the greater the likelihood of that person later hitting his or her spouse (see Chapter 7).

Corporal punishment is deeply traumatic for young children. Most parents, psychologists, parent educators, and authors of child-rearing advice books apparently think that if not overdone, corporal punishment serves to correct misbehavior and has no lasting ill effect on the child. But the opposite might be true. For a child who can barely walk or talk (the age at which children are most likely to be hit), it can be truly traumatic if the most loved and trusted figure in the child's life suddenly carries out a painful attack. The consequence can be a post-traumatic stress syndrome that creates deep, lifelong psychological problems, such as depression and suicidal thinking.

In addition, corporal punishment has tremendous implications for preventing problems such as criminal violence, depression, and poor performance on the job. Ending corporal punishment is an important approach to preventing these problems.

Besides all that, corporal punishment is *inconsistent with humane* values. Regardless of whether corporal punishment has any of the adverse effects just suggested, it contradicts humanitarian values and treatment. We no longer permit the hitting of servants, apprentices, wives, prisoners, and members of the armed forces. All of these were legal until the late nineteenth or early twentieth century. From the standpoint of humanitarian values, hitting children is simply wrong. People should not be hit, and that includes children. Research on corporal punishment of children can result in information that may speed up the process of bringing to children the same protection members of the military, employees, servants, wives, and prisoners now have.

A Conspiracy of Silence

Far too little research has been done on corporal punishment considering how universal it is and its potential adverse effects on children and society. Textbooks on child development barely mention corporal punishment, and there are hardly any discussions of its potentially harmful effects.

The universal and chronic use of corporal punishment and its potentially harmful effects on children is the best-kept secret of American child psychology. It is almost as though there were a conspiracy of silence among those who do research on children or write about child rearing. The discrepancy is so glaring that it is worth considering some of the reasons for the silence.

Taken for Granted and Imperceptible

Corporal punishment is so commonly accepted that it is taken for granted, an unremarkable and almost imperceptible part of the lives of parents and children. Since corporal punishment is so common, it is safe to assume that many social scientists use it on their own children and do not see it as a problem that needs to be studied (see Anderson and Anderson 1976). The same applies to parent educators. At a conference for parent educators in June 1993, I distributed cards and asked the 200 participants to answer yes or no to two questions. Ninety two percent said their parents had used corporal punishment, and 85 percent said they had done the same with their own children.

The matter-of-fact nature of hitting children is probably also one of the reasons why child psychology professors and parents do not demand sections on corporal punishment in the books they buy on child rearing. All such books today contain sections on discipline and control, but, it seems that most authors do not think students need information or parents need advice about corporal punishment. Whatever the reason, students and parents are not getting books that include information on corporal punishment as a method of discipline.

Trivialization, Anxiety, and Moral Opposition

When the question of corporal punishment does arise, most authors and readers seem to regard the topic as trivial because just about everyone uses it and everyone knows that the force used should not be excessive. At the other extreme, if the issue is not how often a child should be spanked, but the idea that children should *never* be spanked or hit in any other way, both authors and readers tend to react with disbelief, anxiety, resentment, or derision. Although there are rare exceptions, even authors and parents who don't believe in spanking generally believe that, *never* spanking a child is unrealistic or impractical.[3]

Now look at it from the perspective of authors who write books for parents. Imagine an author who would like to recommend a policy of "no spanking." If the author brings up the issue in discussions with parents, he or she may soon come to the conclusion that it is a dangerous topic for someone whose livelihood depends on book sales. This is because almost all parents think hitting children is sometimes necessary for the well-being of the child (see Chapter 2). Consequently, advising parents not to spank—ever—is considered off the wall. It worries parents who fear that they will lose a crucial method of correcting serious behavior problems and prompts resentment among many who believe it is morally right and good for children to be spanked. Authors of best selling books have an almost unconscious sense of what readers want to hear. Perhaps they realize that "no spanking" turns off readers, so they avoid the topic.

A similar problem may affect authors of scholarly books, who have to worry about their professional reputations. Peer evaluation can make or break a scientist's career. I speak from experience on this issue. As I became more preoccupied with research on corporal punishment, some of my colleagues wondered aloud why I chose this focus compared to issues they thought had greater theoretical and practical importance.

Lack of Research

Surprisingly few studies have examined corporal punishment, but there are some landmarks in developmental psychology research. Sears, Macoby, and Levin's book, *Patterns of Child Rearing*, is widely cited. Still, the fact that 99 percent of the parents they studied hit their children, and their evidence that frequent corporal punishment produces aggressive children have been largely ignored. To systematically investigate this neglect, I examined 10 widely used textbooks[4] on child development and found that of the 10, 8 did not have an entry in the table of contents for corporal punishment, spanking, or physical discipline. Nevertheless, nine of the books had material on corporal punishment, but very little. It ranged from one sentence to a maximum of four pages. The books that mentioned corporal punishment devoted an average of only 0.3 percent of their pages to that topic. Only one of the 10 unequivocally advised against using corporal punishment.

The problem extends beyond textbooks. Technical books also virtually ignore corporal punishment by parents. An example is the book on punishment by Axelrod and Apssche (1983), which the publisher describes as ". . . the first book in years to approach the subject in a scholarly manner." My first reaction was to question the depth of scholarship of any book on punishment that does not contain a single chapter on the most frequent of all types of punishment—spanking and other corporal punishment by parents. On second thought, I concluded that the omission is characteristic of the profession, not just these two authors.

Amazingly, even books on child abuse fail to discuss the place of corporal punishment in causing physical abuse (see Chapter 5). Such books generally ignore classic studies such as Kadushin and Martin (1981), which show that most cases of physical abuse are the end point of a continuum that began with corporal punishment and got out of hand. One of the few exceptions is Wolfe (1987).

Misleading Research

Many excellent studies in the 1960s and 1970s gathered data on a variety of parent behaviors, including corporal punishment. However, instead of analyzing the corporal punishment data, they lumped it with other components in general categories such as "harsh parenting." These studies tell us a great deal about harsh parenting but almost nothing about corporal punishment itself. They seem to assume that only harsh or inadequate parents use corporal punishment, so it is just incidental or a symptom. There are many reasons why this is not likely to be true. First, consider the fact that more than 90 percent of parents use corporal punishment. No one knows the number of parents that are incompetent, but 90 percent is not plausible. So there must be a sizable number of good parents who spank. When researchers apply data on corporal punishment only to study harsh parenting, they ignore a most important question: whether spanking by "good parents" has harmful side effects (see Appendix C for a more detailed discussion).

Some social scientists have devoted attention to corporal punishment. Some examples are the study of anger in young children by Florence Goodenough (1931); the classic study, *Patterns of Child Rearing*, by Sears, Maccoby, and Levin (1957); the longitudinal studies of Eron et al. (1971); and the cross-cultural studies of Kohn

(1977), Kohn and Schooler (1983), and Pearlin (1971). The earliest study I was able to locate suggests why these are the exceptions and why there is so little attention to corporal punishment in child psychology textbooks.

At the turn of the century, G. Stanley Hall surveyed psychologists and found that almost all endorsed corporal punishment. Three-quarters of a century later, a study of 59 psychologists by Anderson and Anderson (1976) found that 81 percent of them had hit their children. There were no differences between the college psychology teachers and the practicing psychologists in their sample. However, Anderson and Anderson also asked whether they believe that "children need to be spanked sometimes." Forty five percent of the college teachers, compared to 89 percent of practicing clinicians, agreed with that statement. This adds still another irony to the list. The psychologists who work most directly with parents overwhelmingly favor hitting children, but, of course, only "when necessary."

Child-Rearing Advice Books

Books on parenting are also virtually silent on hitting children. Dr. Benjamin Spock, the author of the most widely read book on baby and child care published in the U.S. often is assumed to have advised parents not to spank. In fact, all of the many editions of *Baby and Child Care* through 1992 accepted corporal punishment by saying that it should be avoided when possible. That, of course, implies it is sometimes not possible to avoid hitting a child. It is as though a manual for managers said that slapping employees should be avoided when possible.

Spock is representative of the huge number of parental advice books and magazines published each year. Carson (1986) examined 31 of the most widely read of these books. She found that:

- 35 percent said nothing at all about corporal punishment
- 30 percent encouraged parents to use corporal punishment
- 35 percent discouraged using corporal punishment

A closer look at the publications that discouraged corporal punishment revealed that not a single one unequivocally advised against ever using it. In some, the discouragement took the form of granting permission under certain circumstances. This carries a dual message: it is better not to use corporal punishment, but under certain circumstances it is acceptable.[5]

Many child care experts are probably against corporal punishment in principle, but are ambivalent in practice. Dr. Lewis R. First of Boston Children's hospital, for example, said that ". . . if a child repeatedly runs into traffic,. . . . you may want to play the big card" (Lehman, 1989). Dr. Robert M. Reece, Director of Child Protection there and also at Boston City Hospital, stated he "opposes *all* corporal punishment as ineffective, potentially dangerous, and unfair" (emphasis added). However, he also said "Spanks anywhere but a few light blows on the buttocks or using anything other than an open hand are out of bounds and signal abuse" (Lehman, 1989). In short, the pediatrician responsible for child protection at two of the nation's leading hospitals, in effect, endorsed "light blows on the buttocks with the open hand" at the same time as he opposed all corporal punishment. This ambivalence may also reflect an underlying recognition of the depth of American cultural commitment to corporal punishment, and a fear of losing rapport with parents if it is directly contradicted.

Many of those advocating corporal punishment also believe that the family is in jeopardy and society is in ruin because of permissiveness in bringing up children. They tend to equate this with not using corporal punishment (Guarendi and Eich, 1990; Dobson, 1970 and 1988). Like everyone else, these authors are against child abuse, but, like more than 80 percent of the population, they believe that hitting a "willfully disobedient" child is an act of love and concern, not abuse. They vehemently reject the position that corporal punishment is a type of violence against children.

Dobson and Guarendi differ from most Americans only because they justify corporal punishment on religious grounds. They believe hitting a child is an obligation imposed by God, just as God expects parents to love and nurture children. Indeed, the two must go hand in hand. The child must come to understand that he or she is being hit as an act of love. Fundamentalist Protestants typically cite scriptures to show that children are inherently evil. Parents are responsible for shaping the will of the child, they believe. Like the early Puritans, these latter-day authoritarians generally describe the child as strong-willed and in a constant battle with parents (Greven, 1990).

Hitting a child as an act of concern and love is by no means restricted to Protestant fundamentalists. That is the way most parents think of spanking. Ironically, the fact that children are so often hit out of love and concern is the basis of some of the most damaging effects of corporal punishment. Because the centers of the brain that process love and pain are so close together, such punishment may fuse love and violence. This fusion may later show up as wife beating (see Chapter 7) and sado-masochistic sex (see Chapter 8). Perhaps there is even an unconscious sexual component to the unquestioning acceptance of corporal punishment.

Most of the data used in examining these important issues comes from my studies of family violence, each of which is described in Appendix B. The first of these was done in the late 1960s (Straus, 1971a), and the most recent in 1993. The most important studies are the two National Family Violence surveys (Gelles and Straus, 1988; Straus, Gelles, and Steinmetz, 1980; Straus and Gelles, 1990). A limitation of the National Family Violence surveys is that wife beating and physical abuse of children, rather than corporal punishment, were the main focus. Despite that, it is remarkable how many important aspects of corporal punishment could be addressed.

Plan of the Book

The remaining three chapters in Part I focus on the prevalence and causes of corporal punishment, specifically:

- What proportion of American children who are subjected to corporal punishment, how often it occurs, and whether it has changed in recent years (Chapters 2 and 3)
- What kinds of parents are most likely to use corporal punishment and whether the parents' social class, religion, race, or gender affect the use of corporal punishment (Chapter 4)

Part II focuses on five of the many unwanted side effects identified by the theoretical model in Appendix A. These chapters test the idea that corporal punishment is associated with an increased risk of:

- depression and suicide in later life (Chapter 5)
- physical abuse of children (Chapter 6)
- delinquency and aggression as a teen and wife beating and other crimes as an adult (Chapter 7)
- a fusion of violence with sex (Chapter 8)
- alienation and reduced earnings (Chapter 9)

Part III covers the prospects for ending corporal punishment of children. Chapter 10 focuses on cultural myths about corporal punishment that help perpetuate hitting children as a means of child rearing. The concluding chapter is about changes over the broad sweep of human history. It suggests that changes in the economic structure of society from hunting and gathering to agriculture, industry, and then to a post-industrial social and economic system have influenced the prevalence of corporal punishment. It also argues that ending corporal punishment will have major benefits for society as a whole, not just for individual parents and children.

Certain issues are important in researching corporal punishment and are examined in three of this book's appendices: Appendix A is on the theoretical model that guided the research; Appendix B describes how the data on corporal punishment was obtained; and Appendix C describes the statistical methods.

2

Everyone Does It,
But Less Now

A letter from Susanna Wesley to her son John, the founder of the Methodist Church, described how John and his siblings were reared. Susanna Wesley wrote that, "When they turned a year old . . ., they were taught to fear the rod and to cry softly. . . ." (cited in Miller and Swanson, 1958, p. 10). With the growth of secular education in the nineteenth century, teachers and schoolbooks also taught children to fear the rod. The popular *McGuffey's Eclectic Reader* minced no words in telling children that they would be hit if they misbehaved. Even the rare child whose parents did not hit, saw teachers routinely hitting children.

The Virtuous Violence

Attitudes about corporal punishment have been changing slowly since John Wesley's time. Campaigns against corporal punishment of children date back to pre-Civil War America, but the objectives then were somewhat different. Corporal punishment in that era was carried out with a frequency and severity that we now consider abuse, although at the time it was legally and morally acceptable. The early nineteenth-century campaigns against corporal punishment were not intended to eliminate all hitting of children. They merely wanted to change the dividing line between abuse and punishment. Their objective was to distinguish between moderate and abusive corporal chastisement (Glenn, 1984). Except for groups

19

such as the Shakers and the Transcendentalists, who rejected any corporal punishment of children, nineteenth-century reformers were not completely opposed to parents hitting children.

Over time, interest in ending severe corporal punishment waned. The campaigns and public controversy of the 1830s and 1840s had slipped into obscurity by the mid-1850s (Glenn, 1984). Consider, for example, the fact that the nineteenth century saw the founding of the Society for the Prevention of Cruelty to *Animals* long before the Society for the Prevention of Cruelty to Children.

Concern over corporal punishment re-emerged in the late nineteenth and early twentieth centuries. Charlotte Perkins Gilman, an early twentieth-century feminist and social analyst, campaigned against corporal punishment. However, by the mid-twentieth century, nationally prominent opponents of corporal punishment were few and far between. As we mentioned in Chapter 1, even Dr. Benjamin Spock, the author of the most widely read book on baby and child care published in the United States, did not reject corporal punishment until 1988 (Spock, 1988). While earlier editions of his child-care book did not advocate corporal punishment, neither did they say without equivocation that parents should never hit a child. Before 1988 Spock argued that using corporal punishment is "incidental" to the main issue of whether the parent-child relationship is based on love.

Attitudes Toward Corporal Punishment

The fact that so few books on child rearing clearly advise against hitting a child probably reflects the almost overwhelming approval of corporal punishment by the American public. Study after study shows that almost all Americans approve of hitting children. For example, Owens and Straus (1975) used data gathered in 1968 for the National Commission on the Causes and Prevention of Violence and found an 86 percent approval rate for corporal punishment. In the 1975 National Family Violence Survey, 77 percent of the 2,143 adults surveyed believed that spanking a 12-year-old who misbehaved was normal and appropriate (Straus, Gelles, and Steinmetz, 1980). More recently, the General Social Survey of 1,470 adults found that 84 percent agree that "It is sometimes necessary to discipline a child with a good hard spanking" (Lehman, 1989).

Similar approval rates exist in other Western countries, for example, 83 percent in England (Newson and Newson, 1968) and 93 percent in New Zealand (Ritchie and Ritchie, 1981). Studies done in the 1960s in Denmark, Norway, and Sweden also found almost unanimous approval of corporal punishment, but more recent studies show sharp decreases in approval ratings (Newell, 1989). The most recent studies found that only a small minority of Swedes still believe that children should be corporally punished (Haeuser, 1990). A rapid and dramatic loss of support for corporal punishment in all Scandinavian countries began almost immediately after these countries made it illegal for parents to use any corporal punishment. Unfortunately, there is no data on how many Scandinavian parents actually stopped using corporal punishment, but informal sources suggest that it has indeed declined (Haeuser, 1990; Newell, 1989).

How Much Corporal Punishment?

The studies just mentioned show that almost all American parents endorse corporal punishment. This section reviews research since the 1930s that shows that hitting children is one of the few aspects of child rearing where almost all parents actually do what they say they believe in doing.

One of the earliest studies (Goodenough, 1931, p. 180) found that "Nearly all the parents reported it as an occasional method. . . ." About the same time, Anderson (1936) found that 79 percent of three-year-old children were spanked during the month preceding the interview (Anderson, 1936, p. 214). If the parents had been asked whether they spanked their child in the previous year rather than the previous month, the rate undoubtedly would have been much higher. A 1957 study by Sears, Maccoby, and Levin found that 99 percent of five-year-old children had been hit.

Perhaps even more disturbing is that many parents begin hitting children when they are infants and, as the next chapter will show, most continue even when their children are in their teens. A Los Angeles study revealed that about one-quarter of infants one to six months of age were spanked. By the second half of the first year, nearly half the infants were being spanked (Korsch et al., 1965).

Recent studies of college students also show the overwhelming prevalence of hitting children. Bryan and Freed (1982) found that 95 percent of college students recalled having been hit by a parent, and Graziano and Namaste (1990) found almost the same rate (93 percent). Perhaps even more important, Graziano and Namaste found that more than half (52.2 percent) reported at least one instance that occurred during their teens. It seems clear that being physically attacked by a parent has been an almost universal part of the experience of American children.

Chapter 1 looked at how textbooks on child development and books for parents neglect the problem of corporal punishment. That neglect is remarkable because at least one harmful side effect of corporal punishment—increased physical aggressiveness—has been known for many years. Of course, much more needs to be known to provide a scientific basis for changing this situation. For example, more detailed data is needed on the percent of parents who hit their children and how often they do it. Surprisingly, information on how corporal punishment changes with the age of the child does not seem to be available in any published study. It also is important to know whether corporal punishment is decreasing faster now than the glacial rate of decline from the seventeenth to the twentieth centuries. This chapter will look at several questions including:

- What proportion of children in the United States is hit by parents and how does this change as the children grow older?
- Do fathers hit more or less often than mothers?
- Do boys get hit more than girls?
- Have fewer parents used corporal punishment in recent years?
- Is corporal punishment being used less frequently today?

Corporal Punishment In Two Nationally Representative Samples

The corporal punishment rates in this chapter are based on interviews with parents in two large, nationally representative samples of families known as the National Family Violence surveys. The first survey was conducted in 1975 and the second a decade later in 1985. The first survey did not include children below age three or children in single-parent households, while the second survey included chil-

dren from birth through 17 and also children in single-parent households. Additional information on the surveys is in Appendix B.

How Age Affects Corporal Punishment

Chart 2–1 shows the percent of U.S. parents who use corporal punishment and how the age of the child affects his or her chances of
being hit by a parent.[1] The results of the two surveys are consistent.
Both surveys found that almost all parents in the United States use
corporal punishment with young children—more than 95 percent
of parents of three-year-old children in the first survey and more
than 90 percent of children of this age a decade later. Another
study in 1995 (Straus and Stewart, 1999) found a remarkably similar rate of 94 percent. All of these studies show that hitting toddlers in just about universal.

Chart 2–1 shows that although fewer parents hit children as they
grow older, it often continues for 10 or more years. Even adolescents

**CHART 2–1. Corporal punishment decreases as children get older.
Nevertheless, more than a fifth of parents hit 17 years olds.**

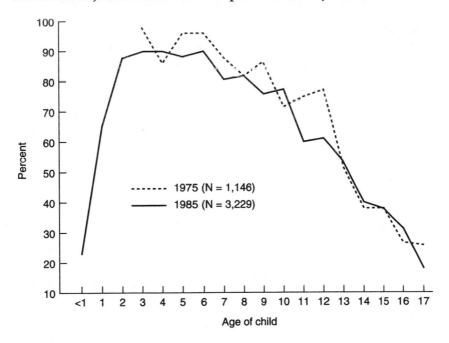

do not escape corporal punishment. More than 60 percent of the parents in these two surveys hit children in the age 10 to 12 range. As late as age 14, 40 percent of American children are still being hit by their parents. Even at age 17, one out of four is still being hit by his or her parents.

These percentages are almost certainly minimum estimates, however. For one thing, we interviewed only one of the parents, despite the fact that all of the children in the first National Family Violence Survey and 83 percent in the second survey were living with two parents. The parent we interviewed might not have hit the child, but the other parent might have.

Another reason these figures are probably minimum estimates is that adolescence is an age when many parents feel that hitting should no longer be necessary. If there are problems with an adolescent that resulted in the parent having to hit the child (to phrase it the way most parents would), it is not something parents are proud of. A number of parents probably did not tell our interviewers about such instances.

Severity and Frequency of Corporal Punishment

The statistics in this section are based on the parents who did use corporal punishment. That is, of the parents who hit children, what percent used more severe types of corporal punishment such as hitting the child with an object, and how often did they hit the child?

SEVERITY

A few rare parents only spank on the bottom. Most others also slap elsewhere. Some use hair brushes or belts, and some throw things at the child. It will come as no surprise that both surveys found that spanking and slapping are the most frequent. Of those who used corporal punishment on children aged 3 through 17 during the 12 months preceding the second National Family Violence Survey, 55.7 percent slapped or spanked, 30.6 percent pushed, shoved, or grabbed the child, 10.4 percent hit with an object such as a hair brush, paddle, or belt, and 3.2 percent threw something at the child.

FREQUENCY

There are huge differences in how often parents use corporal punishment. Twelve percent of those who used corporal punishment said they did it only once during the year covered by the survey, 46 percent two to seven times, and 42 percent reported using corporal punishment eight or more times that year. The average was 8.9 times.

The average of almost nine times per year is even more likely to be a low estimate than the figures on the percentage of parents who hit. Parents know if they have hit the child, even though some may not have told the interviewer. But parents don't realize how often they are hitting their children. Spanking or hitting a child "if necessary" is taken for granted, an unremarkable, everyday event. Parents would have to keep a diary to know how often they really do it. So, rather than saying that the average of 8.9 times is a minimum estimate it is more appropriate to call it a vast underestimate.

One indication of just how everyday an event it is for parents to hit children comes from the National Longitudinal Study of Youth (see Appendix C). To start with, more than 7 percent of the mothers of children under six hit their child right in front of the interviewer. The mothers were asked if they found it necessary to spank the child in the past week. Two-thirds of mothers of children under age six said they had found it necessary that week, and they did so an average of three times. If that week is typical, it means that these children were hit an average of more than 150 times during the year, which is about 17 times more often than the estimate you would get by asking mothers how often a child was hit in the last year. All these numbers get a bit dizzying, but the main point is clear—at least two-thirds of mothers of toddlers hit them three or more times a week.

Trends

Changes in Prevalence

To determine if the rate of corporal punishment had changed between 1975 and 1985, we had to leave out children in one-parent families and children under three. This is because the 1975 survey did not include children under three or children in single-parent

CHART 2–2. Between 1975 and 1985, there was only a small decrease in the percent of parents who used corporal punishment.

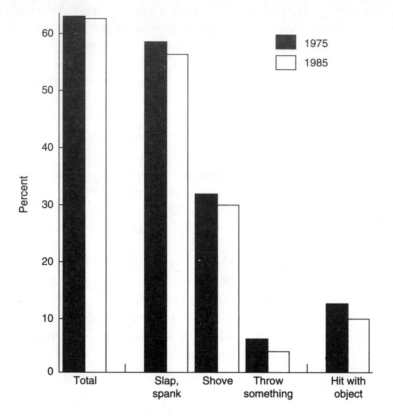

families. Dropping those children for this part of the study made the two surveys comparable.[2]

The first pair of bars in Chart 2–2 shows that the overall rate of corporal punishment hardly changed from 1975 to 1985, which is consistent with Chart 2–1. The remaining pairs of bars show that there was a decrease, but only in the more severe types of corporal punishment—throwing something at a child and hitting the child with an object.

How can there be decreases in the more severe types of corporal punishment, but little change in the overall use of corporal punishment? There are two reasons. First, as explained in Chapter 1, hitting a child with an object was not included in the Overall Corporal Punishment Index because even though hitting a child with a belt or hairbrush is still legal, I think that public opinion has shifted to the point where most people would consider it physical abuse rather than corporal punishment. A second reason is that parents rarely throw something at a child—"only" 5 percent of parents in 1975 and 3 percent in 1985. Consequently, although throwing something at a child dropped by 38 percent between 1975 and 1985, the decrease had little impact on the overall index.

The difference in the rate of change between the more severe and less severe methods of corporal punishment probably also explains what looks like a discrepancy in research on trends in corporal punishment. On the one hand, there is historical evidence that corporal punishment has been declining for at least 200 years (see, for example, deMause, 1984; Miller and Swanson, 1958). But for the most part, what seems to have declined are the more severe forms of corporal punishment, especially what would now be called physical abuse. As pointed out in the introduction to this chapter, the early nineteenth-century campaigns against corporal punishment were really concerned with physical abuse. More recently, there has been wide public concern with both wife beating and physical abuse of children. These more extreme forms of intra-family violence and also murders of spouses decreased markedly from 1975 to 1985 (Straus and Gelles, 1986 and from 1985 Straus and Stewart 1999). The decline was not in the percentage of children who were ever hit, but in the percentage who were victims of abuse and in the legal but more severe types of corporal punishment such as hitting a child with a hair brush.

Change in Frequency

One point is just as important as the decrease in the percentage of parents using the more severe forms of corporal punishment— whether parents are hitting less often. A survey with data on frequency was done for the 1930 White House Conference on Child Health and Protection (Anderson, 1936, p. 215). The parents in that study hit their child 3.2 times per *month*, which implies doing it 38 times a year. If that is correct, there has been a tremendous decrease during the past 50 years in how chronically children are hit. To compare how often parents in the two National Family Violence surveys hit children, we focused on the parents who used corporal punishment at least once during the year of the survey. We then computed the percent of those parents who were chronic hitters.

CHART 2–3. There were large decreases in the percent of parents who hit their child frequently.

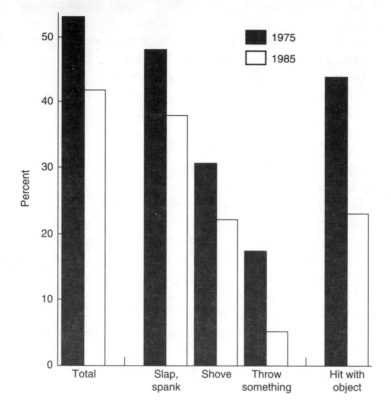

For our purposes, chronic hitters were those who hit more often than the average of eight times a year.

Chart 2–3 shows the percent of chronic hitters in 1975 and 1985. The first set of bars shows that the percentage of chronic hitters went down for the overall Corporal Punishment Index. The remaining pairs of bars in Chart 2–3 show that there was a decrease in the chronic use of every one of the specific types of corporal punishment. The biggest decreases were for the more severe types of corporal punishment, such as throwing something at the child, which dropped to only a third of the rate just 10 years earlier.

Chart 2–4 gives the average number of times children in four age categories were hit during the year of the survey. It shows that at

CHART 2–4. The decrease in how often parents hit applies to children of all ages.

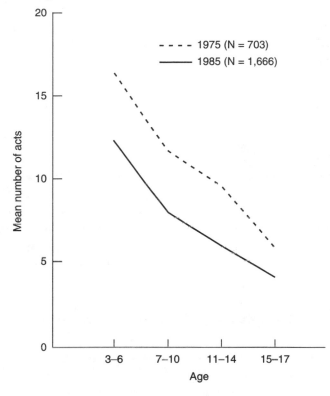

every age, children were hit less in 1985 than in 1975.

Differences Between Boys and Girls

Several studies found that boys are hit more often than girls (Clausen, 1966; Elder and Bowerman, 1963; MacDonald, 1971; Maccoby and Jacklin, 1974; Straus, 1971). Anderson (1936 and 1972) reported no sex differences in the proportions before entering school, but after that, more boys than girls were hit by their parents.

The parents in the National Family Violence surveys also were more likely to hit boys than girls, but not much more. In 1975,

65.8 percent of the boys were hit and 60.1 percent of the girls. In 1985 the figures were 65.3 percent of the boys and 60.6 percent of the girls. Boys also were hit more often: an average of 13.3 times versus 11.5 times for girls in 1975, which is about a 14 percent difference. By 1985, frequency in general had decreased sharply and gender difference decreased slightly: boys were punished about 13 percent more often than girls—an average of 9.4 times compared to 8.3 times for girls. There was also a decrease within each sex from 1975 to 1985. Boys were hit about 29 percent less in 1985 than in 1975, and girls were hit about 28 percent less in 1985 than 10 years earlier.

Why are boys hit more than girls? Conventional wisdom suggests the most obvious answer—they misbehave more. That is probably at least part of the answer because, on the average, boys are generally more active from birth on. In addition, many parents subtly encourage misbehavior by boys. It is very common to tell a young boy, with an approving smile, You little devil. This is part of the process of training boys for anticipated adult roles (Kohn, 1977; Kohn and Schooler, 1983). Another theory is expressed in the cultural principle that boys should be toughened. In one survey, 75 percent of the U.S. population endorsed the idea that it is good for boys to get into fist fights when they are growing up (Stark and McEvoy, 1970). Other studies of U.S. families (Henry, 1974; Miller, 1983) also found that many parents believe that corporal punishment toughens boys. These gender expectations are an important part of the cultural rules affecting corporal punishment by parents. Girls, in contrast, are believed to be more easily injured, and are also not expected to grow up to be tough and able to physically defend themselves (Maccoby and Jacklin, 1974). Even though gender differences are decreasing, more boys than girls in the second National Family Violence Survey continued to be hit by parents, and they continued to be punished more often.

Parents have reduced corporal punishment, or at least told the interviewers about fewer instances. In 1975, traditional differences in bringing up boys and girls were not very large in respect to corporal punishment, but they persisted among the parents in the 1985 survey. The fact that more boys are hit is consistent with traditional expectations for boys and girls. As mentioned, those expectations are partly based on the need to toughen boys. Boys will become men, and men are expected to be more violent. That may be changing, but in the past and with a few exceptions today, only boys are expected to be combat soldiers. This suggests that there is a conflict between the trend to less violence in bringing up children and the belief in the need to prepare boys for a world that expects them to be tough, aggressive, and violent. But the unexpectedly small size of the difference between boys and girls suggests that the principle of hitting children "when necessary" is so firmly established that it largely overrides the principle of bringing up boys to be real men and girls to be ladies.

Cultural Discontinuity in Corporal Punishment

Corporal punishment has been a part of human society for thousands of years. Throughout the centuries, parents have been guided by implicit but readily perceived cultural norms or rules. One of the most fundamental rules is that good parents must be prepared to hit their child to correct misbehavior. The cultural norms about hitting children also distinguish between boys and girls, as suggested in the previous section, and govern the severity of the punishment. In general, the severity of the punishment should fit the severity of the crime.

Although parents are still permitted and expected to hit their children "when necessary," the cultural norms that previously permitted almost any adult to hit a child have changed and are continuing to change. In fast-food chains, managers can't hit their teenaged employees, as used to be the case for teenaged apprentices. Fewer and fewer states in the U.S. permit teachers to hit children (see Chapter 11). These changes also are affecting cultural norms about parents hitting children. As in any period of cultural change, the process does not go forward uniformly, however; some aspects change faster than others. If that is the case, parents should become less consistent in using different types of corporal punishment.

This idea was tested by comparing the correlation between different types of corporal punishment in 1975 and the same correlations in 1985. A high correlation between two different types of corporal punishment, such as spanking and hitting with a belt, indicates consistency because it says that the more parents use one kind of corporal punishment, the more they tend to use other types. The data permitted computing six correlations for corporal punishment of boys and six for girls, making a total of 12 correlations each for the 1975 and 1985 samples. The results support the idea that the rules governing corporal punishment are becoming less consistent in response to changes in cultural norms. The fact that 11 of the 12 correlations between punishment that differed in severity were lower in 1985 than in 1975 indicates that more severe types of corporal punishment were less acceptable in 1985.

Conclusions

This chapter described the extent of and trends in corporal punishment. To recap our findings:

* Almost every American child has been hit by his or her parents.
* Corporal punishment often begins in infancy. It climbs to a peak of at least 90 percent by ages three to four and then declines.
* Even in their late teens (ages 15 to 17), about a quarter of American children still experience some sort of corporal punishment.
* The percentage of parents who used corporal punishment did not change from 1975 to 1985.

Despite the fact that almost all American children have been hit, there are large differences between families in three aspects of corporal punishment:

* The frequency of hitting. For some it is a rare event; for others it occurs daily.
* The severity of the hitting. For some it is a mild slap on the hand or buttocks, for others it is being hit with a belt or paddle.
* The duration of the attacks, that is, the number of years parents continue to hit. Some stop when the child is about school age; others continue to hit for many years.

These differences are crucial to determine the causes and consequences of corporal punishment. For example, by comparing parents who rarely spank with those who do it often, we may find out why some parents spank so often. Differences in frequency, severity, and duration also may be keys in finding out whether increasing amounts of corporal punishment carry a higher risk of harmful side effects.

Although the overall percentage of parents who hit children was about the same in the 1975 and 1985 studies, there also were three important changes in this period.

- The more severe types of corporal punishment declined sharply.
- Parents used corporal punishment less often in 1985—on children of all ages and both boys and girls.
- The decrease was greater for boys, but boys continued to be hit more than girls.

How Real Are the Changes?

It is possible that the changes just described are really the result of the methods used for this study. For example, the changes might really be due to differences in the ages of children in the samples. Parents tend to punish three- and four-year-olds the most, so if there were fewer children that age in the 1985 survey, that might explain the reduction in the proportion of children frequently punished. The percentage of three- and four-year-olds was virtually the same, however. Because boys are hit more than girls, another possibility is that the reduction was due to changes in the sex ratios for 1975 and 1985. But the percentage of boys was about the same in the two surveys

The increased acceptability of divorce as an alternative to an unsatisfactory marriage might also explain some of the changes. When parents are under stress, they tend to hit children more (Straus and Kaufman Kantor, 1987). The two-parent families in the 1985 study may have been under less marital stress, presumably because more of those who were unhappy got divorced. However, as will be shown in Chapter 4, there is very little difference between single-parent and two-parent families when it comes to corporal punishment.

We have just ruled out age, gender, and divorce as the reasons why corporal punishment has declined between 1975 and 1985. At least part of the decrease is likely to be due to another aspect of the method used in this study—the fact that the data depend on the willingness of parents to be honest about the times they have hit their child. So, the decrease in hitting children might be a reporting effect rather than a real decrease. This is especially likely because of the campaign to heighten public concern about child abuse during the years between the two National Family Violence surveys. This may have made more parents reluctant to tell the interviewers about using the more severe types of corporal punishment. There is no way of knowing how much of the decrease was a reporting effect and how much was a real reduction in hitting children. As Straus and Gelles (1986) noted in respect to changes in wife beating, however, even if the entire decrease was due to greater reluctance to report corporal punishment, that reluctance is an important cultural change as well. It is also an important step in reducing the use of corporal punishment because it represents a change in attitudes about whether it is ok to hit children. That is part of the process of changing the behavior.

Corporal Punishment and Interpersonal Violence

The decline in chronic and severe corporal punishment over the last several hundred years may help explain the long historical trend to less interpersonal violence. The findings in Chapter 7 and also a great deal of other research (Bandura and Walters, 1959; Eron et al., 1971; Sears, Maccoby, and Levin, 1957) show that corporal punishment tends to produce physically aggressive children. The theoretical model in Appendix A suggests that corporal punishment helps make many types of violence culturally legitimate.

The differences between hitting boys and girls are also consistent with this theory. It is reasonable to think that the greater likelihood of boys being hit contributes to the greater violence of men. It is time for society to develop ways to alert parents to the harmful side effects of corporal punishment of boys as well as girls. The good news about corporal punishment in the United States is that the long historical trend to reduce violence against children appears to be continuing. The bad news is that most children continue to be hit by their parents.

3

Hitting Adolescents

C orporal punishment is usually thought of as a way of disciplining young children, but it often continues into the teen years.
In 1967 Gerald Bachman found that 61 percent of children in tenth
grade had been slapped by their parents at least once that year. This
is truly astounding considering the fact that tenth graders are about
16 years old. Yet neither Bachman nor anyone else treated it as anything of great importance, and after the original report, that statis-
tic does not seem to have ever been mentioned again. In 1971,
Steinmetz (1971, 1974) and Straus (1971b) found that a quarter of
the university students they studied had been hit during their senior
year in high school. The fact that one out of four high school se-
niors who were doing well enough to be admitted to a college were
still being hit by their parents also has never been mentioned in
popular books and articles on adolescents.

It is remarkable that this information did not result in public
shock or in further research. Now, more than a quarter of a century
later, this chapter and the chapters in Part II finally do that. Part II
focuses on the psychological effects that hitting has on teenaged
children. This chapter looks at corporal punishment of adolescents
in large and nationally representative samples to answer the following questions:

Denise A. Donnelly is co-author of this chapter.

- Are adolescent daughters hit as much as sons?
- Do mothers hit as much as fathers?
- Does social class affect corporal punishment of adolescents?
- To what extent do cultural norms support corporal punishment of adolescents?

The answers to these questions have wide implications. They can, for example, help us understand why some young people are violent. Many studies have shown that the more a child is hit, the greater the chances that he or she will be physically violent (Straus, 1991; Kandel, 1991). The effect is greatest when adolescents are hit frequently (see Part II).

Another reason for focusing on corporal punishment of teenagers involves the adolescent's need to develop independence and an identity separate from parents (Erikson, 1950, 1959; Kohlberg, 1969; Piaget, 1965), but without rejecting them. Corporal punishment may stand in the way of identity formation, independence, and moral development. Adolescents resent authoritarian approaches to solving disputes. They also dislike being disciplined as if they were small children.

This chapter also touches on an important issue that affects how much trust to put in the research on psychologically damaging side effects of corporal punishment. Most of the information on hitting adolescents in chapters 5 to 9 was obtained by asking adults whether they were hit as teenagers. How accurate is this adult recall data? One way of finding out is to compare it with contemporary data obtained by interviewing parents. Both methods were used in the second National Family Violence Survey. Using the two methods makes it possible to compare the results.

Two Measures of Corporal Punishment

The contemporary data on hitting adolescents was obtained by asking parents if they used corporal punishment on one of their children and how often. Adult recall data was obtained later in the same interview by asking the parents whether they themselves had been hit when they were adolescents.

Note that the data differ in two ways. First, the contemporary data is information provided by perpetrators, while the adult recall data is information provided by victims. Second, the contemporary and adult recall data refer to two different generations.

How Many Are Hit and How Often?

How Many?

Despite the long time that had passed since they were adolescents, almost half the adult recall sample (49.8 percent) reported having been hit one or more times during a 12-month period when they were adolescents. The figure based on the contemporary data (46.3 percent) is very similar, even though the contemporary data refers to only one parent, while the adult recall data refers to both parents.

The rates just given should be considered minimum estimates because some respondents did not disclose the information to our interviewers; others simply may have forgotten. So it's safe to say that at least half of American children in early adolescence experience corporal punishment. Although 50 percent seems astonishingly high to some people, it is consistent with previous research (Bachman, 1967; Groziano and Namoste, 1990; Steinmetz, 1971; Straus, 1971b).

Few Americans realize the extent of corporal punishment of adolescents, even though our figures suggest that they themselves probably experienced it. Perhaps the lack of awareness occurs because of what Allport (1933) called "pluralistic ignorance" and Marks (1984) called "false uniqueness." People tend to think their experiences are unique and do not realize that what happened to them actually was very common. Or almost the opposite might be the explanation. Perhaps corporal punishment is such an everyday experience that no one stops to think about it. Whatever the reason, this lack of awareness probably also explains why hitting adolescents has been so rarely investigated.

How Often?

Spanking and slapping a child are well within the legal and publicly accepted levels of corporal punishment (Straus, 1991). However, it can be done so frequently that most Americans today would consider it abuse. Parents are specifically exempted from the crime of assault when it is done to correct and control a child and leaves no injury, but there does not seem to be a public consensus on how much corporal punishment must occur before it is considered abuse. The threshold is probably high because the average number of times that adolescents were hit was 7.9 times per year based on the adult recall data, and 5.9 times per year based on the contemporary data.[1] Remember, these figures should be considered minimum estimates. Even without allowing for the fact that some instances are forgotten and others are deliberately not revealed, it is clear that when an adolescent is hit by his or her parents, it is not an isolated case.

Difference Between Generations in Hitting Adolescents

The contemporary data and the adult recall data refer to two different generations, yet the rate of corporal punishment is similar. Does that mean that there has been no change in corporal punishment of adolescents over the years? The historical evidence and the evidence in the previous chapter make that unlikely. Instead, the similarity probably occurs because older respondents remember fewer of these events. For example, the rate of corporal punishment that participants in the second National Family Violence Survey remembered dropped from 55.4 percent of those aged 18 to 19, down to 40 percent for those 70 and older. Even though older persons may have more difficulty remembering childhood events, even after 60 years, 40 percent still remember being hit by their parents. When it occurs in adolescence, corporal punishment seems to be almost indelibly burned in the minds of many people. Advocates of corporal punishment are likely to see that as a good thing. They will say it shows the lasting effectiveness of corporal punishment because decades later, the recollection of the punishment is still there to deter wrong behavior. Opponents of corporal punishment are likely to see it as showing the lasting damage that results when parents hit teenagers because the painful memories are still there decades later to evoke anger, humiliation, alienation, and depression. The chapters in Part II will provide evidence on which side, if either, is correct.

The Social Context of Hitting Adolescents

Many social and psychological factors could influence whether adolescents will be hit by their parents. We will examine three influences: cultural norms, the gender of the parent and child, and social class.

Cultural Norms Supporting Corporal Punishment of Adolescents

Corporal punishment of adolescents may be encouraged or prohibited by cultural norms. One of the clearest manifestations of cultural norms is the legal system. Every state in the U.S. gives parents the legal right to hit teenagers as well as younger children. Public approval of corporal punishment of adolescents is harder to identify. The survey statistics in Chapter 2 show that almost all Americans believe that corporal punishment is necessary under some circumstances. None of these surveys specified the age of the child, however, and this approval may not extend to hitting adolescents. To find out if it does, David Moore and I surveyed 914 New Hampshire parents (Moore and Straus, 1987). We asked parents if they agreed or disagreed with the statement, "Sometimes it's a good idea for parents to slap their teenaged child who talks back to them." Thirty one percent agreed, 23 percent were neutral or mildly disagreed, and only 46 percent strongly disagreed. In other words, 54 percent did not strongly disagree with slapping a teenaged child. It seems that even in a state with a low level of other types of violence, such as assault, homicide, and child abuse, there is considerable support for parents hitting adolescents.

Turning from cultural norms to individual differences, we tested the idea that the more a parent approved of hitting an adolescent who talked back, the greater the likelihood that the parent would actually hit a child during the 12 months preceding the survey (Straus, 1991). But, as obvious as that sounds, there is no direct link between favoring corporal punishment and actually using it. Many parents who do not believe in the principle of corporal punishment of adolescents did hit their adolescent child, and many who do believe in it did not hit. Some of these discrepancies may be due to characteristics of the parent and the child, which we will examine in the rest of this chapter and in Chapter 4.

Gender of Parent and Child

PREVALENCE

Although the number of women who recalled corporal punishment was remarkably high (44 percent), the rate for men was even higher (58.2 percent). This may reflect a tendency for American parents to follow the traditional pattern in child rearing that makes hitting adolescent sons more appropriate than hitting daughters.

The left side of Chart 3–1 shows that in two-parent families, sons were about equally as likely to be hit by their fathers as their

CHART 3–1. More men than women recall being hit as adolescents.

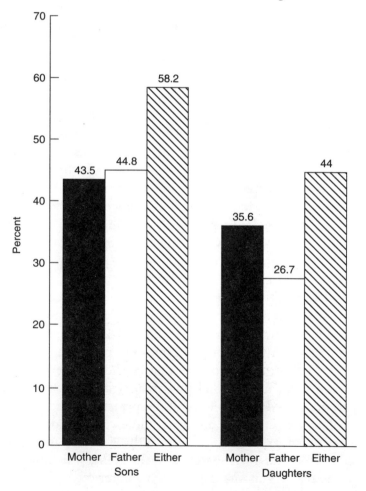

mothers, according to adult recall data. The first two bars in the right side of Chart 3–1, however, show that adolescent daughters were about a third more likely to be hit by their mothers. Chart 3–2, which uses contemporary data, shows the same tendency for mothers to hit adolescent daughters more than fathers; but just a little more than half of both fathers and mothers said that they had hit their adolescent son during the year of the survey.

These statistics indicate that during adolescence, the role of mothers as the main child care-giver and disciplinarian is modified by the idea of woman-to-woman and man-to-man relationships between parents and their adolescents. However, it is important to note that substantial proportions of mothers hit adolescent sons

CHART 3–2. More parents reported hitting adolescent sons than daughters.

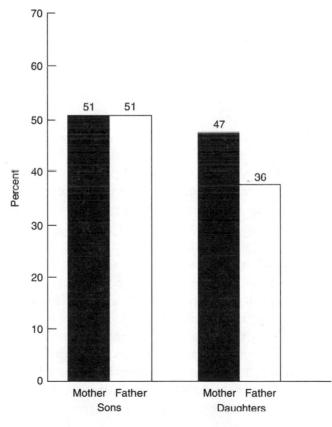

CHART 3–3. When an adolescent is hit, both parents usually do it, especially if the child is a boy.

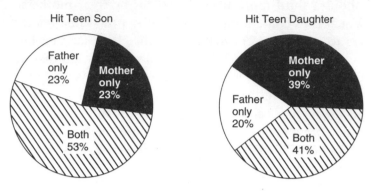

and fathers hit adolescent daughters. So, although there is a tendency toward traditional gender roles, the predominant tendency was for *both* parents to use corporal punishment, regardless of the sex of the child.

CONSISTENCY BETWEEN PARENTS

Chart 3–3 shows the percent of families in which only one of the parents hit and the percent of cases in which both hit. Chart 3–3 can be read as showing that the glass is half full or half empty. On the one hand, just a little more than half of adolescent sons and 41 percent of the girls were hit by both parents. On the other hand, Chart 3–3 also shows a remarkably high percentage of families in which one parent used corporal punishment and the other did not. For sons, when it was only one parent, it was almost equally likely to be the mother or the father who did the hitting. Chart 3–3 shows that when only one parent used corporal punishment on a daughter, it was about twice as likely to be the mother. It seems that the main reason why adolescent daughters are hit less than adolescent sons is because fathers hit daughters less as they grow older.

The differences between fathers and mothers when it comes to hitting adolescent sons and daughters are surprisingly small compared to the huge differences in violent behavior of men and of women outside the family. Although the differences in hitting adolescents are small, they are consistent with other surprising differences between men and women in family violence. These findings show that women tend to initiate physical attacks on husbands at about the same rate as husbands attack wives (see Chapter 7 and also Straus, 1993). There is a match between the statistics in this chapter, which show that there is little difference in the rate of hitting adolescent boys and girls, and the statistics in Chapter 7, which show that having been hit as an adolescent increases the chances of hitting a spouse later in life. If being hit by parents as an adolescent is one cause of hitting a spouse later in life, the almost equally high rate at which parents hit their adolescents may explain the equally high rate at which women and men hit their spouses.

DIFFERENCES IN FREQUENCY OF HITTING ADOLESCENTS

In addition to finding only small differences between the numbers of mothers and fathers who hit and between boys and girls who were hit by their parents, we also found only relatively small differences in how often mothers and fathers hit their sons and daughters.

Detailed statistics on how chronically American parents hit adolescents are in a table in Appendix C. That table shows that mothers and fathers tended to use corporal punishment on adolescent sons and daughters about the same number of times per year. It also shows that the average number of times that parents hit adolescents is similar when adults recall how often they were hit as teenagers and when parents describe what they did in the previous 12 months.

At the same time there are differences worth noting. In the adult-recall data, the lowest average number of times was for fathers hitting daughters. We expected the most chronic hitting would be by fathers hitting sons, and that is what the contemporary data does show. But when frequency was measured by asking adults to recall how often they were hit when they were in their teens, the most chronic pattern is in mothers using corporal punishment on adolescent sons.

The discovery that when adolescents are hit, it is not usually an isolated instance, applies to both parents and to both sons and daughters. Except for fathers hitting daughters, 70 to 90 percent of parents who hit their adolescents did so more than once during the 12 months preceding the interview. The main exception is in fathers hitting daughters, who typically said they had done so "only" once.

It is remarkable that both the adult recall and the contemporary data on fathers hitting adolescent daughters result in almost identical estimates—a little more than 40 percent hit their daughters only once in the year covered by the study. The low frequency of fathers hitting adolescent daughters is consistent with the relatively low prevalence rate for fathers hitting daughters. Regardless of how it is measured, the least corporal punishment is on adolescent daughters by fathers.

Perhaps the most startling statistics are the large percentage of parents, both mothers and fathers, who hit an adolescent son numerous times during the year. Almost everyone who hits an adolescent does it more than once. A third of daughters and 43 percent of sons recalled having been hit six or more times in a year when they were teenagers.[2]

As high as these numbers are, they are even more likely than the prevalence data to be minimum estimates because it is harder for people to remember how many times something happened than it is to remember whether it happened at all during the year.

FREQUENCY OF CORPORAL PUNISHMENT BY MOTHERS

Mothers hit their adolescent children more often than fathers did. Wauchope and Straus (1990), suggested that it reflects the fact that mothers have vastly greater child-care responsibilities than fathers. We did not think that would apply to adolescent children though, because mothers may not spend much more time physically caring for a teenager than a father would. If Wauchope and Straus's suggestion is true, the reason may be because mothers traditionally are responsible for the psychological well-being and moral training of both children and adolescents. Just as wives are traditionally responsible for keeping the family together, so mothers are more responsible for keeping children in line. In the adolescent years mothers may not spend much more time with children than fathers, but they probably would have more occasions to use corporal punishment.

Social-Class Differences

There is a long-simmering controversy over social-class differences in corporal punishment. Bronfenbrenner (1958) found that lower-class people use more corporal punishment than those higher on the

CHART 3–4. A larger percent of middle-class parents use corporal punishment than low- or high-status parents.

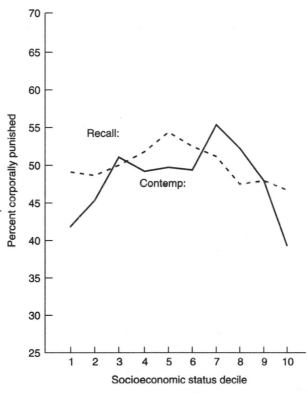

socioeconomic status (SES) ladder, although Erlanger's review of this research (1974) found only small and inconsistent differences. There are several possible reasons why these findings might conflict. One reason may be that previous studies compared only prevalence rates and ignored frequency. Another reason may be that previous studies compared broad groups, such as working class and middle class people, rather than the whole range of social classes.

We avoided these problems by using an SES index to group the families into 10 categories (see Appendix C). Chart 3–4 shows that the highest rate of hitting teens is in *middle-class* families, with lower rates in both higher- and lower-class families. This pattern is clearer in the adult recall data, but it also shows up in the contemporary data. So it appears that corporal punishment of adolescents may be more prevalent in the middle class than in the lower or the upper classes.

CHART 3–5. The higher the socioeconomic status of parents, the less often they use corporal punishment.

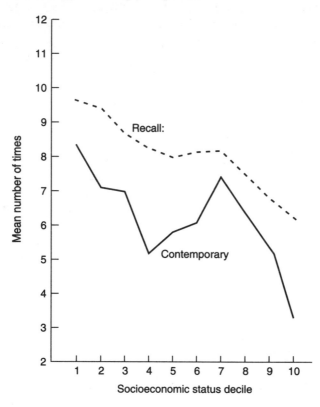

The higher rates by middle-class parents do not necessarily contradict previous studies. Some earlier studies might have divided their sample in the middle to compare the rates of higher- and lower-status groups. In that case, the two halves of a chart such as Chart 3–4 would have equal rates because each half would include some middle-class families with relatively high rates, and some who are either low or the high in status and have low rates of hitting adolescents. It is also important to note that these charts describe hitting adolescents; the relationship between social class and corporal punishment may not be the same for the younger children used in previous studies.

Social-class differences in *how often* parents hit adolescents follow a different pattern. Chart 3–5 shows that the higher the social class, the less chronic the corporal punishment. This means that although fewer lower-class parents hit adolescents, they do it more often. This is an important difference for children. It also might explain why qualitative studies find a class difference, while studies that compare percentages do not. Suppose lower-class parents tend to hit their adolescents about every week or two, but higher-class parents do so only two or three times a year. If that is the case, a researcher who gathers data by observing families would have a much greater chance of seeing a lower-class parent hit a child, even though the percentage of lower-class parents who hit adolescents is relatively low.

Conclusions

Two different methods were used to find out how many parents hit teenaged children and how often they did it. Both methods show that:

- Teens who are hit are not a rare breed; in fact, they are more common than those that are not hit.
- When parents hit teenagers, it tends to happen frequently—an average of six to eight times a year.

Children living with both parents are usually believed to have an advantage over children in single-parent households. While that is correct in many ways (see Mednick, 1989, for a review of the research), this chapter shows that an adolescent with two parents has a greater chance of being hit. For this aspect of family relationships, two parents often means double jeopardy. On the other hand, when an adolescent has two parents, one parent may act as a buffer and intercede on the child's behalf, preventing the other parent from using corporal punishment, especially the more severe types.

There are differences between adolescent sons and daughters in how many are hit and how often that happens, but there is even more similarity:

- Boys tend to be hit more often than girls.
- Fathers tend to hit adolescent girls less than mothers. Despite that, almost half of the daughters were hit during a 12-month period.

- Since so many girls and boys are hit during adolescence, both boys and girls are exposed to the harmful side effects of corporal punishment.

It is widely believed that lower-class parents use more corporal punishment, but past research is inconsistent. In this study, we found that middle-class families were most likely to hit adolescents, but that the lower-class families hit more often.

This chapter shows that more than a quarter of all American children only escape being physically assaulted by their parents when they leave home. Of course, it is hard to think of parents slapping a teenager as an assault in the legal sense, and it is not. A crime is what the law says is a crime (Lincoln and Straus, 1985; Tappan, 1960). Both common law and the legislation in every state of the U.S. exempt parents from being charged with assault for physically attacking a child. Such exemptions are not unusual. The legal system treats families differently in a number of ways. Until recently, every state also had a "marital exemption" for rape (Finkelhor and Yllo, 1985). This means that a husband who physically forced his wife to have sex could not be charged with rape. Although many states have eliminated the marital exemption for rape, no state has eliminated the parental exemption for assault. However, several European countries, led by Sweden, now prohibit corporal punishment by parents (Haeuser, 1988; Chapter 11 of this book).

Although corporal punishment of adolescents is statistically the norm in the United States, some changes are occurring. For example, craftsmen supervising apprentices once had the right to use corporal punishment. Today, in some states the only type of person other than a parent who can legally hit children is a foster parent, a teacher, or other school official; and even that is changing. By 1993, about half the states had banned corporal punishment in schools (Haeuser, 1993; Hyman, 1990). Despite these changes, the majority of adolescents continue to be hit by their parents. Indeed, most adolescents defend corporal punishment, provided it is done in moderation, just as most slaves defended corporal punishment when it was not sadistic. However, neither the fact that corporal punishment is considered normal nor the fact that it is endorsed by its victims is evidence that corporal punishment does no harm. That issue will be examined in the chapters in Part II.

4

Who Spanks the Most?

There is no doubt that almost all American children are hit by their parents at some point. Many people probably would call this an alarmist statement because they believe that it happens to most children only when they are toddlers, and even then not that often. Unfortunately, that is not the case. Most toddlers are hit several times a week (see Chapter 2), and for a majority of American children, physical attacks by parents continue into their teens (see Chapter 3). But even if hitting were rare and confined to the first few years of life, using that as a basis for denying that there is anything wrong only shows how deeply ingrained hitting children is in American culture.

To illustrate the extent of the problem, imagine a study called the National Secretarial Survey. Suppose that study found that more than 90 percent of secretaries had been hit by their bosses. Suppose the National Office Managers' Association challenged the study by pointing out that the punishment was almost all during the first year or two on the job and that in any case, this sort of thing was done only when the secretary would not listen to reason, and it usually happened only once or twice a year. There would be a national outcry. But there is no outrage at the downplaying of studies showing that almost all American children are hit by their

---

Mary M. Moynihan is co-author of this chapter.

parents. If critics label the statements alarmist, they are right. We want to alert people to the pervasiveness of hitting children and the potential harm to which parents unknowingly expose their children when they hit them.

Although hitting children is nearly universal and the frequency of hitting is high, there are large differences between families in how chronic the pattern is, how severe the attacks are, and for how many years they continue. For some it *is* a rare slap on the hand of a toddler who just won't keep his or her hands off something dangerous despite repeated warnings. At the other extreme are parents who get caught up in an ever-growing but increasingly ineffective pattern of hitting, including hitting with belts and hair brushes, and parents who continue hitting until the child moves out of the house. Knowing what accounts for the large differences in the frequency, severity, and duration of hitting children could help change things. If we know the circumstances under which children are likely to be hit, prevention programs can be made more effective by focusing on those circumstances.

Some of the many things that could influence whether and how often parents hit children are given in the theoretical model in Appendix A. This chapter examines the influences that could be studied using data in the Second National Family Violence Survey (described in Appendix B). That study was intended to find out about the *social* causes of family violence. Many other causes also need to be examined, including differences in the temperament of children and differences between parents in personality characteristics that might incline some toward violence, or the chain of interactions that may culminate in hitting a child (Zahn-Waxler and Chapman, 1992).

Although it is a limited focus, the data available for this chapter still touches on a number of important issues, including the influence each of the following has on whether parents hit their children:

• Cultural norms that permit and even encourage corporal punishment
• Age and sex of the child
• Age and sex of the parent
• Family socioeconomic status
• Race/ethnic group

- Violence by parents against each other
- Aggression of parents against non-family members
- Whether the parent was hit as a child

To avoid confusing physical abuse with spanking and other legal forms of corporal punishment, parents who used more severe types of violence, such as punching or kicking, were taken out of the sample before the data were analyzed. This left a total of 2,952 parents, including 1,869 mothers and 1,083 fathers with a child under 18 at home.[1]

Cultural Norms and Attitudes

First we looked at whether social norms and attitudes have an effect on the how often parents hit their children. Almost everyone believes in the principle of "Spare the rod and spoil the child" or some secular version of this idea. In more formal terms, the cultural norms, or rules, of American society encourage and sometimes even require parents to hit children. Barbara Carson (1986) studied parents who had never hit their child. She had a hard time finding such parents, but after screening almost 1,000 parents, she finally found 21. Carson found that parents who never spank tend to be treated as though they are doing something wrong. These parents are doing something wrong. They are violating one of the norms of American society that says misbehaving children should be brought into line—by hitting them if necessary. These parents found they had to defend their child-rearing method against powerful informal pressure to conform to the norms for managing misbehavior. They tended to avoid the problem by recasting things in culturally acceptable language, for example, by saying that they only spank "when necessary" and leaving out the fact that they have never found it to be necessary. Or they may say that the child is so well-behaved that he or she never needs to be spanked. That stops the criticism because very few people nowadays will say that the child should be spanked anyway.

The cultural norm that says parents are morally obligated to hit children "when necessary" is probably the most fundamental reason why so many children are hit. "When necessary" means that the child continues to misbehave after being told to stop or does

CHART 4–1. The more a parent approves of corporal punishment, the more likely the parent is to hit a teenager. Almost everyone hits toddlers, whether they believe in it or not, so attitudes make little difference.

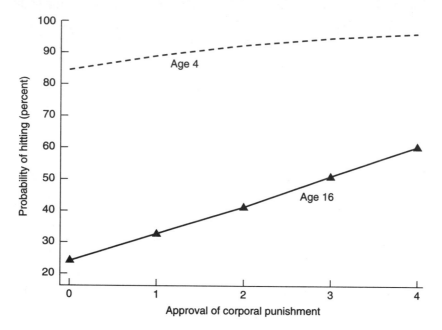

something dangerous. However, two-year-olds are two-year-olds, and it is almost inevitable that there will be situations when they continue to do something the parent does not want them to do, or do something that is dangerous. So, given those cultural definitions, almost all American children are fated to be hit by their parents.

Of course, not everyone follows the rules. And there are always many interpretations of what the rules really require (Embree, 1950; Ryan and Straus, 1954; Straus and Straus, 1951). Cultural norms are only one of many factors behind hitting children. Circumstances also are important. Some parents who believe in corporal punishment may be lucky enough to have such well-behaved children that they rarely "need to spank." Other parents who are strongly opposed to spanking may have a child who is so difficult to manage that they lash out despite their beliefs. In child rearing, as in most aspects of life, people sometimes find themselves doing things they do not believe in, and not doing things that they believe they should be doing. Besides that, a parent's position in the family and in society affects whether he or she uses or spares the rod. A parent's attitude towards corporal punishment may have little effect on whether he or she hits the child.

Chart 4–1 tells us some important things about the relationship between attitudes about spanking and actual spanking.[2] The parents in group O at the far left believed that spanking a 12-year-old was never necessary or appropriate. The parents in groups 1, 2, 3, and 4 expressed increasing amounts of approval of hitting a 12-year-old. Those in group 1 were the quarter with the lowest approval scores, and those in group 4 were the quarter of the parents with the highest approval of corporal punishment.

The top line of the chart is for children aged four. It shows that for children this age, attitudes have very little influence on whether the child was hit by the parent that year. The probability of hitting a four-year-old ranges from a low of 85 percent to 96 percent.[3] In short, almost all parents hit four-year-old children, regardless of whether they believe in corporal punishment.

For older children, however, things are different. The lower line in Chart 4–1 is for 16-year-olds. It shows that the parent's attitude does make a difference for children this old: the higher the score on the Corporal Punishment Approval Index, the greater the chance a parent will actually hit a 16-year-old. Nevertheless, many things besides the parent's attitudes influence whether a child actually will be hit. This can be seen by reading the figures for each triangle in the lower line of Chart 4–1. The triangle at the right side of the line is for parents who most strongly believed that slapping a child is necessary and appropriate, yet they had "only" a 60 percent chance of actually doing it during the 12 months preceding the survey.

The triangle at the left side of that line is for parents who believed that hitting a 12-year-old is *never* necessary or appropriate, yet even parents in this group had a 25 percent chance of actually hitting their 16-year-old. There are many reasons for the difference between believing that it is right to use corporal punishment and actually doing so. For example, some parents are under more stress than others, some children are more difficult than others, and so on.

The Age and Sex of the Child

Chapter 2 showed that boys are somewhat more likely to be hit than girls, and toddlers are much more likely to be hit than older children, even though a majority of children are still hit as late as the early teen years (see Chapter 3). We examine the age and sex of the child in this chapter to see if parental and family characteristics are more important than the age and sex of the child or vice versa.

Parent and Family Characteristics

Age and Sex of Parent

Previous studies have found that older parents are less likely to hit children than are younger parents (Becker et al., 1962; Connelly and Straus, 1992; Straus, 1979; Straus and Smith, 1990). The relationship between the sex of the parent and corporal punishment is less clear, however. The 1975 Family Violence Survey (Straus et al., 1980; Straus, 1983) found higher rates for mothers than for fathers. But Bryan and Freed's (1982) study of college students found no difference in the rates of mothers and fathers. Although participation in child care by fathers has received a great deal of media attention, on the average, fathers still do very little child care (Coverman and Shelley, 1986; Pleck, 1986). Because mothers remain the primary caretakers of children and because of the focus on culturally legitimate hitting of children, we guessed that mothers are more likely to hit children than fathers are.

MOTHERS AND FATHERS

In fact, we did find that mothers hit children more than fathers do. The higher rate by mothers applies to both younger and older children. The difference between mothers and fathers is really small, however, especially considering the huge difference in the number of hours they spend with children. For example, on the average, the chance that a mother would hit a one-year-old child in the previous 12 months was 77 percent, compared to 71 percent for fathers; the chance of hitting a 16-year-old was 43 percent for mothers compared to 37 percent for fathers.[4] Since fathers hit almost as often as mothers but generally spend far fewer hours with their children, it's safe to say that if fathers had as much responsibility as

CHART 4–2. Older parents use less corporal punishment.

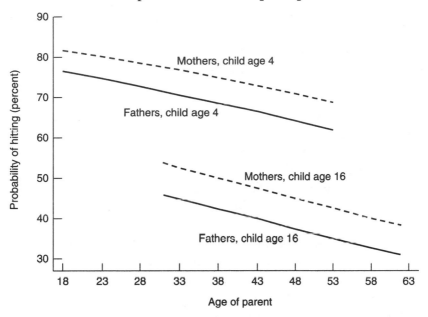

mothers for the care and training of children, the rate of hitting by fathers would be vastly higher. That does not mean that children are better off with fathers doing as little as possible. On the contrary, children probably would be better off (and marriages more satisfying) if fathers did more, provided there were a change in the cultural expectation that men must be tough and aggressive.

AGE OF PARENT

Chart 4–2 shows that older parents hit much less often than younger parents of children who are the same age. The top half of Chart 4–2 shows the decrease with age for parents of four-year-olds, and the bottom half for parents of 16-year-olds. Moving from left to right in Chart 4–2, you will see that as the age of the parent goes up, the percent that use corporal punishment decreases. The decrease is substantial and applies to both mothers and fathers regardless of the age of the child. For example, the lower half of Chart 4–2 shows that the youngest mothers are about a third more likely to hit a 16-year-old than older mothers (53 percent of the youngest mothers versus 30 percent of the oldest mothers), and the youngest fathers are almost half again more likely to hit a 16-year-old child (46 percent versus 31 percent).

Family Socioeconomic Status

A number of studies found that parents in lower socioeconomic classes tend to use corporal punishment more than middle-class parents. As we pointed out in Chapter 3, however, more recent studies have shown no difference, or only very small differences. The contradictions between previous studies, and the fact that most of the studies (such as, Wauchope and Straus, 1990) used only a crude distinction between white-collar and blue-collar families led us to try to clarify the issue. We used a Socioeconomic Status (SES) Index that divided families into 10 or more categories, as we did in Chapter 3. We used the same Socioeconomic Status Index for this chapter to look at this issue for children of all ages. As a result, we found that after making allowances for such things as the age of the parent, ethnic group, and whether there was violence between the parents, there was no relation between the social class of the parent and corporal punishment.

Race and Ethnic Group

Like research on class differences, research on whether ethnic and racial differences affect the use of corporal punishment is contradictory. Some studies find that white parents are more likely to use corporal punishment than are parents of other racial groups. Stark and McEvoy found that about the same proportion of blacks as whites reported spanking their children (Stark and McEvoy, 1970). However, Cazenave and Straus (1990) found that white parents were more likely to report slapping or spanking a child. A study of university students found higher rates of corporal punishment by fathers of white students than by fathers of Hispanic students (Escovar and Escovar, 1985). For these reasons, we expected to find a higher rate of hitting children by white parents compared to minority group parents.

The analyses graphed in Chart 4–3 support this assumption. The upper line shows that, after controlling for a number of other variables, 78 percent of white parents of children age four hit them

CHART 4–3. White parents use more corporal punishment than minority-group parents.

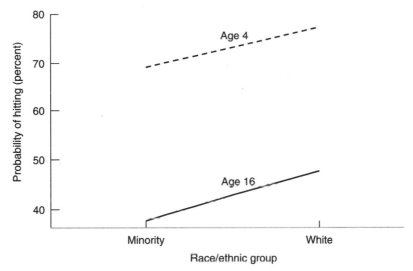

during the year of the survey, as compared to 70 percent of minority-group parents. The lower line shows that 48 percent of white parents hit a 16-year-old, compared to 39 percent of minority parents. These percentages of parents who hit a 16-year-old are higher than the percentages in Chapter 1 because they are based on a statistical analysis that assumed that the child is a boy, the parent is the mother, and the race is white. All of these groups have higher-than-average rates of corporal punishment. So what Chart 4–3 really tells us is the percent of parents who have these characteristics who used corporal punishment.

Parents' Childhood Experiences with Corporal Punishment

Children learn by example, and, as reported Chapter 2, more than 90 percent of parents provide an example of corporal punishment. Studies of college students show that those who were spanked are more likely to approve of corporal punishment and more likely to intend to spank their own children (Graziano and Namaste, 1990; Bryan and Freed, 1982). Those studies are about attitudes and intentions, however, not actual spanking. It is important to know if this also applies to

CHART 4–4. Parents who were hit when they were adolescents are more likely to do the same thing to their own children.

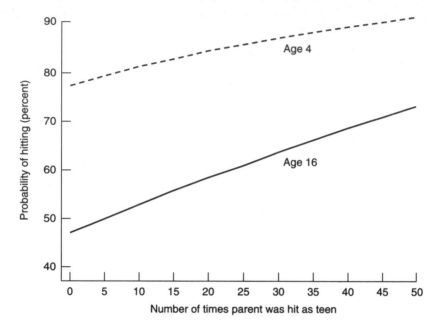

actually hitting children. To find out, we asked parents whether their own parents had hit them when they were teenagers and how often they did it (see Chapter 3 and Appendix B for further information).

Chart 4–4 shows that the more parents were hit by their parents, the greater the percent who hit their own children. In other words, those who were hit the most are the most likely to hit their own child. This applies regardless of the age of the child. The effect is somewhat greater for parents of 16-year-old children. The percent of parents who used corporal punishment on a four year old (the top line) increased from 78 percent for mothers who reported no corporal punishment when they were in their teens, to 90 percent for the mothers who were hit the most when they themselves were teenagers—a difference of 12 percentage points. The probability of using corporal punishment on a 16-year-old (the bottom line of Chart 4–4) increased from 48 percent for mothers who were not hit, to 72 percent for mothers who were hit the most. That is a difference of 24 percentage points—double the increase for mothers of four-year-old children.

Violence By Parents Outside the Home

The idea that one type of violence tends to increase the probability of other types has been put forth under different guises in social science research in the last 50 years (Archer and Gartner, 1984; Baron and Straus, 1989; Baron, Straus, and Jaffee, 1988). Evidence from a wide variety of studies shows that aggression in one sphere of life tends to be generalized to other spheres.

Among children, the effects of watching or taking part in aggressive play tend to spill over to non-play situations. The most famous experiments showing this tendency were done by Albert Bandura. They are called the Bo-Bo Doll experiments because the children watched someone hitting a so-called Bo-Bo doll punching bag (Bandura, 1971 and 1973). Bandura found that children who had seen someone punch the doll tended to become more aggressive to other children and more aggressive than children who had not seen someone punching the doll.

Among adults, Graff (1979) found that violent husbands are more likely than nonviolent husbands to be violent toward non-family members. Hotaling, Straus, and Lincoln (1990) analyzed data from three studies and concluded that "the findings support the notion that assault is a generalized pattern in interpersonal relations. . . ." (1990:467). Although we are not aware of studies linking a parent's aggressiveness outside the home to corporal punishment (as compared to physical abuse) of children, the research just cited suggests that it is possible. We did not, however, find a connection between corporal punishment and whether the parents got into physical fights with non-family adults.

Marital Violence

Although physical fights outside the family did not tend to spill over into corporal punishment within the family, previous analyses using the 1975 National Family Violence Survey found that parents who are violent toward each other are more likely to hit their children than other parents are (Straus, 1983, Straus, Gelles, and Steinmetz, 1980). We retested this idea using the 1985 national survey data and more complete statistical controls.

CHART 4–5. Mothers who have been hit by their husbands are more likely to hit their children.

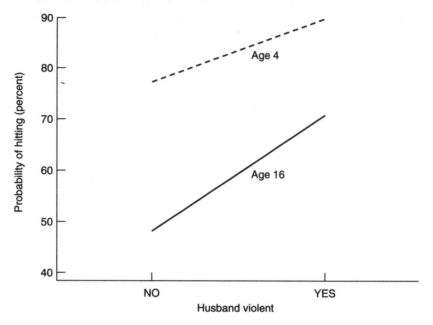

Chart 4–5 shows that mothers are much more likely to hit a child if the mother is a victim of violence by her partner. The line in Chart 4–5 for four-year-old children is higher on the chart than the line for 16-year-olds because the probability of a parent hitting a four-year-old is much greater. However, the line for the 16-year-olds goes up more steeply (from a 48 percent chance to a 71 percent chance). The steeper increase shows that marital violence has a stronger effect on the probability of hitting older children. This is most likely because almost all parents hit toddlers, so it takes a lot to push the rate even higher. Nevertheless, physical violence between the parents increases the probability of a child being hit more than any of the other variables we analyzed.

Other analyses show that the relationship between marital violence and corporal punishment also applies to fathers who are attacked by their partners, and partners who attack one another, which is the most usual pattern of marital violence. (Straus, 1993).

Conclusions

This chapter described the characteristics of parents and family associated with the use of corporal punishment. Some of these characteristics are what we expected to find, but some are not. We expected to find, and did find that, regardless of the age and sex of the child, the more corporal punishment parents experienced as children the more likely they are to do the same to their own children. This finding is consistent with studies showing that people who experienced corporal punishment tend to be the most favorable to it, and also studies showing that parents who were physically abused are more likely to abuse their own children.

We also found that mothers are more likely to hit children than fathers are. This is almost certainly due to the fact that they generally spend more time with their children than fathers do. Coverman and Shelley (1986) found that men spent an average of 14 minutes per day in child care, compared to the 50 minutes per day for women. To compare corporal punishment by fathers and mothers, we must multiply the corporal punishment rate for fathers by at least 3.6 to compensate for the fact that they spend less than a third as much time as mothers do in child care. When that is done, it shows a much higher rate of corporal punishment by fathers than by mothers.

The chapter also showed that the younger the parent, the greater the probability of hitting children of a given age. The lower rate of hitting children by older parents is consistent with the rapid decrease with age in many other types of violence, such as assaults on spouses (Suitor, Pillemer, and Straus, 1990; Stets and Straus, 1990) and homicide (Flanagan and Maquire, 1992).

Evidence also showed that when there is violence between the parents, children are more likely to be hit. Similar links have been found in the study by Jaffe, Wolfe and Wilson (1990) and Straus (1992). One possible explanation is that it reflects the anger and frustration inherent in marital violence. Another possibility is that both violence between parents and corporal punishment are part of a general tendency toward violence that is stronger in some parents than others. Or, it may reflect the in ability to use reasoning and negotiation to solve the inevitable problems of marriage and child rearing.

We also found that almost all parents hit toddlers, regardless of their attitudes toward corporal punishment. This might be because toddlers misbehave so often. When a parent tells a two-year-old not do something, the chances of the child doing it again are probably about 90 percent. This is true regardless of whether the parents simply tell the child No, No or spank the child. But almost everyone thinks that if saying no and explaining do not work, spanking will. So if a parent has said no and explained why, and the child misbehaves again, the parent is likely to spank.

We found no relationship between the socioeconomic status of the family and use of corporal punishment. Our results are consistent with most of the recent studies, which also found no social-class difference in corporal punishment.[5] This is contrary to many earlier studies summarized by Bronfenbrenner (1958) however. Differences between social classes in several aspects of lifestyle have been decreasing, and corporal punishment may be one of the waning differences.

An unexpected finding was that white parents are somewhat more likely than parents of other racial groups to hit their children. Many previous studies found that white parents have a lower rate of physical abuse, although our findings are consistent with studies by Escovar and Escovar (1985) and Cazenave and Straus (1990).

We also noted with some surprise that parents who are violent outside the family are no more likely than other parents to use corporal punishment. Many studies show that violence in one sphere of life tends to spill over to violence in other spheres. The evidence in this chapter, for example, shows that parents who hit each other are much more likely to also hit their children. This is clearly something that needs further study.

One way to bring out the significance of what we found about which parents spank the most is to imagine a public-opinion survey on corporal punishment. Suppose the survey asked participants for their opinion about why parents use corporal punishment. Not many would mention the sort of things described in this chapter. They would be more likely to say that parents use corporal punishment to correct misbehavior and because the child deserved it. That is certainly correct. Those parents are thinking of what criminologists call "deterrence" and "retribution." But this chapter shows that deterrence and retribution are far from the whole story.

Much hitting of children occurs because the parents are angry and out of control (Carson, 1988). That is why almost all parents hit toddlers, regardless of whether the parent believes that corporal punishment is appropriate. For some parents there even may be a certain excitement and emotional high from hitting children (Katz, 1988) and for a substantial number, hitting a child who misbehaves may relieve tension. This increases the chances that the parent will do it again.

The key point is that a child's misbehavior is only a part of the explanation, and perhaps only a small part. Some parents respond to misbehavior by spanking and others do not. Some do so frequently, and others, rarely. This chapter shows that hitting children is a socially patterned behavior. It is used more by parents who are young, and it is used more on boys and young children, and more by white than by minority-group parents. It is used more by parents whose own parents hit them, and whose own parents were violent toward each other. In short, for some parents, corporal punishment is part of a violent way of life. Chapters 6 and 7 further explore the link between corporal punishment and other violence. They show that corporal punishment is related to more severe and dangerous forms of violence, such as physical abuse of children and wife beating, with juvenile delinquency, and with crime as an adult.

Part II

The Price of Virtue

5

Depression and Suicide

The damage to children from physical abuse can involve more than broken bones and burns. There is compelling evidence that physically abused children also tend to suffer from serious psychological problems and are at greater risk of being involved in crime (Egeland, Sroufe, and Erickson, 1983; McCord, 1988; Widom, 1989; Wolfe, 1987). However, seldom heard in the U.S. is the idea that hitting a misbehaving child also may increase his or her chances of delinquency and psychological problems. This should not be surprising because, as we saw earlier, hitting children is a routine event that is legal and, for the most part, expected of parents. There also are deeply ingrained psychological and cultural reasons why the possible harmful effects of corporal punishment are not noticed (see chapters 1 and 11; also Carson, 1986, and Greven, 1991)

As a result, the general public and most social scientists assume that corporal punishment is *not* an important social or psychological problem. This book assumes just the opposite—that corporal punishment puts a child at risk of serious injury, both physical and psychological. This chapter tests the idea that one possible side effect of corporal punishment is an increased chance later in life of being depressed and of having suicidal thoughts.

Depression

Depression is one of the most common mental health problems, requiring clinical intervention for one out of every hundred people, or about a million Americans annually (Charney and Weissman, 1988).

Some estimates put the number as high as 6 percent of the population (Holden, 1991). Less debilitating, but still serious depression affects a much larger number. Depression is a widespread and ancient human problem and has been the subject of much research, but the relationship between corporal punishment and depression seems to have been ignored by psychologists, psychiatrists, and sociologists. Freud's essay, "A Child Is Being Beaten" (1919), for example, is a "Contribution to the Study of the Origin of Sexual Perversions," not the origin of depression. Besides that, the essay is about *fantasies* of being beaten. Freud denied the significance of actual beatings.[1] Nevertheless, Freud believed that ". . . we have long known that no neurotic harbors thoughts of suicide which are not murderous impulses against others re-directed upon himself" (quoted in Greven, 1991: 129).

The lack of research on the link between corporal punishment and depression is probably not accidental. It seems to be a case of selective inattention, similar to the lack of research on wife beating until the women's movement forced the issue into the public arena. In the case of wife beating, the blinders were part of a culturally patterned, selective perception of a male-dominant society. In the case of corporal punishment, Greven (1991) suggests that the perceptual blinders are a result of the fact that almost all of us experience corporal punishment at a young age. Drawing on extensive historical data, Greven (1991) concluded that corporal punishment has been ignored precisely because close to 100 percent of Americans have experienced it. He argues that the morality of corporal punishment is built into the deepest layers of personality when infants and toddlers are repeatedly hit by people they love and depend on for survival. Ironically, the effect might be even more powerful for the fortunate few whose parents stopped spanking by age four because experiences before then are seldom part of conscious memory. The traumatic experience of being attacked by a parent as an infant or toddler might very well become an unconscious, powerful, and continuing part of the inner being.

Social scientists have paid little attention to the possibility that hitting children causes depression in them as adults. It is not surprising, therefore, that little thought has been given to the processes producing that effect. In fact, until recently, there has been no theory explaining why such a relationship is even possible. Greven (1991) presents just such a theory, however, and the conclusion to this chapter presents another.

Greven's theory holds that "depression often is a delayed response to the suppression of childhood anger . . . from being physically hit and hurt . . . by adults . . . whom the child loves and on whom he or she depends for nurturance and life itself" (Greven, 1991, p. 129). Greven's theory and his most compelling evidence involve the religious tradition of Calvinism and evangelical Protestantism. He provides considerable evidence that "Melancholy and depression have been persistent themes in the family history, religious experience, and emotional lives of Puritans, evangelicals, fundamentalists, and Pentecostals for centuries." Greven also provides extensive historical evidence on the frequency and severity of corporal punishment among these devout Protestants. He then argues that:

> The long-sustained persistence of melancholy and depression among twice-born Protestants is clearly no accident, since it has consistently been paralleled by the tradition of assault, coercion, and violence against children committed with the rod, the belt, the hand and other such instruments of parental discipline. . . . From all this historical evidence, it ought to be clear that depression is often the central mood characteristic of adults whose bodies were assaulted, whose wills were broken in childhood, and whose anger was forcibly suppressed. The rage and resentment never disappear; they just take more covert and dangerous forms, dangerous to the self, and potentially to others.
>
> Depression rooted in anger remains so potent because it often begins so early—in the first three years of life, precisely the period corporal punishment advocates have always stressed as critical for the start of physical punishment. . . . The first assaults on children's bodies and spirits generally commence before conscious memory can recall them later. The unconscious thus becomes the repository of rage, resistance, and desire for revenge that small children feel when being struck by the adults they love. . . . Though they cannot remember consciously what happened to them during the first three or four years of life, the ancient angers persist while the adult conscience directs rage inward upon the self. These people hurt themselves just as their parents hurt them. (131–32)

Greven's theory is a highly plausible interpretation of the rich historical evidence he collected. However, although his evidence makes it clear that both corporal punishment and depression were common among fundamentalists, Greven does not provide statistical evidence showing that it is corporal punishment that accounts for the depression, or even that the two are related. It is possible to test Greven's theory using historical evidence, at least in principle, because even fundamentalist Protestants varied widely in their use of corporal punishment and, of course, not all were depressed. So, it might be possible to investigate whether depression occurred at a higher rate among those who experienced the most corporal punishment. Greven does not provide that type of data, though, and it may not be possible to do so. However, his theory can also be tested using data on contemporary families, which is the purpose of this chapter.

CHART 5–1. Adults whose parents hit them as adolescents are more likely to be depressed than those whose parents did not.

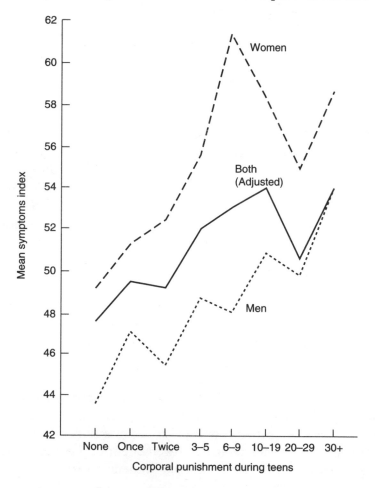

The theory that corporal punishment increases the risk of depression later in life was tested using information on the almost 6,000 participants in the second National Family Violence Survey (described in Appendix B). We asked people in the survey whether their parents had used corporal punishment when they were adolescents and how often. A little more than half had been hit by their parents at that age (see Chapter 3 and Appendix 3); so the effects of corporal punishment described in this chapter apply to a majority of Americans.

Corporal Punishment and Depression

Does it make a difference who hits a child—mother or father, and whether the child is a boy or a girl? Chapter 3, for example, shows that when children reach adolescence, fathers hit girls less, presumably reflecting traditional gender roles. So it could be that the psychological consequences are greater when a father hits an adolescent girl because it also violates cultural norms about how a "young lady" should be treated by a father. For this reason, all the analyses were repeated separately for corporal punishment by fathers and by mothers. We also wanted to take into account other personal and family characteristics that might be linked to corporal punishment and might be the "real" cause of depression, such as poverty or heavy drinking. The statistical analysis was "controlled" for these two variables, and also for witnessing violence between parents as an adolescent and for violence by the husband as an adult (see Appendix C).

Men and Women

Chart 5–1 shows the results of testing the idea that the more corporal punishment, the greater the chances of being depressed as an adult. The lower line is for men. Men who were not hit as teenagers (the lower left") had an average score of 44 on the Depressive Symptoms Index. The score goes up to 47 for those who were hit only once, then goes down a bit, but continues going up as the amount of corporal punishment increases until it reaches 54 for the men who were hit the most when they were adolescents. This is a 23 percent higher score; that is, being hit a lot as an adolescent is associated with 23 percent more depressive symptoms.

For the women in this sample (the upper line in Chart 5–1), the average Depressive Symptoms Index starts at 49 and goes up from there to about 61. Then, for reasons that are not clear, it declines for the highest categories of corporal punishment. The center line, which is for women and men combined, has been adjusted to control for five other variables (see Appendix C, Table C5–1). It tends to be midway between the separate lines for women and men. So, although there are some irregularities in the trend line, the evidence in Chart 5–1 strongly supports the idea that the more corporal punishment experienced as an adolescent, the higher the average score on the Depressive Symptoms Index.

Another point to note in Chart 5–1 is that the chart line for women is higher than the chart line for men, showing that, on the average, women have more symptoms of depression than men. Ironically, this unfortunate fact is helpful here because it shows that the results of this study are consistent with many other studies of differences between men and women where depression is concerned. It increases confidence in the measure of depression that was used for this study.

Sex-of-Parent Differences

In Chart 5–1, hitting by fathers and mothers is combined to get the total amount of hitting by parents. But there might be something unique about the effect of hitting by mothers versus fathers, and different combinations of the sex of the parent doing the hitting and the sex of the child might have a different effect on depression. According to the traditional pattern of gender roles, corporal punishment should be the father's job. If so, physical discipline by a father might not have the same adverse consequences because he would be doing something that fathers are expected to do. To test this, the analyses were repeated separately for corporal punishment by mothers and by fathers. The results were very similar to those shown in Chart 5–1 the more often adolescents are hit, the greater the average score on the Depressive Symptoms Index.

Corporal Punishment and Suicidal Thoughts

Thinking about committing suicide often accompanies depression, but it is a phenomenon that needs to be studied separately. Thinking about suicide is obviously important because of the potential lethal consequences, but it is also important theoretically. The theoretical issues are illustrated by Freud's observation (cited earlier) that suicide is ". . . murderous impulses against others re-directed upon himself." To determine whether the people interviewed had thought about killing themselves, we simply asked if they had thought about taking their own life during the preceding 12 months.

The percent who had thought about committing suicide is represented in Chart 5–2, which is similar to Chart 5–1 in some ways

CHART 5–2. Adults whose parents hit them a lot as adolescents are more likely to have thoughts about killing themselves.

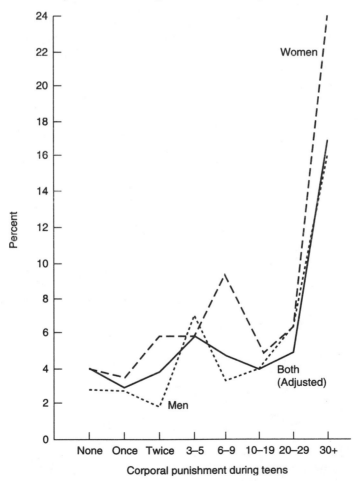

and different in other ways. The similarity is that frequent corporal punishment as an adolescent is associated with a high chance of thinking about suicide as an adult. When the analysis was repeated separately for hitting by mother and by father, the results are very similar in the two charts.

There also are important differences between the relationship of corporal punishment to depression and to suicidal thoughts. One difference is that the lines for men and women who have thought about suicide are much closer. The main difference, however, is that the lines for suicide in Chart 5–2 tend go up slowly or not at all at first, and then at an accelerating rate. This is in contrast to Chart 5–1, which shows an increase in depression starting with even one instance of being hit as an adolescent. In other words, Chart 5–2 shows little or no increase in suicidal thoughts until the two highest categories of corporal punishment are reached. After that, the frequency of thinking about suicide jumps sharply. Perhaps

CHART 5–3. The more corporal punishment, the greater the chances of being depressed as an adult, regardless of whether the parents were violent to each other.

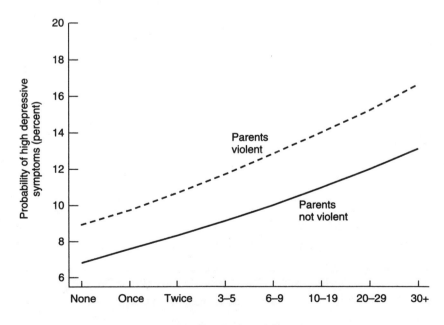

this is because suicide is such an extreme step that it can only be prompted by truly chronic attacks by a parent.

Another Statistical Approach

When studying the effects of corporal punishment, it is important to allow for other factors that coincide with corporal punishment. Different statistical methods do this in a variety of ways. The method used up to now takes competing explanations for depression into account by holding them constant statistically. The method used for this section allows us to look at the effects of *combinations* of corporal punishment and the other variables. For example, it can answer the question of whether the effect of corporal punishment is different for people whose parents were also physically violent to each other. When there is violence in a marriage, there is also more likely to be violence to children, that is, more corporal punishment. If hitting a teenager is strongly related to whether the parents hit each other, then what seems to be the effect of being hit by parents might really be an effect of having witnessed your parents physically attacking each other. That is also very traumatic for children (Straus, 1992b; Jaffe, Wolfe and Wilson, 1990).

The statistical method used for Chart 5–3 allows for the overlap of witnessing violence between parents and experiencing corporal punishment by showing the relationship between corporal punishment and depression separately for people who witnessed violence between their parents and those who did not. The upper line in Chart 5–3 is for people who witnessed violence between their parents, and the lower line is for those who did not. Both chart lines show that the more an adolescent child was hit, the greater the probability of being depressed later in life. For example, the lower line shows that people whose parents were not violent to each other and who were not themselves hit when they were adolescents have about a 7 percent chance of being depressed as an adult (see the circle at the left of the lower line). The chances of being depressed go up with each increase in the amount of corporal punishment, reaching 13 percent for people who were hit the most as adolescents. This rate is almost 1.9 times greater than the rate for those who were not hit as adolescents. None of the people represented by the lower line in Chart 5–3 witnessed violence between his or her parents. In their case, corporal punishment seems to increase the chances of depression regardless of whether the parents were violent to each other, and also regardless of the many other things that the statistical analysis controlled.

What about the effect of corporal punishment on thinking about committing suicide? We have already seen that for both men and women, the more corporal punishment, the greater the percent who thought about killing themselves during the year of the survey (Chart 5–2). Chart 5–4 adds data for the women in the sample. There are separate lines for women who were physically attacked by their husbands (upper line) and those who were not (lower line).

The fact that the line for "Husband Violent" starts at a 10 percent chance of thinking about suicide, whereas the line for "Husband not Violent" starts at 3 percent is consistent with studies showing that women who were attacked by their partners have a

CHART 5–4. Women married to violent husbands are three or more times more likely to think about suicide than women whose husbands are not violent. Within both groups, women who were hit a lot as adolescents are twice as likely to think about suicide than women who were not hit at that age.

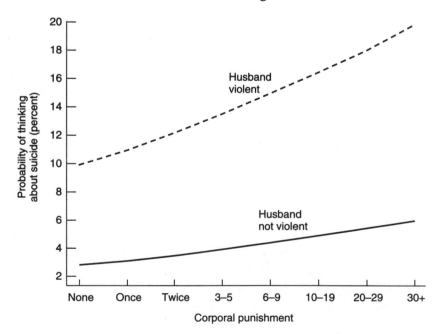

much higher rate of depression and suicide attempts (O'Leary, Beach, and Sandeen, 1990; Stets and Straus, 1990). Most important in Chart 5–4 is that both lines go up as the amount of corporal punishment increases. In both cases, the chances of being suicidal are double for women who were hit the most by their parents as adolescents compared to those who were not hit by their parents. The upper line (women who were attacked by their husbands) goes from 10 percent to 19 percent; the lower line (women who were not married to violent men) also doubles, from 3 percent to 6 percent.

Summary

This chapter examined the idea that the harmful psychological effects of being physically attacked by a parent are not restricted to the sort of severe attacks that are labeled as physical abuse. The results show that even when the attack is in the form of ordinary and legal corporal punishment, it may have serious and harmful psychological side effects, including an increased chance of being depressed or suicidal as an adult.

About half the respondents in this nationally representative sample recalled having been hit by their parents when they were adolescents (see Chapter 3). This rate is consistent with other studies. The fact that half of all teenagers are hit by their parents is important because it indicates that the relationship between corporal punishment and depression does not just occur in the small number of cases that fall outside the realm of ordinary corporal punishment. Consider the following:

1. Regardless of sex, socioeconomic status, drinking problems, marital violence, or whether children witnessed violence between their parents, the fact is the more people were hit by their parents in their early teens, the higher their scores on the Depressive Symptoms Index and the greater the percent who thought about committing suicide.

   This does not say that gender, socioeconomic status, marital violence, and witnessing violence as a child are unrelated to depression. Far from it. The results of this study show that women, people of low socioeconomic status, Dohrenwand et al., (1992) people in violent marriages, (Stets and Straus,

1990), and people who witness violence between their parents (Straus, 1992b) have a significantly higher level of depressive symptoms. Nevertheless, after taking into account the overlap of corporal punishment with these variables, corporal punishment by itself remains related to depression.

2. The analyses were repeated separately for boys and girls with no important differences. So, for both men and women, being hit as teenagers is associated with essentially the same increase in depressive symptoms and suicidal thoughts, even though men have fewer depressive symptoms.

3. The results of separate analyses of corporal punishment by fathers and mothers are very similar. Regardless of whether it is the father or mother who does the hitting, being hit by a parent increases the probability of depression and thinking about killing yourself later in life.

4. All the analyses were repeated using two other measures of marital violence—violence by the wife and couple violence. The results are essentially the same as those shown in the charts in this chapter.

Why Does Corporal Punishment Produce Depression?

Philip Greven's theory that depression is a delayed response to suppressing childhood anger at being hit by parents is a plausible explanation of what links corporal punishment with depression and suicidal thoughts. That is not the only theory that needs to be studied, however. Another theory about the processes linking corporal punishment and depression is suggested by research on the neurobiology of depression.

At a 1991 conference attended by specialists on depression, there was wide agreement that depression is a mental health problem with many causes, but that it probably involves a biological process in which there are lasting changes in the structure and chemistry of the brain (Holden, 1991). A speaker at the conference reported that "One fact that could play a role in such long-term changes is stress. Both animals and people who experience chronic stress respond by secreting 'stress hormones' [that are] the most robust biological concomitant of depression—showing in up to 50 percent of cases, especially severe ones" (Holden, 1991, p. 1,451). Several other *permanent* changes in brain function were reported in both animals and humans who experience continuing stress.

For children, one such continuing stress may be corporal punishment by their parents. It often begins in infancy and is particularly frequent for toddlers, many of whom are hit almost daily. Moreover, we have seen that corporal punishment continues into the teen years for a majority of American children. The changes in brain structure and function associated with the stress of having been physically assaulted for 13 or more years might explain the link between corporal punishment and depression reported in this chapter. This theory could be tested relatively easily by obtaining information which parents readily provide, on how often they use corporal punishment, and information on the level of stress hormones produced by children subjected to varying levels of corporal punishment.

There is an urgent need for more definitive studies of corporal punishment and depression, especially experiments that can provide better evidence of cause and effect, and studies that investigate the processes that link corporal punishment and depression. Finding answers is urgent because so many American children are hit by their parents and because so many Americans suffer from depression. If the more definitive studies also show that being hit by parents causes depression and suicide, or if neurobiological studies find that the more a child has been hit by parents, the greater the level of depression, it would have far-reaching implications for preventing depression and suicide.

6

Physical Abuse

Ricky LeTourneau "was disciplined to death" by foster mother Deborah Wolfenden after she lost control of her temper and beat him in January 1990. . . . [She] lost the battle for control. She lost control of herself. She lost control over her temper and her ability to discipline reasonably.
(The Times Record, *Brunswick, Maine, April 27, 1992, p. 1*)

Ricky's death illustrates the tendency for physical discipline to become physical abuse. There is a fine line between physical abuse and legal, socially approved spanking and other modes of disciplining children. A number of leading researchers argue that spanking and other legal forms of corporal punishment of children are some of the major causes of physical abuse. Despite this, the idea that spanking increases the risk that a parent will go too far and cross the line to physical abuse has been largely ignored. Corporal punishment is not mentioned as a possible cause of physical abuse in the many publications of the National Center on Child Abuse and Neglect or in reports of the U.S. Advisory Board on Child Abuse and Neglect (1993). The U.S. Advisory Board on Child Abuse recommended that federal funds be denied to *organizations* that permit corporal punishment of children, and the National Committee to Prevent Child Abuse and Neglect (a major national voluntary organization) mounted a campaign against corporal punishment *by teachers*. Neither organization has said that *parents* should never hit children.[1]

These omissions illustrate the extent to which corporal punishment has been ignored by major agencies concerned with the

---

Carrie L. Yodanis is co-author of this chapter.

81

prevention and treatment of child abuse. Is the same omission made in scholarly books on physical abuse? This chapter will look at that question.

Past research on the link between corporal punishment and physical abuse also will be examined. We need to see if corporal punishment has been ignored because the research evidence is not very convincing. We will also identify some of the processes that might link corporal punishment to physical abuse. Finally, the chapter will describe a study to test the possible link between corporal punishment and physical abuse.

Another Conspiracy of Silence

Chapter 1 showed that the authors of textbooks on child development and advice books for parents almost totally ignore the research on corporal punishment. They are not the only ones. The authors of books on the causes and prevention of physical abuse also largely ignore corporal punishment, even though its connection with physical abuse has been pointed out by highly respected social scientists for many years. As long ago as 1970, David Gil wrote:

> Since culturally determined permissive attitudes toward the use of physical force in child-rearing seem to constitute the common core of all physical abuse of children in American society, systematic educational efforts aimed at gradually changing this particular aspect of the prevailing child-rearing philosophy, and developing clear-cut cultural prohibitions and legal sanctions against the use of physical force as a means for rearing children, are likely to produce over time the strongest possible reduction of the incidence and prevalence of physical abuse of children (p. 141).

Others (Feshbach, 1980; Gelles and Straus, 1988; Haeuser, 1991; Maurer, 1976; Steinmetz and Straus, 1974; Straus, Gelles, and Steinmetz, 1980; and Williams, 1983) also concluded that reducing corporal punishment is essential to reducing physical abuse.

The authors just mentioned, as well as others such as Greven (1991), argue that physical abuse is rooted in cultural norms that make many types of violence acceptable or desirable, including, of course, corporal punishment. Doing something about physical abuse, therefore, requires changing the larger social context, including corporal punishment. Zigler and Hall (1989), for example, say that "ultimate control of the abuse problem lies in changing our societal attitudes towards and acceptance of aggression as an appropriate mechanism for problem solving." Bybee (1979) argues that the strong support for corporal punishment sets the psychological stage for other types of violence and escalation of that violence. Parke (1982, p. 39) concludes that "Just as the availability of and prior experiences in using a gun make murder more likely under conditions of stress and anger, so previously experiencing and utilizing violent child-rearing tactics make child abuse more likely." Daro's discussion of the "environmental theory" of child abuse (1988, p. 49) holds that social tolerance of corporal punishment is a likely precondition of physical abuse.

Despite the fact that these and other well-respected scholars have argued that corporal punishment increases the risk factor of physical abuse, this idea is missing in the publications of leading agencies concerned with child abuse. To find out if the same holds true for books on child abuse, we analyzed 120 of them (see Appendix D for the list). More than half (57 percent) had nothing on spanking as a risk factor for physical abuse. An additional 22 percent, although mentioning spanking as a possible risk factor, did not discuss whether parents should avoid spanking children. Nine percent recommended avoiding physical discipline, but qualified it by phrases such as "if possible." Only 12 percent of the 120 books unambiguously stated that corporal punishment is never appropriate.

The Research Evidence

Perhaps corporal punishment is absent from books and articles on preventing physical abuse because the research evidence is not convincing. Lets' look at that evidence.

Corporal Punishment by Abusive Parents

Lynch and Roberts (1982) studied 33 physically abusive families and found that corporal punishment was the most commonly used means of punishment, with 72 percent of the families frequently hitting their children. But since they did not have a comparison group of non-abusive parents, there is no way of knowing if the abusive parents used more corporal punishment than other parents.

Other studies however, did use comparison groups and found that abusive parents tend to use corporal punishment more than non-abusive parents. Smith (1975) compared 214 abusive and 76 non-abusive parents and found that 50 percent of abusive mothers and 37 percent of abusive fathers frequently used corporal punishment on their children, compared to 13 percent of the non-abusive mothers and 10 percent of the non-abusive fathers. Similarly, Oates (1980) compared 56 abusive and 56 non-abusive parents and found that 54 percent of abusive mothers frequently used corporal punishment versus only 11 percent of the non-abusive mothers.

Not all studies have supported the idea that abusive parents use corporal punishment more than non-abusive parents. Elmer (1967) compared 11 abusive and 12 non-abusive families and concluded that whipping and spanking were the most frequent forms of discipline in both the abusive and non-abusive families. Baher et al., (1976) found that of 25 abusive mothers, 12 used corporal punishment, which is probably less than the general population rate. Trickett and Kuczynski (1986) compared 20 abusive and 20 non-abusive families and found that corporal punishment was the main form of discipline used by both abusive and non-abusive parents. They found, though, that 40 percent of abusive parents, but no non-abusive parents, used severe forms of corporal punishment, such as striking child with an object or in the face, pulling hair, or spanking the child with pants down.

Corporal Punishment in the Childhood of Parents

This approach is based on the escalation theory, but tests it indirectly. It assumes that the more parents were themselves hit as children, the more likely they are to be heavy users of corporal punishment on their own children, increasing the risk that it will escalate into physical abuse. Three studies by Straus and his colleagues have taken this approach. Straus (1980) studied the parents in the first National Family Violence Survey (see Appendix B). Moore and Straus (1987) studied a sample of 958 New Hampshire parents, while Straus and Smith (1990, p. 360) studied the Hispanic-American parents in the second National Family Violence Survey. All three studies found that the more the parents themselves were corporally punished as adolescents, the greater the percentage who went beyond ordinary corporal punishment with their own children and engaged in attacks severe enough to be classified as physical abuse. However, none of these studies used enough statistical controls for characteristics that overlap with corporal punishment and might be the "real cause" of the physical abuse.

Non-Compliance and Escalation

Clinical work with abusive parents has shown that much physical abuse starts as an attempt to correct and control through corporal punishment. When the child does not comply or, in the case of older children, hits back and curses the parent, the resulting frustration and rage leads some parents to increase the severity of the physical attack and kick, punch, or hit with an object. Kempe and Kempe (1978), for example say:

> [Abusive parents] . . . may be discouraged when spanking obviously brings no result, but they truly see no alternative and grow depressed both by their own behavior and their babies responses. Helplessly, they continue in the same vicious circle: punishment, deteriorating relationship, frustration, and further punishment (p. 27).

Wolfe et al., (1981) call this sequence "child-precipitated" abuse because it begins when a child misbehaves. If corporal punishment is not effective, abusive parents increase the severity of the punishment until the point where a child may be injured. Devenson (1982) and Marion (1982) reached similar conclusions on the basis of clinical evidence. Marion also points out that corporal punishment creates a false sense of successful discipline because of the temporary end it puts to undesirable behavior. She also cites research that shows the corporal punishment tends to *increase* undesirable behavior in children. So, parents who rely on hitting to control the child's behavior have to continually increase the intensity. Besides the clinically based conclusions we just mentioned, there has been some research on this increasing intensity, or escalation. Frude and Gross (1980) studied 111 mothers and found that 40 percent were worried that they could possibly hurt their children.

These tended to be the mothers who used corporal punishment frequently. Gil (1970) studied 1,380 abused children and found that 63 percent of the abuse incidents were an "immediate or delayed response to specific [misbehavior] of the child."

The research by Kadushin and Martin (1981) on 66 abusive parents is probably the most direct test of the escalation theory. They describe a number of specific situations in which escalation occurs, such as a child who fails to respond to the punishment, attempts to fight back or run away, or the parent who becomes frustrated and then enraged when using corporal punishment, as in the following two examples:

> Then I started to spank her and she wouldn't cry—stubborn, she's just like I am, she wouldn't cry—like it was having no effect, like she was defying me. So I spanked her all the harder (p. 173).

> It all started when Camille [age 14] slammed the door on her little sister's leg. Camille was in the bathroom and realized there was no toilet tissue. She asked her little sister, the 9 year old, to get some tissue, which she did do, and apparently her sister wasn't rushing out of the bathroom fast enough and Camille kind of pushed the door, and in the process, she caught her sister's leg in the door, and with the child screaming as she did from the pain, it got me very angered . . . And I think at that moment I lost control completely, and I went over and I swatted Camille with my—you know, my hand, and Camille turned around and she swung back to strike me, which she did do and that got me even more aggravated. And before I know what really was going on, I had pounded Camille several times. She had run a tub of bath water to take a bath, and suddenly I realized I had knocked Camille into the bathtub. And apparently I had struck her in the face, which by no means was intentional. But she had a swollen eye, and she didn't say anything to me that night (p. 175).

Evaluating the Evidence

Three of the five studies that compared abusive and non-abusive parents found that abusing parents were more prone to use corporal punishment or severe corporal punishment. Three out of five studies is far from conclusive. On the other hand, the clinical evidence, the indirect tests of the escalation theory by Straus et al. and the only scientific study that directly tested the idea that corporal punishment tends to escalate into physical abuse (Kadushin and Martin, 1981) strongly supported the findings of the three studies.

A hard-nosed evaluation would point out that there has not been a definitive experimental study showing that corporal punishment causes physical abuse. On the other hand, that also can be said about every other presumed cause. The research evidence on corporal punishment is as strong or stronger than the evidence on other causes of physical abuse that have been studied, such as poverty or teenaged motherhood (Connelly and Straus, 1992). Yet I have never heard or read a demand for definitive experimental evidence before teenaged motherhood or poverty can be considered causes of abuse.

At a 1993 conference to plan a national agenda on reducing family violence, many causes of family violence and how to prevent them were discussed. When I brought up corporal punishment, there was an instant demand for me to cite the evidence—something that had not been requested in the previous day and a half of the conference during which many potential causes of family violence were mentioned. I then outlined the evidence just presented and also the results of the research in this chapter. The rejoinder essentially was, It's all correlational evidence, and We need evidence based on randomized field trials. I agreed, but then pointed out that *none* of the strategies for preventing child abuse mentioned in the previous day and a half had been tested by a randomized trial experiment, yet no one objected. Those who demanded experimental evidence on whether reducing corporal punishment will reduce the rate of physical abuse were correct. Their error was in not demanding the same level of evidence for other presumed causes of physical abuse.

Reasons for Ignoring
Corporal Punishment

The evidence that corporal punishment leads to physical abuse is at least as good as the evidence implicating other presumed causes of physical abuse. Moreover, this evidence has led some respected scholars to conclude spanking is a major cause of physical abuse. If that is the case, why has corporal punishment been virtually ignored in efforts to prevent physical abuse? We will consider three possibilities.

Contradicts Deeply Embedded Cultural Norms

Probably the main reason for ignoring the idea that corporal punishment is one of the causes of physical abuse is because the concept conflicts with cultural norms supporting corporal punishment. These norms influence social scientists, child-abuse professionals, parent educators, and parents. Almost everyone is against teenagers having children regardless of whether it is a cause of child abuse, so there is consensus that reducing teenaged pregnancy would be a good way to reduce physical abuse and other social problems, such as welfare dependency. Corporal punishment, however, is something that 84 percent of the population thinks is necessary. So, both the general public and social scientists demand definitive evidence before concluding that corporal punishment is one of the causes of child abuse. At the national conference mentioned earlier, many potential causes were discussed. The *only* cause of physical abuse about which questions were raised because of lack of experimental evidence was corporal punishment. There seems to be a double standard concerning the evidence that is needed, and this leads many social scientists and almost all agencies concerned with preventing or treating physical abuse to dismiss corporal punishment. The same applies to agencies that fund research, and that reduces the chances of more definitive research being done.

There are many indicators of the degree to which corporal punishment is a culturally expected aspect of parent behavior:

- Corporal punishment, as defined in Chapter 1, is legal in every state of the U.S.
- At least 84 percent of Americans believe that "a good hard spanking is sometimes necessary" (Chapter 2).
- More than 90 percent of American parents use corporal punishment on toddlers (Chapter 2), and more than half continue this into the early teen years (Chapter 3).
- The laws permitting corporal punishment are not forgotten features of an earlier period. The child-abuse legislation passed in

all 50 states of the U.S. in the 1960s reconfirmed them by explicitly excluding use of corporal punishment from what is prohibited. Ironically, if the theory is correct that corporal punishment increases the risk of physical abuse, this legislation may have put children at *increased* risk of physical abuse by legally reinforcing the traditional appropriateness of corporal punishment.

- A study by Carson (1986) found that non-spanking parents tend to be perceived as ineffective and their children as badly behaved. Their neighbors, friends, and relatives offer indirect and sometimes direct suggestions to spank, such as, "What that child needs is a good spanking."

Misperception of Typical Abuse Cases

Another reason corporal punishment may be ignored as a cause of physical abuse is a distorted perception of physical abuse. This perception comes from the fact that newspapers and television—to attract more readers or viewers—tend to show only cases involving sadistic and mentally ill parents who burn, maim, and kill children. By contrast, 95 percent of physical-abuse cases do not involve severe injuries (Garbarino, 1986) and typically are rooted in corporal punishment rather than psychopathology. This matches the conclusion reached by pioneer child-abuse researchers such as Gelles (1973), and Kempe and Kempe (1978), who argued that psychopathology is involved in no more than 10 percent of physical-abuse cases. It is possible that the horrifying image of extreme but not typical cases diverts attention from the typical case, which is most often rooted in corporal punishment.

Absence of Linking Processes Theory

Still another reason books and agencies concerned with child abuse would ignore corporal punishment might be if there were no satisfactory explanations of how or why corporal punishment leads to physical abuse. Without an explanation, people tend to think the idea is preposterous. But there are, in fact, numerous theories about the link between corporal punishment and child abuse. Every author who has written about corporal punishment as a cause of physical abuse has offered an explanation. We have already considered one of these theories—the idea that much physical abuse occurs when parents escalate the level of the attack when their children continue to misbehave or strike back at them. The following section reviews three additional theories and presents a theoretical model integrating all four.

Theories that Might Explain the Link

Cultural Spillover Theory

The idea behind the cultural spillover theory is that cultural norms that make violence legitimate for socially approved purposes, such as corporal punishment of children or capital punishment of murderers, tend to be applied to non-legitimate purposes, such as use of physical force and violence to obtain sex, namely, rape (Baron and Straus, 1987, 1989).

The results of a study of 958 New Hampshire parents are consistent with the cultural spillover theory because they show that parents who approved of corporal punishment had a much higher rate of going beyond that and severely assaulting their children than did parents who did not approve of corporal punishment (Straus, 1991). However, a study of 171 abusive parents by Shapiro (1979) did not support cultural spillover theory because a majority of the parents did *not* believe that spanking is the best form of discipline.

Depression

Another theory that might explain the link between corporal punishment and physical abuse involves depression. Chapter 5 showed that the more corporal punishment a person experienced as an adolescent, the greater the chance of being depressed as an adult. At first this may seem to contradict the long tradition of conceptualizing depression and suicide as internally directed aggression, with some people directing aggression inward and others outward in hostile acts towards others. But recent research shows that many depressed people do both (Berkowitz, 1993). So, depression could be a link between having been a victim of corporal punishment and physically abusing a child.

Marital Violence

The third theory was suggested by research showing that the more corporal punishment experienced as a child, the greater the chance of physically assaulting a spouse later in life (Straus, 1991; Straus, Gelles, and Steinmetz, 1980). Putting this together with research showing that marital violence greatly increases the chance of physical abuse (Kaufman-Kantor, 1990; Straus, Gelles, and Steinmetz, 1980) suggests that violence between the parents is the link between corporal punishment and physical abuse of children.

The three theories just described and the escalation theory presented earlier probably complement each other. Chart 6–1 brings them together in a model that can be tested using a powerful statistical technique called "path analysis" (see Appendix C). This model was used to guide the research in the balance of this chapter. Specifically, we tested the idea that part of the reason why corporal punishment increases the risk of physical abuse is because parents who were hit by their own parents tend to be more accepting of violence as a means of correcting wrongdoing, are more likely to be involved in a violent marriage, and are more likely to be depressed.[2]

Characteristics of Abusing Parents

Before using more complicated statistical methods, it is a good idea to compare parents who physically abused a child with those who did not. The table giving those statistics is in Appendix C. It shows that, consistent with the theory, the abusing parents:

CHART 6–1. Why does corporal punishment lead to child abuse?

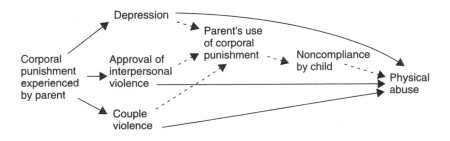

- Were more often hit by their own parents
- Had more symptoms of depression
- Were more likely to believe that there are occasions when it would be all right for a husband to hit his wife or a wife to hit her husband
- Were more likely to have actually experienced marital violence

In addition, comparing the abusing parents to the non-abusing parents showed that the abusing parents:

- Were the same age as the non-abusing parents
- Were slightly lower in socioeconomic status
- Had substantially higher conflict with their spouses
- Were more likely to be a minority-group family
- Had somewhat more children living at home
- Had abused a somewhat younger child
- Were about equally divided between fathers and mothers

Each of the characteristics just listed could overlap with the four characteristics in the theory. If that is the case, one or more of them could be the "real" explanation. For example, abusing parents had more conflict with each other, and that might be the real cause. So some method is needed that can answer the question of whether corporal punishment makes a difference when the amount of conflict between the parents is held constant. Path analysis does just that. It tells us the extent to which corporal punishment makes a difference over and above the amount of conflict. It shows the net effect of corporal punishment after allowing for each of the variables just listed.

Corporal Punishment and Physical Abuse

The results of the path analysis are in Chart 6–2. Each of the arrows in the chart shows that there is a statistically dependable relationship between the variable at the left and the variable it points to. The coefficients (which range from 0 to 1), such as .13, show how strong the relationship is.

The top left arrow shows that corporal punishment experienced by parents is related to depression, as predicted (see Chapter 5 for a more detailed analysis of the links between corporal punishment

CHART 6–2. The size of the numbers indicates the strength of the link between corporal punishment and physical abuse.

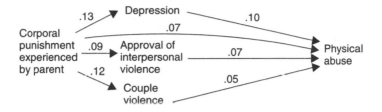

and depression). The arrow at the top right shows that depression is related to physical abuse. The coefficient of .10 indicates that the connection between depression and physical abuse is almost as strong as the connection between corporal punishment and depression (.13).

At the middle of Chart 6–2, the arrow from "Corporal Punishment Experienced by Parents to Approval of Interpersonal Violence" shows that the more corporal punishment, the greater the approval of interpersonal violence. This in turn is related to physical abuse. The path coefficients of .09 and .07 are slightly lower than the other coefficients, which shows that whether parents approve of violence is somewhat less important than whether the abusing parent suffers from depression or whether there is violence between the parents.

At the bottom of Chart 6–2, the arrow between corporal punishment and "Couple Violence" (.12) shows that the more corporal punishment these parents were subjected to when they were adolescents, the more likely they are to end up in a violent marriage. This, combined with the path from "Couple Violence" to "Physical Abuse" shows that one of the reasons corporal punishment increases the chances of physical abuse is because it increases the chances of a violent marriage, and parents who are violent to each other are more likely to be violent to their children.

Finally, the arrow that goes directly from corporal punishment to physical abuse shows there is a connection between these two in addition to the connection through the three variables from the theory (depression, violent attitudes, and couple violence) and in addition to the seven control variables.[3]

CHART 6–3. The more a parent was hit as an adolescent, the greater the chances the parent will physically abuse his or her own child.

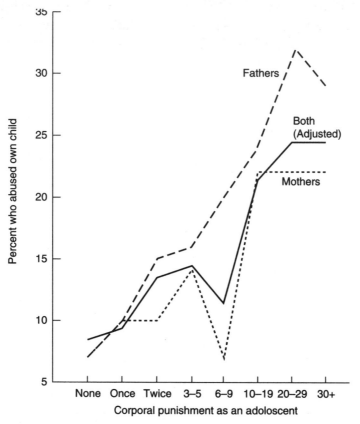

The path analysis clearly supports the theory that corporal punishment is related to physical abuse, even after many other variables are taken into consideration. The trouble is that path coefficients are not very clear to anyone except those who deal with these sorts of statistics every day. But Chart 6–3 may be clearer because rather than showing coefficients, it shows the percentage who physically abused their children. The top line is for fathers, the bottom dashed line is for mothers, and the center line is for both parents. The middle line is adjusted to hold constant all the other variables.

The most important point to note about Chart 6–3 is that the percent of parents who physically abused a child goes up strongly with increasing amounts of corporal punishment. The rate for parents who were not hit by their own parents—the "None" group at the left side—is high (about 7 percent), but not nearly as high as the rate of abuse by parents who were hit the most—the 30-or-more group at the right side (about 24 percent). So the chance of physically abusing a child is more than three times greater for parents who were hit the most when they were teenagers.

Several other things need to be mentioned about Chart 6–3. First, the lines for mothers and fathers separately are similar. That means corporal punishment has a similar effect on men and women.

Second, the relationship shown is a net effect, after controlling or standardizing for seven other variables.

Third, Chart 6–3 does not show that everyone who was hit a great deal as a teenager will abuse a child. On the contrary, although a rate of 24 percent is astounding, it also needs to be read the other way around—it shows that 76 percent of parents who were hit a lot did *not* seriously attack their children. The opposite is also true. Just because parents were not hit as teenagers there is no guarantee that they will avoid physically abusing their children. In fact, about 7 percent did. That is an extremely high rate of abuse, even though it is a third of the rate for parents who were hit the most.

Finally, even though the highest rate of physical abuse is for the parents who were hit many times as teenagers, being hit even once at that age increases the chance that a person will abuse his or her own children. The risk is very small, but it is still there.

Conclusions

During the past 25 years, many well-respected scholars have argued that corporal punishment by parents increases the chances that they will go too far and physically abuse their children. The scientific evidence showing that corporal punishment is a risk factor for physical abuse, although not conclusive, is as good or better than the evidence for other suspected causes. Despite the evidence and the prestigious backing of this theory, corporal punishment has been virtually ignored as a cause of physical abuse by government and private agencies, and by authors of books on child abuse.

The main reason corporal punishment is neglected is probably because hitting children to correct and control them is so deeply ingrained in American culture that the idea of eliminating it is regarded as ridiculous, outrageous, or impractical. One purpose of this chapter was to make that idea seem less ridiculous by setting forth a possible theory and testing that theory.

Our review of previous studies and our analysis suggest that corporal punishment can lead to physical abuse by a process that works at several levels. At the *immediate incident* level, escalation occurs in a specific sequence between a parent and child: a parent spanks a child, the child rebels rather than complies, and the now even-angrier parent attacks the child in a way that crosses the boundary between legal corporal punishment and physical abuse.

Viewed *developmentally*, the more corporal punishment is used, the greater the risk of escalation because corporal punishment does not help a child develop an internalized conscience and leads to more physically aggressive behavior by the child (see Chap. 7 and Sears, Maccoby, and Levin, 1957; Marion, 1982; Straus, 1991). So the more parents rely on hitting, the more they will have to do it over time, and the greater the chance of the child hitting back (Straus, Gelles, and Steinmetz, 1980), further increasing the risk that corporal punishment will lead to physical abuse.

At the *macro-cultural* level, corporal punishment creates a social climate that approves of violence to correct wrongdoing and to achieve other socially desirable ends. This makes the public, and parents themselves, more tolerant of physical abuse. Cultural approval or tolerance of this sort is illustrated by a 1993 New Hampshire Supreme Court decision, which said that a child had not been physically abused even though he had welts visible five days after being beaten with a belt by his mother.

At the *inter-generational* level of analysis, corporal punishment increases the chance that when the child is an adult he or she will approve of interpersonal violence, be in a violent marriage, and be depressed. Thus, corporal punishment is one way physical abuse is transmitted from generation to generation.

The research in this chapter was at the inter-generational level. We found that more than half of the parents remembered being hit one or more times during their early teens (see Chapter 3), and that the parents who experienced corporal punishment were more likely to physically abuse their own children. Even one instance of being hit by parents at that age increased the chances of later being physically abusive. Parents who were hit the most had the greatest chance of physically abusing their own child.

Why does being hit as a child increase the chances of physically abusing your own children? We found three reasons: corporal punishment is tied in with attitudes favoring violence, with an increased chance of violence between the parents, and with an increased chance of depression. Each of these three reasons is associated with physical abuse.

Although the results in this chapter indicate that corporal punishment fosters physical abuse, there are important limitations to keep in mind. First, our study is about corporal punishment of parents when they were in their early teen years, and may not apply to parents who were hit only when they were younger. Second, the research used recall data, whereas experimental and prospective data is needed for a more definitive conclusion. Third, our study tested only part of the model developed in the theoretical section of this chapter.

Even with these limitations in mind, the research has important implications. At the very least, it suggests that more progress toward preventing physical abuse can be made if researchers and organizations concerned with reducing physical abuse stop ignoring corporal punishment. There is a certain irony in this conclusion because it is doubtful that any of the agencies mentioned in the introduction approve of parents hitting a teenaged child, yet they are silent on the issue. To start with, there should be programs to alert parents of teenagers to the risks they unknowingly subject their children to by hitting them even once. In the long run, we believe future research will show that this same principle applies to children of all ages.

7

Violence and Crime

Hitting a child who persists in some wrong behavior will usually, but not always, stop it. The long-term effect may be very different, however. In the long run, corporal punishment may *increase* the chances of misbehavior and even crime. The violent and criminal behavior this chapter examines includes violence against other family members, such as severe attacks on siblings, wife beating, and child abuse; and crime outside the family, such as delinquency, robbery, assault, and homicide.

I think that corporal punishment is really just a milder, culturally permissible form of physical abuse. Since this is the case, the research on "real" physical abuse (severe and illegal violence against a child) also should apply to corporal punishment. One reason to think that corporal punishment tends to make things worse in the long run is because many studies have shown that physically abused children have high rates of violence and crime later in life (Widom, 1989).

Ironically, the thought that corporal punishment increases rather than decreases crime escapes almost all parents because psychologists and authors of parental-advice books have been silent for so long on the research showing these effects. As a result, parents do not know about the many studies linking corporal punishment to an increased chance of the child being aggressive, even violent. With rare exceptions, child psychologists and authors are unaware of the irony. Their conspiracy of silence is a conspiracy of American culture, not a consciously devised effort to suppress the truth. In fact, to the extent that authors of these books have thought about it at all, they believe they are applying normal scientific standards by not presenting questionable research. They ignore the research showing that hitting children teaches children to hit because very little of it is based on experimental evidence (see Chapter 11). The problem is that this also applies to hundreds of studies of other issues that are mentioned in child psychology textbooks and in books for parents. Most child psychologists probably are aware of the book *Patterns of Child Rearing* (Sears, Maccoby, and Levin, 1957). This classic study clearly shows that children who are spanked the most are more aggressive and have less fully developed consciences. Some of what they found is shown in Chapter 9 (Charts 9–1 and 9–2). But even textbooks that mention other aspects of the study rarely point out the link between corporal punishment and aggression. Some authors go out of their way to deny the evidence. For example, Burton L. White, in his highly regarded *The First Three Years of Life* (1985), implicitly gives permission to spank children "after they entered the second year." White says, "The research done on this issue is far from conclusive." That is true, but then he goes on to say something that is not true: "There is *no evidence* that children who have been spanked (not abused) when they were young became either aggressive older children or abusive parents" (p. 253). On the contrary, a relatively large amount of research has been done on the link between corporal punishment and aggression and delinquency. Almost all of those studies show that children who are hit by their parents tend to have higher rates of hitting and other aggression (see the summary in Kandel, 1991. Some of the many specific studies include Agnew, 1983; Glueck and Glueck, 1950; Bandura and Walters, 1959; Hirschi, 1969; Sears, Maccoby, and Levin, 1957). Although none of the individual studies is conclusive, the cumulative weight of the evidence is probably stronger than that for most of the recommendations in White's book. We will return to this evidence in the concluding chapter.

This book extends the previous research on the effects of corporal punishment by looking into whether it is associated with violence and crime by adults. Chapter 6, which is on physical ouse, showed that the higher rate of aggression shows up wh. a these children are parents themselves. As parents, they have a ┠ gher rate of severely attacking their own children than the parents who were not hit when they were adolescents. This chapter adds wife beating, arrests, and other crimes to the scenario and introduces a theoretical principle that can help explain why corporal punishment is related to adult violence, including murder.

Corporal Punishment and Family Violence

Still another irony is revealed by a national survey that showed that parents are most likely to use corporal punishment when a child hits another child. Of the parents surveyed, 9 percent said they would hit if the child ignores a request to clean his or her room and 27 percent said they would hit for stealing something, while 41 percent would hit if the child hit another child (Lehman, 1989). If hitting the parent had been included in that study, the percentage could be double that. Although the irony of those figures seems obvious, it is not to most parents.

When parents are told that corporal punishment teaches the child the very thing they are trying to correct, the typical reactions are: "Children need to learn that they can't do that;" "But hitting a parent is really serious and I have to do something about it;" "Spanking is different—it's for when he does something really wrong." Few parents realize that children use exactly the same reasons for hitting other children. It is extremely rare for a child to just walk up to another child and hit him or her. Children hit other children when, in their minds the other child is doing something seriously wrong and won't listen to reason, as when a child says: She took all the toys and won't give me one; or He's squirting water at me and won't stop. This parallels the sort of things that lead parents to hit children. So, contrary to what most parents think, it is not different when parents hit children. When they spank and, ironically, when as good parents they explain why, they are teaching the child just what to do and what to say when he or she hits another child. In short, children learn from corporal punishment the script to follow for almost all violence. The basic principle of that script is what underlies most instances of parents hitting children—that when someone does something outrageous and won't listen to reason, it is morally correct to physically attack the offender. That principle, which is taught by corporal punishment,

CHART 7–1. Children whose parents used corporal punishment are more than twice as likely to severely attack a brother or sister than children whose parents did not. Physically abused children are even more likely to severely attack a sibling.

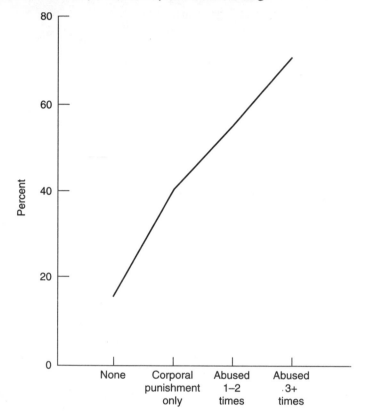

explains most instances of violence, ranging from a parent hitting a child, to a child hitting a sibling, to a husband or wife slapping his or her partner, to a man stabbing someone who makes a pass at his girlfriend or wife, to capital punishment and war. Lost along the way is the principle that all differences must be dealt with without violence (except where physical self-defense is involved).

Assaults on Siblings

Chart 7–1 is based on the 1,141 children in the 1975 National Family Violence Survey (as reported in Straus, 1983). It shows that "only" 18 percent of the "None" group (no corporal punishment in the previous year), repeatedly and severely attacked a sibling (kicked, bit, punched, or hit with an object three or more times during the year). The next group to the right in Chart 7–1 includes children whose parents used corporal punishment that year and did *not* physically abuse their child. Of this "corporal punishment only" group, 41 percent repeatedly and severely attacked a sibling. The rate of severe attacks goes up even further for children who were physically abused. It reaches an astounding 78 percent for children who were severely attacked by a parent three or more times that year. Although violence against siblings is greatest for children who were physically abused, the rate of repeated, severe violence against siblings by children who were "only" corporally punished is still more than double the rate of children whose parents did not hit them at all that year.

Of course, much of the corporal punishment occurred precisely because the child hit a sibling. Granted that, these findings suggest that hitting children to get them to stop hitting a brother or sister does not work. In fact, we believe that in the long run (a few weeks, a month, or a year later), corporal punishment *increases* the probability that the child will be physically violent. That idea could not be tested with the children we studied because there was no follow up in the National Family Violence surveys to see what the children were like a few months or a year later. However, we have begun to study the children in another large national survey who were followed up (the National Longitudinal Survey of Youth). The preliminary results show just what we expected—the children whose parents hit them to correct misbehavior had higher rates of misbehavior two years later than did children whose parents did not use corporal punishment.

Assaults on Spouses

Chart 7–2 is also based on the first National Family Violence Survey, but it uses data on all adults who were interviewed, not just those with children. The chart is based on the experiences of slightly less than 2,000 husbands and wives. It clearly shows that the more the participants were hit by their parents as adolescents, the higher the percentage who assaulted their *spouses* during the year of the survey. This effect applies to both men and women. It is important to remember that being hit as an adolescent is not a rare event. A

CHART 7–2. Adults who were hit as adolescents are more likely to hit their spouses.

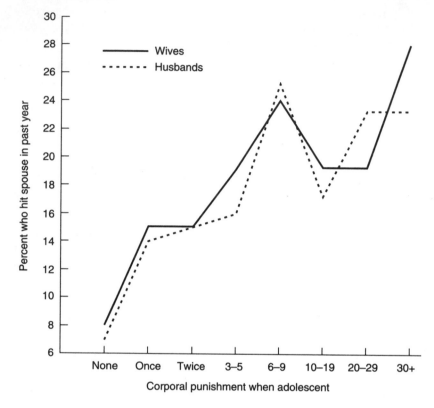

Corporal punishment when adolescent

majority of American adolescents are hit by their parents, which probably helps explain the high rate of violence between spouses in the United States.

Although Chart 7–2 shows that people who were hit a great deal as adolescents are more than three times as likely to hit their spouses when they are adults (25 percent compared to 7 percent), that is only part of the story. It is also important to keep in mind that most people who were hit as adolescents are not violent. The rate of assaults on spouses of those hit the most is about 25 percent, which means that 75 percent of those who were hit the most as adolescents did *not* hit their wives or husbands during the year covered by this study.

CHART 7–3. The more a parent hits a child, the greater the chances that the parent will also hit his or her spouse.

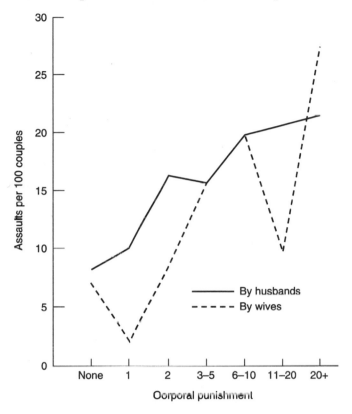

Effects of Hitting Children on Parents

Up to now, we have examined the effect that being a victim of corporal punishment has *on children*. This section examines the possibility that hitting children has an effect *on parents*. We looked into the idea that when a parent hits a child, it makes the parent more likely to hit others. The idea behind this is that parents who hit children are getting practice in the role of being physically violent. The more people practice this role, the more likely they are to generalize hitting to other situations in which people misbehave.

The process probably also operates at the cultural level through what is called "cultural spillover." The cultural spillover theory says that when a society makes violence legitimate in one sphere of life,

CHART 7–4. Teenagers who were hit by their parents are more likely to steal and physically assault someone.

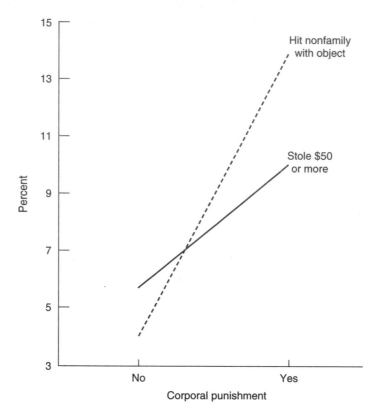

some people will apply that authorization to situations for which society does not authorize violence. The effect is presumably strongest for people who are engaged in culturally legitimate violence such as spanking. The combined effect of the cultural spillover and practice may be even stronger when the violence is required or expected, as it is for members of the armed forces. Shwed and Straus (1979) tested this theory by comparing military personnel in combat commands, where violence is a required part of the job, and in non-combat commands, which provide goods and services to the combat units. They found a higher rate of physical abuse among parents in combat units, even though most were in non-combat roles, including mechanics, truck drivers, and cooks.

Hitting your children is a type of violence that is legitimate and expected. True, the law only permits parents to hit children; it does not require them to do so. But, there are a number of reason why, in practice, corporal punishment is virtually required. As shown in Chapter 2, there is an almost universal belief that the welfare of the child and society requires hitting children "when necessary." These attitudes help explain why the non-spanking parents studied by Carson (1986) were under pressure to spank from relatives and friends.

This reasoning led us to expect that the more a parent uses corporal punishment on his or her child, the greater the probability of also hitting *a spouse*. Chart 7–3 shows this is true for both parents. A more refined statistical approach showed that it applies only to mothers, however. One possible explanation why is that violence is much less a part of the normal life experience and values of women than it is for men. Men do not "need" the role practice in violence provided by hitting children because the willingness to hit "if necessary" is so imbedded in male values and male culture in the United States. For women, however, carrying out a violent behavioral script in the form of hitting a child may provide an important learning experience. Children are not the only family members who misbehave and won't listen to reason. When a husband does something outrageous (as the wife sees it), wives who hit children frequently may be more inclined to also apply the Johnny, I've told you ten times script to their husbands.[1]

Corporal Punishment and Street Crime

A number of studies have shown that physical abuse in the family relates to violence and crime outside the family. For example, wife beaters and physically-abusing parents are more likely to also have committed crimes against non-family members (see the review in Hotaling, Straus, and Lincoln, 1989; Straus, 1985a). Other studies show that abused children, that is, children whose parents did things like kick, punch, or burn them, are more likely to engage in crime (Widom, 1989). But what about children whose parents restricted their violence to spanking and other legal forms of corporal punishment? Do those children have a high rate of delinquency and, when they grow up, are they more likely than others to be involved in crime? This important issue has rarely been studied

CHART 7–5. Regardless of whether the parents are violent to each other, the more corporal punishment parents use, the greater the chances of delinquency.

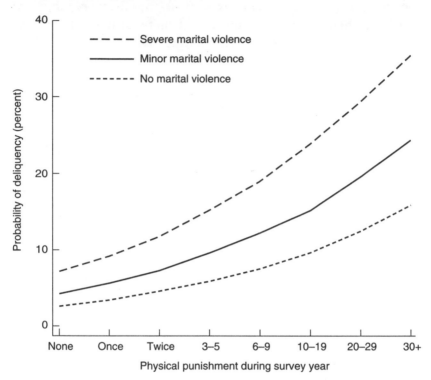

before (see McCord, 1988, for one of the exceptions). We therefore looked at whether corporal punishment is associated with an increased risk of juvenile delinquency, physical assaults later in life, and criminal arrest.

JUVENILE DELINQUENCY

Chart 7–4 is based on a survey of 385 college students. The students completed a questionnaire that included questions on corporal punishment by their parents and also questions on whether they had committed any of a list of typical juvenile crimes (see Appendix C). Chart 7–4 shows that students who were hit were more likely to be involved in both violent crime and property crime. Similar results were found for the other delinquent acts.

We also studied delinquency among the children in the second National Family Violence Survey (see Vissing et al., 1991, for the measure of delinquency). Unlike the college student data, the National Family Violence Survey covered children from birth through age 17. This made it possible to examine the relationship between corporal punishment and delinquency for children of all ages, not just corporal punishment of adolescents. We focused on children aged 8 through 17. Even more important, the survey contained data that could be used to control for the overlap of spanking with several family characteristics that might be the real cause of a relationship between spanking and these crimes. These included whether the parents were violent to each other, whether there was a drinking problem, and whether they were otherwise competent parents, as well as other family characteristics that are related to delinquency. We found that, even after controlling for the overlap between corporal punishment and other family characteristics, corporal punishment by itself is related to delinquency.

Chapter 4 showed that parents who are violent with one another also hit their children more than other parents. There is also evidence that growing up in a family where the parents physically attack each other increases the probability that the child will have psychological and social-relationship problems such as violence (Jaffe, Wolfe, and Wilson, 1990; Straus, 1991b). So, what seems to be an effect of corporal punishment might really be the effect of growing up in a family where the parents physically assault each other. Chart 7–5 was computed to see if the overlap of violence between parents and corporal punishment is the real explanation for the link between corporal punishment and delinquency. Chart 7–5 is consistent with previous research showing that children who grow up witnessing violence between their parents are more likely to be delinquent. The line for children whose parents severely assaulted each other is highest on the chart, indicating that they had the highest delinquency rate, while the line for "No Marital Violence" is lowest on the chart. However, all three of the lines in Chart 7–5 go up as corporal punishment increases. So, for children whose parents were not violent to each other and those whose parents were violent to each other, the more corporal punishment the parents used, the greater the chances of the child being delinquent.

CHART 7–6. Adults who were hit as adolescents are more likely to physically assault someone outside the family.

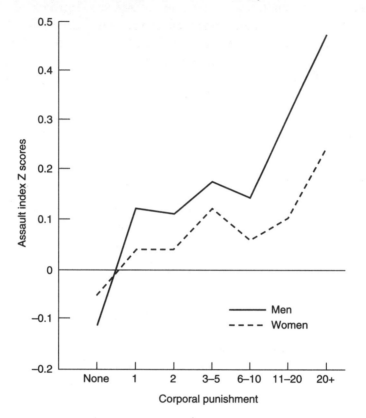

ASSAULTS AND ARRESTS

Chart 7–6 is based on the adults in the second National Family Violence Survey. It shows that the more a participant in the survey had been hit by his or her parents, the higher the proportion who committed physically aggressive acts outside the family in the year covered by the survey.

Corporal Punishment and Violence in Schools

No state in the U.S. has a law against parents hitting children, but the number of states that forbid it in schools is growing. In 1979, only four states prohibited corporal punishment in schools (Hyman and Wise, 1979).

Analysis of the national surveys of schools conducted by the federal Office for Civil Rights since 1979 and other data lead Hyman (1990) to conclude that at least 2 million to 3 million incidents of corporal punishment occur each year. Only one state—Hawaii—reported no instances of corporal punishment, but this also must be regarded with some caution since corporal punishment occurs even in states that prohibit it. Nevertheless, there are important differences between regions. The data for 1985 through 1986 indicates that the 12 Southern states accounted for about 80 percent of the incidents of corporal punishment in the nation's schools (Hyman, 1990).

The use of corporal punishment in schools is declining, however, or at least official permission to hit children is being withdrawn. By 1999, the states prohibited corporal punishment in schools. There also is considerable opposition today to ending corporal punishment in schools. The extent to which corporal punishment is used does not match the legal situation. It occurs in some schools despite legal prohibitions, while other schools in states that permit corporal punishment never use it, despite the nearly unanimous support of corporal punishment by parents.

The most vocal advocates of corporal punishment in schools are fundamentalist Christians (Greven, 1991), teachers' organizations, and school boards (Hyman, 1987). Many teachers and a large percentage of the public believe that, just as parents must have the right to use corporal punishment "when necessary," teachers also need a similar right to maintain discipline and order in schools. The hypothesis we tested is the opposite: that corporal punishment in schools increases rather than reduces violence.

Research most often shows that corporal punishment and aggression are linked because of "social learning," that is, when children imitate the parent's violence. As explained earlier, the cultural spillover theory argues that part of the explanation is to be found in characteristics of society. The cultural spillover theory was developed to explain the differences in violence rates between societies, such as the huge differences in the rates for murder and rape from one U.S. state to the next (Baron and Straus, 1987, 1988, 1989;

Baron, Straus, and Jaffee, 1988). Baron and Straus (1989) found that differences in criminal violence rates between societies can be explained somewhat by differences in the extent to which violence is used to punish criminals or to achieve other valued ends.

The concept behind the cultural spillover theory is that the more a society uses force for socially legitimate ends (using corporal punishment to correct misbehavior or to maintain order in schools, capital punishment to deter criminals, or wars to defend against foreign enemies), the greater the tendency for those engaged in illegitimate behavior to also use force for their own purposes. The following section applies the cultural spillover theory to the question of whether corporal punishment in schools deters or promotes crime.

State-to-State Difference

In 1979 there were large differences between states in the extent to which corporal punishment was permitted in schools. Some states permitted only the principal to hit children, others permitted the principal and teachers, but only under certain circumstances. At the extreme, some states permitted any school employee to hit a child and imposed no restrictions on the circumstances. At the time, Florida even prevented school districts from forbidding corporal punishment.

CORPORAL PUNISHMENT PERMISSION INDEX

Information on these state-to-state differences, listed by Hyman and Wise (1979), was used to give each state a Corporal Punishment Permission Index score. One point was given for each type of school employee who could legally hit students and one point for each circumstance. So, the higher the score, the more circumstances under which a child could be hit and the more school employees who could legally hit children. The states were divided into four categories: 0 (prohibits any corporal punishment), 2 to 4 points, and 5 to 9 points. The last category includes the states that permit corporal punishment in the largest number of situations or in *any* situation, that is, that had no legislation restricting hitting children in school.

The dotted line in Chart 7–7 is for the rate of assault within schools by students (from the National Safe School Study, 1978). It

CHART 7–7. States in which teachers are allowed to hit children have a higher rate of student violence and a higher murder rate.

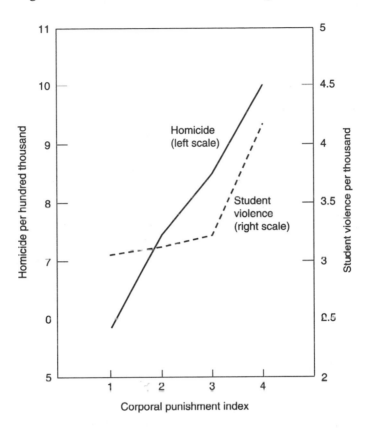

Corporal punishment index

shows that the more school personnel are authorized to use corporal punishment, the higher the assault rate by children with in schools. Of course, the reverse could also be true—the higher the rate of student assaults, the greater the authorization for corporal punishment by school personnel. These statistics, at a minimum however, show that hitting children does not reduce the level of in-school violence to the level found in schools without corporal punishment. We think that it actually increases the amount of student violence because teachers set an example and students tend to follow that example. Before we see how that works, let us assume that almost all teachers who use corporal punishment do so only for some serious problem. Note that research shows that when students are violent, it is also almost always for some reason that *they* think is a serious problem, such as stealing a prized and expensive piece of clothing.

Corporal Punishment in Schools and Homicide

The solid line in Chart 7–7 is the 1980 murder rate for the state as a whole. It shows that the more hitting of children that is permitted in the schools of a state, the higher the state's murder rate. Of course, very few of the murders in 1980 were committed by children. If that is the case, why is hitting children in school related to the number of murders? The murders in 1980 could have been committed by people who were hit in school a decade or more earlier, but such a direct link is not likely. A more likely explanation is that corporal punishment in schools and murders reflect state-to-state differences in an underlying tendency to use violence to correct problems. Corporal punishment in schools is an example of using violence to correct a problem, and so are most murders. About 60 percent of murders occur as part of a dispute or argument (Federal Bureau of Investigation, 1988). Both corporal punishment in schools and murders reflect an underlying culture of violence.

In a violent society, violence is used to control violence. This applies to corporal punishment and also to tough treatment of criminals, including using capital punishment and passing laws such as those recently enacted in Colorado and other states that allow citizens to use deadly force to protect their property. The question from the perspective of the cultural spillover theory is whether such laws will tend to legitimize violence and increase rather than decrease violent crime. When crime and violence flourish, even ordinarily law-abiding citizens can become caught up in that milieu. This is what happened in the New York subway when Bernard Goetz was menaced by four youths and shot and paralyzed one from the waist down (*Times Dailey*, 1985).

If the set of underlying cultural and social characteristics reflected in Chart 7–7 help to maintain and reinforce each other, that is immensely important. It suggests that one way to eventually reduce the murder rate is to reduce as many legitimate uses of violence as possible, including corporal punishment of children.

CHART 7–8. Nations where teachers favor corporal punishment have a higher rate of murder rate for infants.

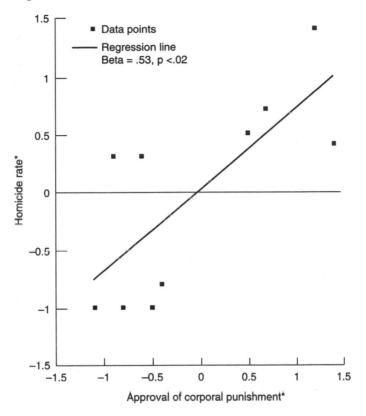

*Z Scores 10 Nations

Differences Between Nations

The final question we will look at in this chapter was tested by comparing 10 European countries. We used data on the attitudes of teachers to see if countries in which teachers are more favorable to corporal punishment have higher infant homicide rates. This hypothesis is important because it seems to defy common sense. Teachers who favor hitting children "when necessary" certainly do not favor murdering infants. Yet the cultural spillover theory predicts a higher infant homicide rate.

Nancy Burns and I tested this hypothesis using data on the degree to which teachers in 10 nations approved of corporal punishment (see Appendix C). The homicide rate for infants was the outcome variable. However, both the infant homicide rate and attitudes favoring corporal punishment tend to overlap with other variables that could be the real cause. Specifically, high military expenditures per capita were found to be related to a higher corporal punishment approval score; while wealth (Gross National Product per capita), educational expenditures, and the availability of physicians were associated with a lower infant homicide rate. To make sure that the analysis really tells us something about attitudes on corporal punishment, we used a statistical method called multiple regression to account for the overlap of these variables with each other (see Appendix C). After removing the overlap with the other variables, the results show the net effect of each variable. The results, given in Chart 7–9, show an association between attitudes favoring corporal punishment and an increase in the infant homicide rate.

These results are evidence of cultural spillover because approval of corporal punishment by teachers in no way implies that teachers approve of murdering infants. Such approval, however, creates the social conditions for increasing the rate of infant homicides. First, approval of corporal punishment increases the likelihood that corporal punishment will be used at all age levels, including infancy. The statistics in Chapter 2 showed that at least a fifth of American parents hit their infant children. Second, infants are extremely vulnerable. Shaking a six year old will rarely produce an injury, but shaking a six month old can be fatal. So, the more a society favors corporal punishment, the more frequently it will be used and the earlier in life it is likely to be used. The combination of starting early, hitting a lot, and vulnerability means that more infants are at risk of being killed in a society that favors corporal punishment, even though no one favors killing infants.

Socio-Cultural Context

At the 1993 annual meeting of the Eastern Sociological Society, two of the most respected African-American social scientists, Elija Anderson and Charles Willie, both said, "I was whupped, and I'm OK." Anderson, went on to say that "If you live in a society in which respect means willingness to be violent to uphold one's principles and be respected, how can parents who are not willing to whup a child be respected?" Many, if not most, African-Americans, both lay persons and social scientists, also argue that "strong discipline" in the form of corporal punishment is necessary to keep children out of trouble in an environment where trouble lurks on every block. Some also argue that corporal punishment is part of black culture.

Corporal punishment has become a part of black culture in response to slavery and oppression (Alvy and Marigna, 1987), and the continuation of that aspect of black culture interferes with progress towards equality (see Chapter 9). Corporal punishment is not a necessary part of strong discipline. Violence does not help people defend their honor or gain respect. In fact, the more a child is taught to "defend himself," the more likely he or she is to end up dead.

Anderson, Willie, and many other African-Americans who have "made it" were whupped. Their parents did use strong discipline, including hitting their children, but in my opinion, they made it despite being hit. Clear standards, consistency, monitoring the child's activities and whereabouts, and parental warmth and support made the difference. To attribute the success of such children to corporal punishment is equivalent to a "spurious correlation" (see section statistical controls in Appendix C). A person has to be aware of the misbehavior to punish for misbehavior. The "real" cause of their success is the standards and monitoring part of that package, not the hitting part. One of the most important things a parent in a high-crime environment can do to protect his or her child from being sucked into crime is to have clear rules and to monitor the child's activities. Many parents in that environment do not or cannot effectively monitor their children. Hitting without clear and consistent rules will not help, and it is likely to increase the chances that the child will get into trouble (Agnew, 1984). Since hitting without consistent standards and monitoring is so common, it is no wonder that what we reported in this chapter applies regardless of socioeconomic status—to African-American and Hispanic-American children, as well as to Euro-American children (Straus and Lauer, 1992).

Conclusions

It is virtually certain that part of the link between corporal punishment and crime occurs because "bad" children are hit and then go on to have a higher rate of criminal activity than other children.

CHART 7–9. Several processes affect whether corporal punishment increases violence and other crime.

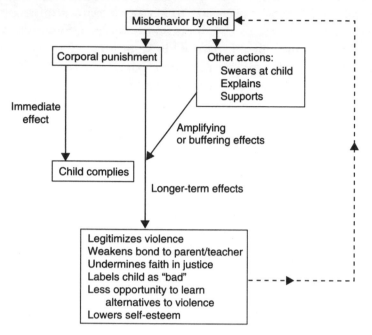

The important question is not whether misbehaving children are spanked, however, but whether spanking for misbehavior, despite stopping the misbehavior in the short run, tends to make things worse in the long run.

To find out if corporal punishment does make things worse over the long run, children who have been spanked need to be followed up over a period of months or years. Not many studies have done that. But the research that has been done shows that this is what tends to happen. Nagaraja (1984), Patterson (1982), and Patterson et al. (1987) studied children with severe behavior problems. They found that when the parents of these children used corporal punishment or verbal aggression to control the child's misbehavior, the child tried to use similar coercive tactics with the parents. The parents, of course, regarded this as more misbehavior and punished even more; and in turn the children became more coercive and hostile. This escalating feedback loop, in which parents unintentionally legitimize violence, is diagramed in Chart 7–9. Patterson and his colleagues have had a high rate of success in ending that vicious circle. Their approach included getting the parents of these highly aggressive and disruptive children to stop all use of corporal punishment.

Patterson's research is highly regarded by psychologists. But it has an important limitation because it applies only to children who were extremely disruptive and aggressive. People who favor corporal punishment argue that most children don't respond to it the way these children did. While that may be true, it is remarkable that one of the steps that got these difficult children back on track was to stop using corporal punishment.

This is one of many reasons why the idea that corporal punishment *increases* violence and delinquency needs the support of a long-term follow up of a representative cross-section of children. As mentioned earlier in this chapter, that is what my colleagues and I are now doing. The preliminary analyses show that corporal punishment does increase behavior problems.

Assuming that the preliminary results of the long-term study hold up, most people will find the evidence hard to believe. This is because they know that most children who are spanked do not become criminals. In fact, a typical American can say to himself or herself, "I was spanked and I wasn't a delinquent and I'm not a criminal." That is probably correct, but it does not show that corporal punishment is harmless. The confusion occurs because not everyone is harmed. Take a look at Chart 7–2 again. It shows that the rate of hitting a wife or husband goes up from about 7 percent for people who were not hit when they were adolescents to about 25 percent for people who were hit the most at that age. So, corporal punishment can more than triple the rate of marital violence. However, we also noted that this same figure of 25 percent means that 75 percent of people who were hit the most did *not* physically assault their wives or husbands during the year covered by our survey. This is parallel to what has been found by research on smoking. About a third of people who smoke more than a pack of day will die of lung cancer or some other smoking related disease (Mattson et al., 1987). However, that same figure also means that two thirds of very heavy smokers can say "I've smoked all my life and I'm ok," just as 75 percent of married men can say, "I was hit and I'm not a wife beater." (See the chapter on Myths That Perpetuate Corporal Punishment).

Why do some people who have been hit by their parents become violent and others do not? It is because many other characteristics and circumstances are involved in addition to corporal punishment. Chart 7–9 lists some of the circumstances that result in violence in some cases and not others. Two examples can illustrate this process. Both refer to the Other Actions box of Chart 7–9. First, violence is more likely if corporal punishment is accompanied by verbal assaults because this adds to the risk of damage to the child's self-esteem (Vissing et al., 1991). Second, violence is less likely if corporal punishment is administered along with reasoned explanations (Larzelere, 1986). Reasoning and explaining to the child reduces but does not eliminate the relationship between corporal punishment and child's aggressiveness.

Although Chart 7–9 shows that many factors are involved, research shows that hitting children to correct misbehavior has the opposite effect in the long run. Several family characteristics that could really account for the higher rate of violence and crime among those who were spanked were statistically controlled, which means that the relationship between corporal punishment and violence and crime is very real. Nevertheless, the research methods we used cannot definitively prove the theory because they do not establish whether hitting children causes the aggressiveness and delinquency, or the aggressiveness and delinquency causes the child to be hit. On the other hand, these methods could have falsified the theory. That is, they could have resulted in finding no relationship between corporal punishment and violence and other crime. Many analyses that could have falsified the theory instead found a clear link between corporal punishment and crime. This strengthens the case for the basic proposition of our theory—that although corporal punishment may produce short-term conformity, over the long run it increases the chances of violence and crime.

8

The Fusion of Sex and Violence

The popularity of Madonna's song "Hanky Panky (A Little Spanky)" and the rash of TV news-magazine shows recently on masochistic sex and bondage and discipline clubs, may reflect society's intrigue with those who enjoy pain, humiliation, or domination during sex. Of course, Americans may just be interested in sex of any kind or, possibly, anything that is taboo.[1]

How many people actually take part in masochistic behavior? Barbach and Levine (1980) concluded from a study of a sizeable but non-random sample of women that their most frequent sexual fantasies were about being dominant or submissive, including forms of bondage or spanking. Actual bondage was by far the most popular acted-out fantasy (p. 124). As one woman put it:

> One of my sexual fantasies that I always wanted to live out was having some sadomasochistic sexual experiences. Although I didn't want to be whipped and permanently damaged, I did want to feel that my partner was controlling the sex and that his control came in the form of physical demands, by either hitting me, tying me up, handcuffing me, or mild beatings. My lover at the time was also into that so it was great! It made our sex intense and arousing. I eventually outgrew the fantasy, but I really enjoyed it when I was going through it. (pp. 124–25)

Denise A. Donnelly is co-author of this chapter.

121

Kinsey et al. (1953) estimated that 12 percent of females and 22 percent of males became sexually aroused by masochistic stories. In response to one mild masochistic activity—biting—55 percent of women and 50 percent of men became sexually aroused, according to Kinsey. That was two generations ago, and many aspects of sex have changed since then. One of the purposes of this chapter is to provide a more recent estimate, but the main purpose is to try to understand why some people enjoy this type of sex. We theorize that the more a person was spanked by presumably loving parents as a child, the greater the chance that he or she will link love and violence and, therefore, want to be dominated, humiliated, or spanked as part of sex. The fusion is greatest when the parents are warm and affectionate.

A link between spanking and masochistic sex is not a new idea. Jean-Jaques Rousseau (*Confessions*, 1928) attributed his need to be spanked for sexual arousal to being spanked as a child. Rousseau was sent off to school at age eight and boarded with a minister and his sister. The minister's sister, Miss Lambercier, was a very loving and affectionate woman who nevertheless frequently used corporal punishment. As Rousseau puts it:

> She had often threatened it [spanking], and this threat of a treatment entirely new, appeared to me extremely dreadful; but I found the reality much less terrible than the idea, and what is still more unaccountable, this punishment increased my affection for the person who inflicted it. All this affection, aided by my natural mildness, was scarcely sufficient to prevent my seeking, by fresh offenses, a return of the same chastisement; for a degree of sensuality had mingled with the smart and shame, which left more desire than fear of a repetition. . . . Who would believe this childish discipline, received at eight years old, from the hands of a woman of 30, should influence my propensities, my desires, my passions, for the rest of my life, and that in quite a contrary sense from what might naturally have been expected? . . . When I became a man, that childish taste, instead of vanishing, only associated with the other. (pp. 19–23)

Freud (1961) saw childhood experiences and conflicts as contributing to adult masochistic preferences but did not specifically implicate corporal punishment. He saw masochism as a "need for punishment at the hands of a parental power" (p. 169), thus suggesting a link between corporal punishment and masochism.

Gibson (1978), Krafft-Ebing (1895), and Money (1986, 1987) also argued that being spanked as a child can lead to an adult interest in sexual activities that incorporate pain and humiliation similar to those experienced at the hands of parents. Philip Greven makes the same argument on the basis of historical data.

In the 1970s, when I first began to study why physical assaults were so common among married and cohabiting couples, this was my line of thinking:

> Learning about violence starts with corporal punishment, which is nearly universal. When corporal punishment is used, several things can be expected to occur. First, and most obviously, is learning to do or not do whatever the punishment is intended to teach. Less obvious, but equally or more important are three other lessons that are so deeply learned that they become an integral part of one's personality and world view.
>
> The first of these unintended consequences is the association of love with violence. Corporal punishment typically begins in infancy with slaps to correct and teach. Mommy and Daddy are the first and usually the only ones to hit an infant. And for the most part this continues throughout childhood. The child therefore learns that those who love him or her the most are also those who hit.
>
> These [and other listed] indirect lessons are not confined to providing a model for later treatment of one's own children. Rather, they become such a fundamental part of the individual's personality and world view that they are generalized to other social relationships . . ." (Straus, 1978: 453–4)

While the connection between childhood spanking and an adult interest in pain, bondage, or flagellation has been argued theoretically and is supported by some clinical case evidence, we have not been able to locate research that tested this proposition in a segment of the general population. This chapter makes a start on filling that gap in knowledge. It is only a start, however, because it is very difficult to establish a cause-and-effect link between spanking and certain adult behavior, such as masochistic sex. Definitive evidence requires an experiment in which parents agree beforehand to be assigned to one of two groups, but without knowing which one. Half of the parents, chosen randomly, would be put into a group that is assigned to spank under certain conditions. The other half would be in a group instructed to never spank or hit in any way. When the children are adults, their level of interest or participation in masochistic sex could be compared. Obviously, no one would conduct an experiment like that because of the serious ethical, technical, and practical problems. Fortunately, the question of whether spanking leads to masochistic sexual interests, or whether masochistic sexual interests lead to spanking is not as critical as whether spanking leads the child to be aggressive or the child's aggression leads the parents to spank. Parents do spank children who hit other children, so it is important to find out the cause and the effect, that is, to determine whether spanking to control aggression tends to make the child even more aggressive in the long run. Cause and effect also is important when it comes to the relationship between spanking and masochistic sex. We think it is less important however, because parents are not likely to know about whether their children are engaging in masochistic sex and it is therefore not something for which they are likely hit their child.

Lovemaps

Money (1986 and 1989) introduced the term *lovemaps* to refer to the routes that an individual's mind must follow to arrive at sexual pleasure and satisfaction. The lovemap is a template in the mind that determines what is erotic, pleasurable, and sexually satisfying. Under average childhood conditions, the lovemap is heterosexual and relatively uncomplicated. But when lovemaps are "vandalized," the child comes to connect erotic arousal with acts that for most people have no sexual connotations. Money considers lovemaps most vulnerable from ages four to nine. He believes they can be vandalized by adults who punish and humiliate the child for engaging in sexual rehearsal play or when the child is prematurely introduced to sexual play, especially with infliction of harm or pain (Salkin, 1990).

Money argues that because the centers of the brain that process feelings of sexual arousal and feelings of pain are in such close proximity, when they are stimulated simultaneously many times over a long period of time, the brain can no longer separate the two. So feelings of sexual arousal and pain become forever woven together. This fusion is especially likely because the most common age for spanking is two to six, which substantially overlaps the age that Money regards as most vulnerable for lovemap vandalism.

Sexual Scripts and Other Influences

Money's theory hinges on a neurological link between brain centers that process feelings of sexual arousal and feelings of pain, but to date there is no direct neurological evidence. Even if there were such evidence, it would not mean that spanking and neurological fusion are the only ways of producing masochistic sex. For example, Gagnon (1977) argues that sexual behavior is based on learned sexual scripts, or mental scenarios for behavior. These are mental plans that take into account past, present, and planned actions. Scripts help determine which course of behavior we will take and set standard ways of behaving in given settings (Byer and Shainberg, 1991). As people mature, they develop sexual scripts through their sexual experiences and erotic contacts with others. Sexual activity generally follows these scripts, which tell them what is exciting sexually. So, if a person learns to associate pain or humiliation with love or pleasure, sexual scripts may develop that require pain or humiliation to become sexually aroused.

Glickauf-Hughes and Wells (1991) attribute the development of masochism to growing up in a hostile, intrusive, and unpredictable environment. They argue that masochism is caused by two types of influences. The first is early deprivation, such as erratic nurturing, a weak parent-child attachment, and the parent's inability to meet the child's needs. The second is growing up in an unpredictable environment where the child is punished and praised for the same behavior, where parents are ambivalent or inconsistent, and where parents are more concerned with their own needs than those of their child. In these households, children often are treated badly under the guise of love. They may come to associate mistreatment with love, regardless of whether the parents spanked.

Lynn Chancer (1992) argues that masochism is a product of a society, such as that in the United States, that is characterized by domination and subordination in most spheres of life. Chancer's theory suggests that masochism is more likely to occur in a society with a rigid class system, male dominance, and other unequal social relationships. This type of society produces masochistically inclined people regardless of whether they have been subjected to experiences, such as spanking, that fuse love and violence.

There also is the possibility that inherited behavior patterns can lead a child who was spanked to masochism as an adult. Imagine a parent who is genetically inclined toward being masochistic. If this tendency can be inherited, his or her child is more likely to have those traits than the children of other parents. If masochistically inclined parents tend to spank more, that might be a part of the link between spanking and a tendency to masochism.

There are probably other processes that might explain masochism as well. For this book, however, the most relevant theory is the effect of spanking and other legal forms of corporal punishment.

Masochistic Sex Among College Men and Women

This chapter is based on questionnaires completed by 455 students (163 men and 292 women) in sociology and psychology classes at three universities and colleges in the Northeast (see Appendix C for more information on the sample). The questionnaires asked the students about relationships with parents while growing up, including how often their parents used corporal punishment. They also were asked about their current sexual practices and interests, including whether and how often they had been sexually aroused by thinking about or doing a number of masochistic sexual acts.

When this study was planned, we were worried about using a college student sample. We were afraid that given their age, there would be too few who had been aroused by a masochistic act or fantasy to provide enough cases for reliable statistics. Our worry turned out to be unnecessary. In fact, the opposite occurred—the numbers were unbelievably high. An amazing 61 percent of the students said that they had been sexually aroused while imagining or doing one or more of the three activities in the Masochistic Sex Index (see Appendix C for information on that measure). Then we remembered that a little more than half of the people studied by Kinsey had been aroused by one mild masochistic activity—biting.

In view of the Kinsey study findings, our finding concerning another mildly masochistic activity, being sexually aroused by "Engaging in playful fights and being physically rough with a partner,"

CHART 8–1. More men than women are aroused by masochistic sex.

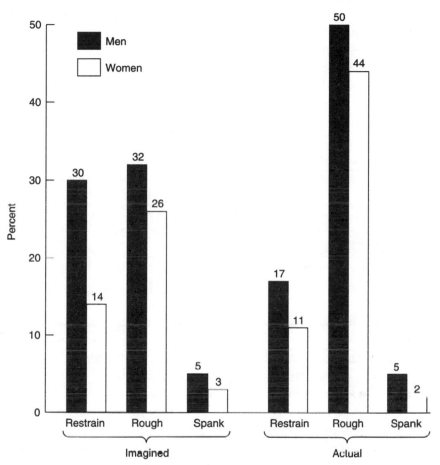

is not out of line. Almost half the students we studied (46 percent) reported being sexually aroused by a play fight. A much lower but still very large number—29 percent—said that they had become excited by imagining a play fight.

Nor did we find a large difference between the number who had been sexually aroused by imagining and those by engaging in the other two activities in the Masochistic Sex Index. Twenty percent of the sample became sexually aroused while imagining "Having a partner restrain me as part of sex play" and almost the same percentage—13 percent—became excited while actually being restrained.

The least-frequent type of masochistic activity was "Having a partner spank me as part of sex play." Just over three percent of the students were sexually aroused by being spanked, and an equal number were aroused by fantasies of spanking.

Chart 8–1 compares men and women on mildly masochistic behaviors and indicates that more men than women had been sexually aroused by imagining or doing each of the three. The differences between men and women are somewhat greater for fantasizing about masochistic sex (shown in the left half of Chart 8–1) than for actually taking part in it. That is, men are more likely to fantasize about masochistic sex than women, but when it comes to actual behavior (the right side of Chart 8–1), there is less of a difference between men and women. The biggest difference is in fantasizing about being restrained. Almost a third of the men became sexually aroused fantasizing about being restrained, compared to one out of seven women. The smallest differences between women and men were in actually engaging in rough sexual play. The rate for men (50 percent) is only 14 percent greater than the rate for women (44 percent).

The percentages in Chart 8–1 also can be used to calculate the ratio of men to women in fantasizing or imagining masochism. These calculations show that men are 2.1 times more likely to fantasize about being restrained than women, but only 1.5 times more likely to become excited by activity engaging in this behavior. Men are 1.2 times more likely to fantasize about playful fights or rough sex play than are women, but only very slightly more likely (1.1 times) to become excited while engaging in playful fights and rough sex play. Finally, men are 1.7 times more likely to fantasize about being spanked than women, and 2.5 times more likely to become excited by actually being spanked as part of sex.

Chart 8–2 which uses all six questions in the Masochistic Sex Index, provides more information on the extent of masochistic interest by the men and women. A score of zero means that the student reported never having been aroused by either imagining or doing any of the three activities. A score of one means that the student reported having been aroused in response to only one of the activities. Scores of 2, 3, 4, and so on mean that the student reported sexual arousal in 2, 3, 4, or more of the six questions. Chart 8–2 shows that men are more likely than women to imagine or engage

CHART 8–2. A much larger percentage of women than men have never been aroused by masochistic sex. However, for those who have been, there is not much difference in the the number of kinds of arousal.

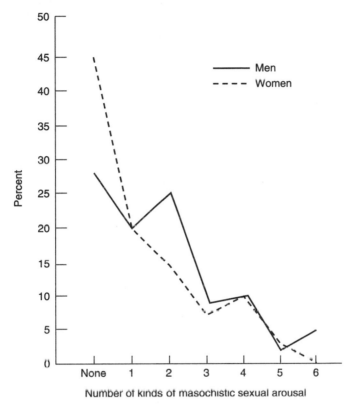

Number of kinds of masochistic sexual arousal

in masochistic behavior: only 28 percent of the men did not become aroused by any of the masochist acts, compared to 45 percent of the women. Putting it the other way, 72 percent of the men were sexually aroused by at least one masochistic behavior, compared to 55 percent of the women. These are important differences, but they should not obscure the fact that the majority of women as well as men had been sexually aroused by masochistic sexual fantasies or acts. Perhaps this reflects the fact that very large percentage has experienced corporal punishment at the hands of those they loved as children and adolescents.

Corporal Punishment and Masochistic Sex

The different statistical figures for men and women and the fact that a majority of these college students had become sexually aroused by masochistic sex are important. But, the main issue for this book is whether there is a relationship between corporal punishment and masochistic sex. Chart 8–3 gives the results of testing this theory (see Appendix C for the details). To create this chart, the students were divided into groups based on the amount of corporal punishment they experienced. Group 1 at the left side of the chart is the fifth of students who experienced the least corporal punishment. The upper line is for men, and the lower line is for women. It is evident that among both men and women, those in group 1 at the left side had the lowest chance of having been sexually aroused by one or more of the masochistic sexual activities we studied—about a 40 percent chance for women and a 46 percent chance for men. Reading Chart 8–3 from left to right shows that

CHART 8–3. As corporal punishment increases, so does the chance of masochistic sex as an adult.

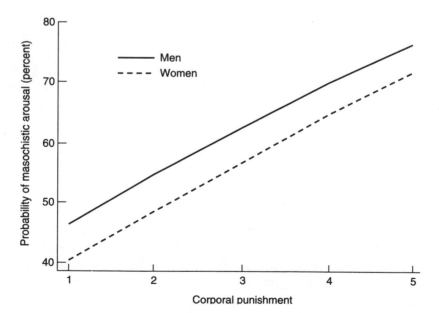

increases in the amount of corporal punishment are associated with substantial increases in the probability of being sexually aroused by masochistic activities. Students in the group who were hit the most (group 5 at the right) were the most likely to become aroused by masochistic activities. The chance of arousal for women goes up from 40 percent at the left side of the chart to 71 percent at the right side, which included women in the high-scoring group. Similarly, for men, the chance of being aroused by a masochistic sexual activity increases from 46 percent for the least-punished group to 75 percent for the most frequently hit group. These percentages hold true even after statistically removing the effects of five types of parent behavior that might explain the increase better than corporal punishment: parental warmth, consistency, monitoring, reasoning, and severe violence or physical abuse. Appendix C describes how each was measured.

In general, Chart 8–3 shows that the more children were hit by their parents, the greater the probability they were sexually aroused as adults by imagining or engaging in certain masochistic activities. Chart 8–3 also shows that, even though more men than women have an interest in masochistic sex, the relationship between this interest and corporal punishment is almost identical for men and women.

So far, we have focused entirely on spanking. Parental warmth and love, also have a lot to do with masochistic sex. Of the six parental behaviors we studied, warmth and corporal punishment are the only two that are related to masochistic sex. The upper line in Chart 8–4 is for students who were in the highest group for corporal punishment. The lower line is for students in the lowest group of corporal punishment. This indicates that high corporal punishment is linked to masochistic sex.

The downward slope of the lines in Chart 8–4 shows that the more warmth and affection by parents, the *lower* the chances of masochistic sex. Both lines slope down, which shows that warmth helps insulate children from masochism regardless of whether they experienced little or no corporal punishment (the lower line) or a great deal of it (the upper line). In fact, lack of parental warmth is more closely related to sexual masochism than anything else we studied.

CHART 8–4. Warmth by parents decreases the chances of masochistic sex as adults for children who were spanked and not spanked.

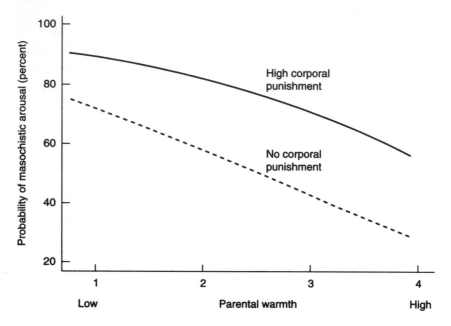

The idea that parental warmth protects children from masochism may at first seem inconsistent with our theory that the effect of spanking is worst when the parents were also warm and affectionate. Actually, we found support for both propositions.[2] Chart 8–4 seems to be inconsistent with our theory because it shows the effect of warmth when the effect of all the other possible causes that we studied are held constant. When the *combination* of high warmth and spanking is considered, as in Chart 8–5, then the findings on warmth and spanking are consistent with each other.

Chart 8–5 refers to male students. The upper line shows the effect of spanking on masochism when the parents are very low in warmth. The fact that the line is so high up in the chart indicates that these students have an extremely high rate of arousal by masochistic sex. However, reading from left to right, that line does not increase very much as corporal punishment goes up. It goes from about 82 percent at the left to about 91 percent on the right, a difference of only 9 percentage points.

CHART 8–5. The link between corporal punishment and masochistic sex is greater when the parents are warm and loving.

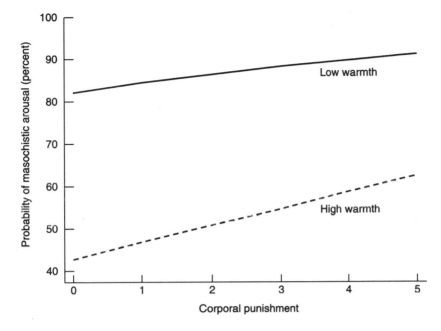

The lower line in Chart 8–5 represents the effect of spanking when the parents are very warm and affectionate. The line is lower on the chart because parental warmth lowers the risk of developing a masochistic sexual interest. On the other hand, if these warm and loving parents also spank, the spanking has a strong effect on the risk of becoming sexually masochistic. The rate goes up from 43 percent at the left to 62 percent at the right. This is a difference of 19 percentage points, which is more than double the difference that is associated with spanking by cold and indifferent parents. What this boils down to is that when parents are cold and indifferent, spanking does not make much difference. Their children are the ones most likely to be masochistic because they do not have much of a chance to know what love and affection are really like. Similarly, children whose parents were the most warm and loving generally had the lowest chance of being attracted to masochistic sex. Among the children whose parents were warm and affectionate, however, the more the parents spanked, the more likely the child was to be aroused by masochistic sex. Or, as Rousseau put it, when there is "All this affection . . .," each increase in the amount of spanking is associated with a relatively large increase in the probability of masochistic sex. To put this in perspective, Chart 8–5 also shows that being brought up parents who lack warmth and affection produces a higher rate of masochistic sex than any combination of warmth and spanking.

A chart similar to Chart 8–5 was computed for women, and the results are very similar to those just presented for men. However, both lines are somewhat lower on the chart because as adults, fewer women than men were sexually aroused by masochistic sex.

Conclusions

According to the diagnostic manual of the American Psychiatric Association, masochistic sex is ". . . not part of normative arousal-activity patterns. . . ." (DSM III-R, p. 279). That may be true in the sense of cultural norms, but it seems to be off the mark statistically. Almost two-thirds of the college students we studied were sexually aroused by at least one of the activities in the Masochistic Sex Index. It appears that at least some masochistic fantasies or behaviors are a common part of the sexual repertoire of the majority of college students, not a rare form of sexual deviance.

There is also the stereotype that women are more inclined toward masochism than men. For sexual masochism, we found the opposite. We found that more men than women have an attraction to sexual masochism.

The most important result of this study is not so much what we found out about the effect of spanking on masochistic sex. It is that lack of parental warmth is even more strongly related to masochistic sex than spanking. Nevertheless, we did find that spanking is linked to how much corporal punishment a child experienced, regardless of whether the parents were cold, or warm and loving. For both men and women, the more a child was hit by parents, the greater the probability of being aroused by masochistic sex. Our research suggests that the widespread use of corporal punishment on American children is one reason for today's interest in sexual masochism, as shown in this chapter.

These statistics do not mean that spanking and lack of warmth are the only causes, or even necessary causes, of masochistic sex. If that were the case, there would be no masochistic sex among students whose parents were warm and caring and who rarely or never used corporal punishment. In fact, Chart 8–4 shows that these children have about a 27 percent chance of being aroused by imagining or engaging in masochistic sex. One of the reasons may be that reward for good behavior and punishment for bad behavior are just about inevitable in bringing up children. This can lead children to believe that they are worthy of love only after punishment for being "bad."

In future research, we plan to explore what is behind the relationship between corporal punishment and masochism. Money (1986) believes that this connection exists because of connections established in the brain cells as a result of experiencing love and pain simultaneously during a critical period in the brain's development. This is probably correct, but there is no reason to think that those brain linkages are any different than the brain linkages associated with learning anything else.

Regardless of whether sexual masochism involves a unique type of change in the brain cells, changes that occur with ordinary learning, or inherited predispositions, not everyone who is hit a great deal by his or her parents becomes a sexual masochist. We already know that the warmth and affection of parents affect whether a person becomes a sexual masochist.

We also already know that whether the child is a boy or a girl makes a difference. The statistics in this chapter show that men have higher rates of fantasizing about and participating in masochistic sex. One explanation for the higher rate harks back to the Kinsey studies (1948, 1953). That research uncovered statistical evidence for what everyone assumed—that men have more interest in *every* type of sexual activity than women. Perhaps, as Kinsey suggested, there is a biological basis for this. Or, perhaps it is simply that men and women are socialized differently. Men are encouraged to be more sexual, more daring, and to take more chances than women. So the higher arousal rate by men from masochistic sex may be just another manifestation of their greater interest in sex in general. An equally likely and intriguing possibility is that boys are at greater risk for developing sexual masochism because boys are spanked somewhat more than girls (see Chapter 2). Finally, boys may get less affection from parents, and we have seen that the lack of warmth and affection as a child is associated with masochistic sex as an adult.

The higher rate of sexual masochism among men raises some interesting questions. For example, as mentioned earlier, popular wisdom has it that women are more likely to fantasize about being tied up and sexually ravaged than are men. Consider the so-called "bodice-ripper" novels, for example, which are read almost exclusively by women. It is true that many women in our sample were sexually aroused by masochistic sex, but even more men were aroused, however. Almost twice as many men as women were sexually aroused while fantasizing about being restrained. Perhaps the greater risk of being raped makes these fantasies less palatable for women than for men.

Another interesting difference between men and women is that the gender differences are greater for fantasizing about masochistic sex than for actually taking part in it. This is contrary to the idea that women are more likely to fantasize about sex, and men more likely to do it. However, this may simply reflect the fact that fewer college women than men engage in any kind of sexual act.

Among the many other issues that need to be investigated are whether corporal punishment is also linked to more severe forms of masochism, whether corporal punishment is also related to sadism, and if so, whether the circumstances are similar. We suspect the circumstances are not. Our research so far suggests that when corporal punishment is combined with love, masochism is the result. Perhaps an equal amount of hitting by cold and indifferent parents will more likely result in sadism than masochism. This speculation is an example of how important it is for research on corporal punishment to take into account a variety of other parent behaviors.

Most parents probably precede or follow corporal punishment with declarations of love for their children, at least occasionally. They do not realize the confusing message that they send. Of course, spanking with love is preferable to spanking without love. Corporal punishment without love puts the child at risk of profound damage to self-esteem and for developing a resentful, cold, and aggressive personality, and sometimes even murderous aggression. Fortunately, it is not necessary to choose between styles of parenting that increase the probability of masochistic tendencies (corporal punishment with love) and those that increase the probability of aggression (corporal punishment without love). The alternative is to keep the love and affection, but stop hitting.

9

Alienation and Reduced Income

The American Dream is the hope that children will rise higher on the social ladder, earn more, and enjoy a life-style better than their parents. This chapter looks at the idea that hitting children to correct and control their behavior *reduces* their chances of attaining the American Dream. Occupation and income, of course, involve far more than the dreams of parents for their children. They also affect mental health. Americans tend to evaluate themselves and others on the basis of income and occupation, so a person's position on the occupational ladder and earnings influence his or her self esteem.

The idea that corporal punishment affects how high up the occupational ladder a person climbs and how much money he or she earns is probably something that most people think is even more ridiculous than the idea that spanking causes depression or violence later in life. But if it is true, it might be the one thing that will convince American parents to stop hitting their children.

The connection between corporal punishment and economic achievement was suggested by a study showing that women who were sexually abused as children had lower incomes than those who were not abused. This was the case even after taking into account other characteristics that also affect occupational and economic attainment, such as how much education they had completed (Hyman, 1993).

Holly S. Gimpel is co-author of this chapter.

CHART 9–1. Why does corporal punishment leads to lower economic achievement?

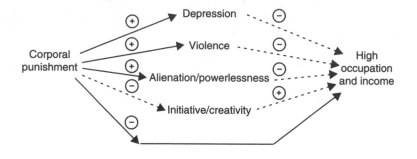

Hyman assumes that sexual abuse is an experience that traumatizes many victims and impairs their physical and mental health, which in turn lowers economic achievement. That assumption also probably applies to the effects of corporal punishment.

It is not too far fetched to believe that when a child is hit by someone he or she loves and depends on, it can be traumatizing. A severely traumatic experience can have wide-ranging effects that might spawn characteristics that could impair occupational success. Besides that, children cannot escape the parents who punish them. So, even if no single instance is traumatizing, they may be similar to the laboratory animals in Seligman's experiments on "learned helplessness" who became passive and withdrawn as a way of adapting to punishment they could not escape (Seligman and Garbor, 1982).

We already have seen that corporal punishment is related to an increased probability of depression and violence. Being passive, depressed, or physically violent are not traits that endear a person to an employer or fellow employee. Future research might reveal still other types of psychological injury that could interfere with moving up the occupational ladder.

Of course, there is no simple, one-to-one link between corporal punishment and economic achievement. If there is a relationship, it might have a number of causes. Chart 9–1 lists some of the effects of corporal punishment that might interfere with occupational and economic achievement. The solid lines represent links for which the evidence was given in previous chapters or will be given in this chapter. The dashed lines are for links that are important parts of the theory but for which we have no data.

The two characteristics at the top of the chart, "Depression" and "Violence," were talked about in previous chapters. Depression has been proven to be an important factor in impaired economic achievement. Several studies have shown that mental health problems result in substantially lower income (Bartel and Taubman, 1979, 1986; Benham and Benham, 1981; Frank and Gertler, 1991). The effect of violent tendencies on income has not been documented in previous research, but it could be similar. After all, a person who is about to fly off the handle and hit someone is not likely to be highly regarded, especially in high-level occupations.

Data on the middle variable, Alienation/Powerlessness," will be presented in this chapter. Alienation was included in Chart 9–1 because correcting misbehavior by using corporal punishment carries a high risk of creating a sense of powerlessness and alienation in the developing child. Alienation in turn may interfere with later occupational success and income. If this is true, alienation may be a key to understanding why corporal punishment may cause lowered occupational and economic achievement. To see if corporal punishment is linked to feeling alienated and powerless as an adult, we used data from a survey of 238 students in two New England colleges (see Appendix C).

Our surveys do not have data on the "Initiative/Creativity" part of Chart 9–1, which deserves future study. However, we believe future research will show that corporal punishment decreases initiative and creativity. Corporal punishment teaches children what to think, not how to think.

Finally, the line at the bottom of Chart 9–1 represents a major point this chapter will make—that corporal punishment is linked to lowered prospects for occupation and income. The idea was tested using the experience of the people who participated in the 1975 National Family Violence Survey (see Appendix B)

Chart 9–1 deliberately leaves out some key points that were in the statistical analysis in Appendix C (such as gender and socioeconomic status) in order to focus attention on the unique parts of the theory. To keep Chart 9–1 from getting too complicated, we omitted other logically possible paths between variables.

A more adequate test of the theory would need data for each person on all the characteristics listed in Chart 9–1. Getting this data is part of our plans for future research. In addition, there are no doubt other processes that might produce a relationship between corporal punishment and a lower probability of high economic achievement. For example, Brian and Freed (1982) found a link between corporal punishment and lower grades in college, and poor grades are a handicap in landing a first job that has good prospects for the future. Despite the limitations of data used for this chapter, the issue is so important that it was worth trying to piece together an answer using the data that was available.

Corporal Punishment and Achievement

Occupational and economic achievement was measured by occupational prestige, or how high up the occupational ladder a person had climbed, and how much money he or she earned in the previous year. High occupational and economic achievement was defined as being in the upper fifth of the sample (see Appendix C). Since the sample is large and representative of married couples and people living together, this means that the high group is the top fifth economically of the United States. For brevity, instead of referring to them as being high in occupational and economic achievement, from here on, we will use the term *economic achievement*.

The results of analyzing data on the 1,377 men and women who participated in the first National Family Violence survey are in Chart 9–2. This chart shows that the adverse effect of corporal punishment on economic achievement depends on how many years of education a person has finished.

The bottom line in Chart 9–2 represents people who did not finish high school. Contrary to our theory, the chance of high economic achievement does not go down with increasing amounts of corporal punishment. For men and women with less than a high school education, there is almost no relationship between corporal punishment and high occupational and economic achievement. The second line up in Chart 9–2 is for people with a high school diploma. The line slopes slightly downward, indicating that the more corporal punishment, the lower their chances of high economic achievement. The effect of corporal punishment is very small, how-

CHART 9–2. The more corporal punishment in adolescence, the lower the chances of being in the top fifth economically, especially for college graduates.

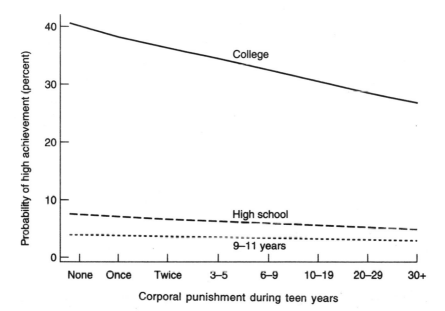

ever. The top line is for people who completed college. For this group, there is a clear tendency for corporal punishment to be associated with a lower chance of high occupational and economic achievement.

These findings raise the intriguing question of why the adverse effect of corporal punishment on economic achievement applies mainly to people with a college education. One guess is because different occupational and economic opportunities are available to people with different levels of education. People who did not finish high school, probably face a ceiling effect that limits their chances, no matter what their personal characteristics. People who did not complete high school have very limited chances of landing a high-prestige job or earning a high income, regardless of whatever personal characteristics they may have from corporal punishment.

High school graduates have somewhat greater opportunities, but the slight downward slope of the middle line in Chart 9–2 suggests that those who suffer from the effects of corporal punishment are slightly less able to take advantage of those opportunities. College-educated people have the greatest opportunities and the greatest possibility that a personal or social problem such as depression could interfere with their economic achievement.

A number of other possible causes of low economic achievement were taken into account, such as having parents of low socioeconomic status or parents who physically attacked each other. The main reason for including them was to make sure that the effect of corporal punishment on economic achievement is something that persists after accounting for these variables. Their relation to economic achievement is important even though they were not directly diagramed in Chart 9–1.

In brief, the people who were in the top fifth of our study (see Appendix C):

• Had a father in a high-level occupation
• Were college graduates
• Were older
• Had parents who were physically violent to each other

The first three of these points are hardly surprising because they have been found in dozens of previous studies. They are important in this context because they indicate that the results of the survey are consistent with established knowledge. On the other hand, the finding that people whose parents were violent to each other have an *increased* probability of high economic achievement is puzzling and needs to be studied in future research.

Alienation

The theory diagramed in Chart 9–1 argues that corporal punishment limits economic achievement mainly for those who have or aspire to high-level jobs because it promotes the development of characteristics that interfere with success in that type of job. One of these characteristics is a feeling of being powerless and alienated. This is the opposite of what is needed for many, if not most high-level jobs. They demand a person who is involved rather than turned off, someone who feels empowered to take charge and do what is necessary to get the job done.

CHART 9–3. The more corporal punishment as an adolescent, the greater the chances of being alienated as an adult.

To measure alienation, we used a standard test—the alienation scale developed by Dwight Dean (see Appendix C). This test includes two aspects of alienation: a feeling of powerlessness and a "normlessness," a belief that there really are no firm moral standards—that anything goes. The normless aspect may seem surprising since most people believe that spanking can and should be used to instill moral standards. According to out theory, however, spanking often does the opposite. It teaches that might makes right.

The data summarized in Chart 9–3 are consistent with our alienation theory. Chart 9–3 shows that the more corporal punishment of a teenager by the father, the greater the chances he or she will be highly alienated. Similar results were found for corporal punishment by the mother. The fact that the lines in Chart 9–3 for men and women are parallel to each other shows that the relationship between corporal punishment and alienation is almost identical for men and women. At the same time, the fact that the line for men is higher on the chart shows that men are more likely to be alienated.

The higher rate of alienation among men raises an important question: If men tend to be more alienated, and if alienated people have lower economic achievement, why aren't women in charge of the American economy? The answer is important for understanding almost everything in this book because the same principle applies. The principle is that something as complex as economic achievement or depression has multiple causes. There is no one explanation. In this case, alienation is only one of many things that influence occupational and economic achievement. Many other factors affect women's economic achievement, and these outweigh the effect of being less alienated than men. Some of the most important influences are culturally embedded differences between men and women in roles and occupational interests, and culturally embedded discrimination in the labor market.

The findings in Chart 9–3 suggest that although corporal punishment may force people to conform to rules, it comes at the cost of giving the child a sense of being powerless and undercutting the development of conscience. Thirty-five years ago, a classic study of American parenting, *Patterns of Child Rearing* (Sears, Maccoby, and Levin, 1957), also found that corporal punishment was linked to an impaired development of conscience (see Chapter 10). Piaget's work also suggests that "corporal punishment may arrest moral development. . . ." (Worr, Zax, and Banner, 1983, p. 251).

One important feature of the analysis done to produce Chart 9–3 is that it also tested the widely held belief that if the hitting is done by loving parents who explain what they are doing, there will be no adverse side effects. So, measures of nurturance and reasoning were included in the analysis. The table in Appendix C shows that the link between corporal punishment and alienation occurs regardless of whether the father was loving and reasoning. The same analysis was done for mothers and had similar results.

Conclusions

The survey results in this chapter are consistent with the theory that hitting a child lowers the chance that he or she will eventually be in a high-level occupation with a high income. The dampening effect of corporal punishment applies mainly to those who completed college, however. This probably happens because hitting children increases the probability that later in life they will have one or more characteristics that are especially damaging to success in high-level occupations—depression, an inclination to physical violence, a sense of powerlessness, and a lack of internalized moral standards.

The analyses allowed for the fact that corporal punishment, violence, depression, and alienation may overlap with such things as socioeconomic status and violence between parents (see Appendix C). This type of analysis shows the net effect of corporal punishment, after subtracting out the overlap of these variables. This underscores the idea that corporal punishment impairs economic achievement. It shows that the relationship of corporal punishment to alienation and economic achievement remains after other parental characteristics are removed.

Although the sophisticated statistical analyses presented in Appendix C support our theory, they do not "prove" it. The methods we use are limited, and do not provide conclusive support for a cause and effect relationship. For example, we used information from three separate surveys to test the theory presented in Chart 9–1. A more accurate test could be done if all the questions had been asked of one group of people, rather than three. In addition, we asked adults to recall how many times they were hit by their parents as adolescents. Some people—especially those who are angry or alienated—may find it easier to recall being hit than people who are not angry or alienated, even when no differences actually exist. To overcome these limitations we would need to do longitudinal or experimental research, both of which are expensive and time consuming. Our results suggest however, that a research investment of this magnitude is in order.

It may take even more evidence to get social scientists to conduct research on the relationship between spanking and economic achievement because the idea seems so unbelievable to almost everyone. One example illustrates the point. When Batya Hyman's research (1993) showing that sexually abused women had lower earnings was presented at the weekly Family Research Laboratory seminar, it was received with enthusiasm. A year later, I presented another aspect of this study to the same group. It too was received with enthusiasm, but also with a skepticism that was not evident for the previous study. One possible reason for the difference in reaction is because one presentation dealt with sexual abuse and the other with corporal punishment. Everyone knows that sexual abuse of children is harmful. They knew this long before research showed the adverse effects. Conversely, almost everyone thinks that spanking children is not harmful, despite the studies showing that it is. Eighty four percent of American adults, including most practicing psychologists, believe that corporal punishment is sometimes necessary. The remarkable thing is that the members of the Family Research Laboratory seminar are social scientists who, presumably, are against hitting children. Yet the idea that "moderate corporal punishment" is harmless is so deeply ingrained in American culture that even this group was more skeptical of the idea that it could adversely affect a person's occupation and income.

If subsequent research confirms what is in this chapter, the implications are profound because the side effects of corporal punishment are wide ranging and significant. The particular side effects described here are likely to have even more serious consequences as the transformation to a post-industrial society proceeds. More than 20 years ago Kohn argued in *Class and Conformity* (1969) that corporal punishment tends to produce adults who are adapted to low-level occupations in which obedience rather than initiative and creativity are the key requirements, but poorly adapted to high-level occupations that demand initiative and creativity. The demand for workers in low-level occupations who can adapt to the monotony of unskilled factory work is disappearing. Jobs that require a strong back and obedience to authority are becoming so rare that men and women who, in the past, could have a stable place in society may find no place whatsoever in the post-industrial labor market. Corporal punishment, which helped socialize previous generations of factory workers, now may be helping to create the next generation of the chronically unemployed.

Part III

The Future

10

Ten Myths That Perpetuate Corporal Punishment

C hapter 1 pointed out that hitting children is legal in every state of the United States and that 84 percent of a survey of Americans agreed that it is sometimes necessary to give a child a good hard spanking. Chapter 2 noted that almost all parents of toddlers act on these beliefs. Study after study shows that almost 100 percent of parents with toddlers hit their children. There are many reasons for the strong support of spanking. Most of them are myths.

Myth 1: Spanking Works Better

There has been a huge amount of research on the effectiveness of corporal punishment of animals, but remarkably little on the effectiveness of spanking children. That may be because almost no one, including psychologists, feels a need to study it because it is assumed that spanking is effective. In fact, what little research there is on the effectiveness of corporal punishment of children agrees with the research on animals. Studies of both animals and children show that punishment is *not* more effective than other methods of teaching and controlling behavior. Some studies show it is less effective.

Ellen Cohn and I asked 270 students at two New England colleges to tell us about the year they experienced the most corporal punishment. Their average age that year was eight, and they recalled having been hit an average of six times that year.[1] We also asked them about the percent of the time they thought that the corporal punishment was effective. It averaged a little more than half of the times (53 percent). Of course, 53 percent also means that corporal punishment was *not* perceived as effective about half the time it was used.

LaVoie (1974) compared the use of a loud noise (in place of corporal punishment) with withdrawal of affection and verbal explanation in a study of first- and second-grade children. He wanted to find out which was more effective in getting the children to stop touching certain prohibited toys. Although the loud noise was more effective initially, there was no difference over a longer period of time. Just explaining was as effective as the other methods.

A problem with LaVoie's study is that it used a loud noise rather than actual corporal punishment. That problem does not apply to experiments by Day and Roberts (1983) and Roberts and Powers (1990). They studied three-year-old children who had been given "time out" (sitting in a corner). Half of the mothers were assigned to use spanking as the mode of correction if their child did not comply and left the corner. The other half put their non-complying child behind a low plywood barrier and physically enforced the child staying there. Keeping the child behind the barrier was just as effective as the spanking in correcting the misbehavior that led to the time out.

A study by Larzelere (1998) also found that a combination of non-corporal punishment and reasoning was as effective as corporal punishment and reasoning in correcting disobedience.

Crozier and Katz (1979), Patterson (1982), and Webster-Stratton et al. (1988, 1990) all studied children with serious conduct problems. Part of the treatment used in all three experiments was to get parents to stop spanking. In all three, the behavior of the children improved after spanking ended. Of course, many other things in addition to no spanking were part of the intervention. But, as you will see, parents who on their own accord do not spank also do many other things to manage their children's behavior. It is these other things, such as setting clear standards for what is expected, providing lots of love and affection, explaining things to the child, and recognizing and rewarding good behavior, that account for why children of non-spanking parents tend to be easy to manage and well-behaved. What about parents who do these things and also spank? Their children also tend to be well-be-haved, but it is illogical to attribute that to spanking since the same or better results are achieved without spanking, and also without adverse side effects.

Such experiments are extremely important, but more experiments are needed to really understand what is going on when parents spank. Still, what Day and Roberts found can be observed in almost any household. Let's look at two examples.

In a typical American family there are many instances when a parent might say, "Mary! You did that again! I'm going to have to send you to your room again." This is just one example of a non-spanking method that did *not* work.

The second example is similar: A parent might say, "Mary! You did that again! I'm going to have to spank you again." This is an example of spanking that did *not* work.

The difference between these two examples is that when spanking does not work, parents tend to forget the incident because it contradicts the almost-universal American belief that spanking is something that works when all else fails. On the other hand, they tend to remember when a *non* spanking method did not work. The reality is that nothing works all the time with a toddler. Parents think that spanking is a magic charm that will cure the child's misbehavior. It is not. There is no magic charm. It takes many interactions and many repetitions to bring up children. Some things work better with some children than with others.

Parents who favor spanking can turn this around and ask, If spanking doesn't work any better, isn't that the same as saying that it works just as well? So what's wrong with a quick slap on the wrist or bottom? There are at least three things that are wrong:

- Spanking becomes less and less effective over time and when children get bigger, it becomes difficult or impossible.
- For some children, the lessons learned through spanking include the idea that they only need to be good if Mommy or Daddy is watching or will know about it.
- As the preceding chapters show, there are a number of very harmful side effects, such as a greater chance that the child will grow up to be depressed or violent. Parents don't perceive these side effects because they usually show up only in the long run.

Myth 2: Spanking Is Needed as a Last Resort

Even parents and social scientists who are opposed to spanking tend to think that it may be needed when all else fails. There is no scientific evidence supporting this belief, however. It is a myth that grows out of our cultural and psychological commitment to corporal punishment. You can prove this to yourself by a simple exercise with two other people. Each of the three should, in turn, think of the most extreme situation where spanking is necessary. The other two should try to think of alternatives. Experience has shown that it is very difficult to come up with a situation for which the alternatives are not as good as spanking. In fact, they are usually better.

Take the example of a child running out into the street. Almost everyone thinks that spanking is appropriate then because of the extreme danger. Although spanking in that situation may help *parents* relieve their own tension and anxiety, it is not necessary or appropriate for teaching the child. It is not necessary because spanking does not work better than other methods, and it is not appropriate because of the harmful side effects of spanking. The only physical force needed is to pick up the child and get him or her out of danger, and, while hugging the child, explain the danger.

Ironically, if spanking is to be done at all, the "last resort" may be the worst. The problem is that parents are usually very angry by that time and act impulsively. Because of their anger, if the child rebels and calls the parent a name or kicks the parent, the episode can escalate into physical abuse. Indeed, most episodes of physical abuse started as physical punishment and got out of hand (see Chapter 5, and Kadushin and Martin, 1981). Of course, the reverse is not true, that is, most instances of spanking do not escalate into abuse. Still, the danger of abuse is there, and so is the risk of psychological harm.

The second problem with spanking as a last resort is that, in addition to teaching that hitting is the way to correct wrongs, hitting a child impulsively teaches another incorrect lesson—that being extremely angry justifies hitting.

Myth 3: Spanking Is Harmless

When someone says, I was spanked and I'm OK, he or she is arguing that spanking does no harm. This is contrary to almost all the available research. One reason the harmful effects are ignored is because many of us (including those of us who are social scientists) are reluctant to admit that their own parents did something wrong and even more reluctant to admit that we have been doing something wrong with our own children. But the most important reason may be that it is difficult to see the harm. Most of the harmful effects do not become visible right away, often not for years. In addition, only a relatively small percentage of spanked children experience obviously harmful effects.

The delayed reaction and the small proportion seriously hurt are the same reasons the harmful effects of smoking were not perceived for so long. In the case of smoking, the research shows that a third of very heavy smokers die of lung cancer or some other smoking-induced disease. That, of course, means that two-thirds of heavy smokers do *not* die of these diseases (Mattson et al., 1987). So most heavy smokers can say, I've smoked more than a pack a day for 30 years and I'm OK. Similarly, most people who were spanked can say, My parents spanked me, and I'm not a wife beater or depressed.

Another argument in defense of spanking is that it is not harmful if the parents are loving and explain why they are spanking. The research does show that the harmful effects of spanking are reduced if it is done by loving parents who explain their actions. However, chapters 8 and 9 and a study by Larzelere (1986) show that although the harmful effects are reduced, they are not eliminated. The chapters in Part II have shown that the harmful side effects include an increased risk of delinquency as a child and crime as an adult, wife beating, depression, masochistic sex, and lowered earnings.

In addition to having harmful psychological effects on children, hitting children also makes life more difficult for parents. Hitting a child to stop misbehavior may be the easy way in the short run, but in the slightly longer run, it makes the job of being a parent more difficult. This is because spanking reduces the ability of parents to influence their children, especially in adolescence when they are too big to control by physical force. Children are more likely to do what the parents want if there is a strong bond of affection with the parent. In short, being able to influence a child depends in considerable part on the bond between parent and child (Hirschi, 1969). An experiment by Redd, Morris, and Martin (1975) shows that

CHART 10–1. Few children of parents who use a lot of corporal punishment have a well-developed conscience.

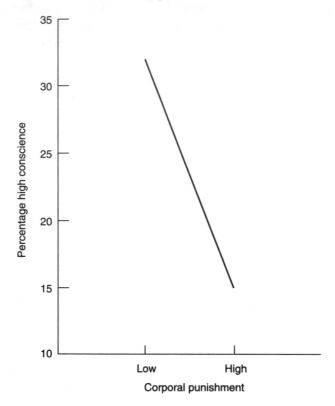

children tend to avoid caretaking adults who use punishment. In the natural setting, of course, there are many things that tie children to their parents. I suggest that each spanking chips away at the bond between parent and child.

Part of the process by which corporal punishment eats away at the parent-child bond is shown in the study of 270 students mentioned earlier. We asked the students for their reactions to "the first time you can remember being hit by one of your parents" and the most recent instance. We used a check list of 33 items, one of which was "hated him or her." That item was checked by 42 percent for both the first and the most recent instance of corporal punishment they could remember. The large percentage who hated their parents for hitting them is important because it is evidence that corporal punishment does chip away at the bond between child and parent.

Contrary to the "spoiled child" myth, children of non-spanking parents are likely to be easier to manage and better behaved than the children of parents who spank. This is partly because they tend to control their own behavior on the basis of what their own conscience tells them is right and wrong rather than to avoid being hit (see Chart 10–1).[2] This is ironic because almost everyone thinks that spanking "when necessary" makes for better behavior.

Myth 4: One or Two Times Won't Cause Any Damage

The evidence in this book indicates that the greatest risk of harmful effects occurs when spanking is very frequent. However, that does not necessarily mean that spanking just once or twice is harmless. Unfortunately, the connection between spanking once or twice and psychological damage has not been addressed by most of the available research. This is because the studies seem to be based on this myth. They generally cluster children into "low" and "high" groups in terms of the frequency they were hit. This prevents the "once or twice is harmless" myth from being tested scientifically because the low group may include parents who spank once a year or as often as once a month. The few studies that did classify children according to the number of times they were hit by their parents are illustrated in chapters 5, 6, and 7. They show that even one or two instances of corporal punishment are associated with a slightly higher probability of later physically abusing your own child, slightly more depressive symptoms, and a greater probability of violence and other crime later in life. The increase in these harmful side effects when parents use only moderate corporal punishment (hit only occasionally) may be small, but why run even that small risk when the evidence shows that corporal punishment is no more effective than other forms of discipline in the short run, and less effective in the long run.

Myth 5: Parents Can't Stop Without Training

Although everyone can use additional skills in child management, there is no evidence that it takes some extraordinary training to be able to stop spanking. The most basic step in eliminating corporal punishment is for parent educators, psychologists, and pediatricians to make a simple and unambiguous statement that hitting a child is wrong and that a child *never*, ever, under any circumstances except literal physical self-defense, should be hit.

That idea has been rejected almost without exception everytime I suggest it to parent educators or social scientists. They believe it would turn off parents and it could even be harmful because parents don't know what else to do. I think that belief is an unconscious defense of corporal punishment. I say that because I have never heard a parent educator say that before we can tell parents to never *verbally* attack a child, parents need training in alternatives. Some do need training, but everyone agrees that parents who use *psychological* pain as a method of discipline, such as insulting or demeaning, the child, should stop immediately. But when it comes to causing *physical* pain by spanking, all but a small minority of parent educators say that before parents are told to stop spanking, they need to learn alternative modes of discipline. I believe they should come right out, as they do for verbal attacks, and say without qualification that a child should *never* be hit.

This is not to say that parent education programs are unnecessary, just that they should not be a precondition for ending corporal punishment. Most parents can benefit from parent education programs such as The Nurturing Program (Bavolek, 1983 to 1992), STEP (Dinkmeyer and McKay, 1989), Parent Effectiveness Training (Gordon, 1975), Effective Black Parenting (Alvy and Marigna, 1987), and Los Ninos Bien Educado Program (Tannatt and Alvy, 1989). However, even without such programs, most parents already use a wide range of non-spanking methods, such as explaining, reasoning, and rewarding. The problem is that they also spank. Given the fact that parents already know and use many methods of teaching and controlling, the solution is amazingly simple. In most cases, parents only need the patience to keep on doing what they were doing to correct misbehavior. Just leave out the spanking! Rather than arguing that parents need to learn certain skills *before* they can stop using corporal punishment, I believe that parents are more likely to use and cultivate those skills if they decide or are required to stop spanking.

This can be illustrated by looking at one situation that almost everyone thinks calls for spanking: when a toddler who runs out into the street. A typical parent will scream in terror, rush out and grab the child, and run to safety, telling the child, No! No! and explaining the danger—all of this accompanied by one or more slaps to the legs or behind.

The same sequence is as effective or more effective *without the spanking*. The spanking is not needed because even tiny children can sense the terror in the parent and understand, No! No! Newborn infants can tell the difference between when a mother is relaxed and when she is tense (Stern, 1977). Nevertheless, the fact that a child understands that something is wrong does not guarantee never again running into the street; just as spanking does not guarantee the child will not run into the street again.

If the child runs out again, nonspanking parents should use one of the same strategies as spanking parents—repetition. Just as spanking parents will spank as many times as necessary until the child learns, parents who don't spank should continue to monitor the child, hold the child's hand, and take whatever other means are needed to protect the child until the lesson is learned. Unfortunately, when non-spanking methods do not work, some parents quickly turn to spanking because they lose patience and believe it is more effective. But spanking parents seldom question its effectiveness, they just keep on spanking.

Of course, when the child misbehaves again, most spanking parents do more than just repeat the spanking or spank harder. They usually also do things such as explain the danger to the child before letting the child go out again or warn the child that if it happens again, he or she will have to stay in the house for the afternoon, and so on. The irony is that when the child finally does learn, the parent attributes the success to the spanking, not the explanation.

Myth 6: If You Don't Spank, Your Children Will Be Spoiled or Run Wild

It is true that some non-spanked children run wild. But when that happens it is not because the parent didn't spank. It is because some parents think the alternative to spanking is to ignore a child's misbehavior or to replace spanking with verbal attacks such as, Only a dummy like you can't learn to keep your toys where I won't trip over them. The best alternative is to take firm action to correct the misbehavior without hitting. Firmly condemning what the child has

CHART 10–2. Children of parents who use a lot of corporal punishment tend to be aggressive, especially if the parents ignore their aggression.

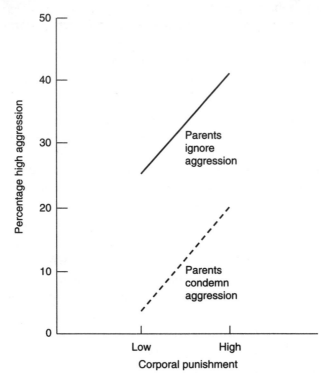

done and explaining why it is wrong are usually enough. When they are not, there are a host of other things to do, such as requiring a time out or depriving the child of a privilege, neither of which involves hitting the child.

Suppose the child hits another child. Parents need to express outrage at this or the child may think it is acceptable behavior. The expression of outrage and a clear statement explaining why the child should never hit another person, except in self defense, will do the trick in most cases. That does not mean one such warning will do the trick, any more than a single spanking will do the trick. It takes most children a while to learn such things, whatever methods the parents use.

The importance of how parents go about teaching children is clear from a classic study of American parenting—*Patterns of Child Rearing* by Sears, Maccoby, and Levin (1957). This study found two actions by parents that are linked to a high level of aggression by the child: permissiveness of the child's aggression, namely ignoring it when the child hits them or another child, and spanking to correct misbehavior. The most aggressive children in Chart 10–2 are those at the upper right. They are children of parents who permitted aggression by the child and who also hit them for a variety of misbehavior. The least aggressive children are at the lower left. They are children of parents who clearly condemned acts of aggression and who, by not spanking, acted in a way that demonstrated the principle that hitting is wrong.

There are other reasons why, on the average, the children of parents who do not spank are better behaved than children of parents who spank:

- Non-spanking parents pay more attention to their children's behavior, both good and bad, than parents who spank. Consequently, they are more likely to reward good behavior and less likely to ignore misbehavior.
- Their children have fewer opportunities to get into trouble because they are more likely to child-proof the home. For older children, they have clear rules about where they can go and who they can be with.
- Non-spanking parents tend to do more explaining and reasoning. This teaches the child how to use these essential tools to monitor his or her own behavior, whereas children who are spanked get less training in thinking things through.
- Non-spanking parents treat the child in ways that tend to bond the child to them and avoid acts that weaken the bond. They tend to use more rewards for good behavior, greater warmth and affection, and fewer verbal assaults on the child (see Myth 9). By not spanking, they avoid anger and resentment over spanking. When there is a strong bond, children identify with the parent and want to avoid doing things the parent says are wrong. The child develops a conscience and lets that direct his or her behavior. That is exactly what Sears et al. found (see Chart 10–1).

Myth 7: Parents Spank Rarely or Only for Serious Problems

Contrary to this myth, parents who spank tend to use this method of discipline for almost any misbehavior. Many do not even give the child a warning. They spank before trying other things. Some advocates of spanking even recommend this. At any supermarket or other public place, you can see examples of a child doing something wrong, such as taking a can of food off the shelf. The parent then slaps the child's hand and puts back the can, sometimes without saying a word to the child. John Rosemond, the author of *Parent Power* (1981), says, "For me, spanking is a first resort. I seldom spank, but when I decide . . . I do it, and that's the end of it."

The high frequency of spanking also shows up among the parents described in this book. The typical parent of a toddler told us of about 15 instances in which he or she had hit the child during the previous 12 months. That is surely a minimum estimate because spanking a child is generally such a routine and unremarkable event that most instances are forgotten. Other studies, such as Newson and Newson (1963), report much more chronic hitting of children. My tabulations for mothers of three- to five-year-old children in the National Longitudinal Study of Youth found that almost two-thirds hit their children during the week of the interview, and they did it more then three times in just that one week. As high as that figure may seem, I think that daily spanking is not at all uncommon. It has not been documented because the parents who do it usually don't realize how often they are hitting their children.

Myth 8: By the Time a Child Is a Teenager, Parents Have Stopped

As we have seen, parents of children in their early teens are also heavy users of corporal punishment, although at that age it is more likely to be a slap on the face than on the behind. The charts in Chapter 3 show that more than half of the parents of 13 to 14-year-old children in our two national surveys hit their children in the previous 12 months. The percentage drops each year as children get older, but even at age 17, one out of five parents is still hitting. To make matters worse, these are minimum estimates.

Of the parents of teenagers who told us about using corporal punishment, 84 percent did it more than once in the previous 12 months. For boys, the average was seven times and for girls, five times. These are minimum figures because we interviewed the mother in half the families and the father in the other half. The number of times would be greater if we had information on what the parent who was not interviewed did.

Myth 9: If Parents Don't Spank, They will Verbally Abuse Their Child

The scientific evidence is exactly the opposite. Among the nationally representative samples of parents in this book, those who did the least spanking also engaged in the least verbal aggression.

It must be pointed out that non-spanking parents are an exceptional minority. They are defying the cultural prescription that says a good parent should spank if necessary. The depth of their involvement with their children probably results from the same underlying characteristics that led them to reject spanking. There is a danger that if more ordinary parents are told to never spank, they might replace spanking by ignoring misbehavior or by verbal attacks. Consequently, a campaign to end spanking must also stress the importance of avoiding verbal attacks as well as physical attacks, and also the importance of paying attention to misbehavior.

Myth 10: It Is Unrealistic to Expect Parents to Never Spank

It is no more unrealistic to expect parents to never hit a child than to expect that husbands should never hit their wives, or that no one should go through a stop sign, or that a supervisor should never hit an employee. Despite the legal prohibition, some husbands hit their wives, just as some drivers go through stop signs, and a supervisor occasionally may hit an employee.

If we were to prohibit spanking, as is the law in Sweden (see Chapter 11: Deley, 1988; and Haeuser, 1990), there still would be parents who would continue to spank. But that is not a reason to avoid passing such a law here. Some people kill even though murder has been a crime since the dawn of history. Some husbands continue to hit their wives even though it has been more than a century since the courts stopped recognizing the common law right of a husband to "physically chastise an errant wife" (Calvert, 1974).

A law prohibiting spanking is unrealistic only because spanking is such an accepted part of American culture. That also was true of smoking. Yet in less than a generation we have made tremendous progress toward eliminating smoking. We can make similar progress toward eliminating spanking by showing parents that spanking is dangerous, that their children will be easier to bring up if they do not spank, and by clearly saying that a child should *never*, under any circumstances, be spanked.

Why Do These Myths Persist?

Some of the myths we just presented are grounded in society's beliefs that spanking is effective and relatively harmless. Let's turn to some of the reasons these two types of myths persist.

The Myth of Effectiveness

There are a number of reasons why almost everyone overestimates the effectiveness of spanking, but a central reason is what has been called "selective inattention." This occurs when people do not remember the times when spanking fails because it contradicts what they believe to be true, namely, that spanking works. On the other hand if someone knows that the parents do *not* spank, it is assumed that the child must be spoiled or wild. So there is a tendency to overlook the good behavior of the child and to attribute the inevitable instances of misbehavior to the lack of spanking. This provides the evidence that parents who don't spank "when necessary" have spoiled children. These all-too-human errors in information processing create the perception that spanking is much more effective than it really is. This error may be the main reason for the persistence of the effectiveness myth. The reality is that although all children misbehave, the behavior of children who are not spanked, although far from perfect, is on the average better than the behavior of children whose parents spank.

The idea of selective inattention raises the question of why the "necessity" of spanking is such a deeply held belief. Why do most Americans have a vested interest in defending spanking? The following are some of the possible reasons:

- Almost all have been spanked as children, so it is part of their normal life experience.
- Even if someone is suffering from one of the harmful side effects, such as depression, he or she may not realize that having been spanked may be one of the reasons why. He or she continues to believe that spanking is harmless.
- Almost all parents slap or spank toddlers. So, if a parent accepts the idea that spanking is wrong, it implies that he or she is a bad parent, at least in this respect. That is difficult to admit.
- Almost everyone has been hit by his or her parents. So, to say corporal punishment is wrong is to condemn your own parents. Few people are comfortable doing that.
- These beliefs and attitudes have been crystallized as part of American culture and the American view of what a good parent owes a child. There is abundant evidence that people tend to misperceive things that are contrary to basic tenants of their culture and beliefs (Higgins and Bargh, 1987).
- Most spanking occurs when parents are frustrated and angry. In that context parents tend to get emotional release and satisfaction from spanking, which is confused with effectiveness in changing the child's behavior.

There is almost always a kernel of truth behind myths and stereotypes. The belief in the usefulness of spanking is no exception. The truth is that some parents who do not spank also do not attempt to correct misbehavior. As explained earlier, children of these extremely permissive or neglectful parents do tend to be out of control. However, such parents are a minority of non-spanking parents. Their children tend to be difficult to deal with or sometimes even to be around. These few and unrepresentative cases get burned into memory.

The Myth of Harmlessness

Probably the most important reasons for the myth of harmlessness are because the harmful effects do not become visible right away, often not for years, and because only a relatively small percentage of spanked children experience obviously harmful effects.

It is now widely accepted that smoking causes lung cancer, but that fact was hotly disputed only a generation ago. The research on spanking children associates it with delinquency, wife beating, depression, and other problems later in life. But just as the research on smoking a generation ago, the evidence is not conclusive. Those favoring spanking can dismiss it, just as those favoring smoking dismissed the early inconclusive evidence.

When there is more conclusive evidence on the harmful effects of spanking, it may be harder to get people to give up spanking than it was for them to give up smoking. Spanking may be more firmly entrenched because almost everyone was spanked or is a spanker, but not everyone was a smoker.

Another reason spanking will be hard to eliminate is because the chance of falling victim to one of the harmful effects of spanking is much lower than the risk of experiencing the harmful effects of smoking. For example, Chapter 7 shows that spanked children are about four times more likely to be highly aggressive and about twice as likely to hit their spouses later in life. These are large risks, but the effects of smoking are much larger. A high rate of smoking tends to increase the chances of lung cancer by 34 times, even though two-thirds of very heavy smokers do not die of a smoking-related disease (Mattson et al., 1987).

Spanking is associated with a two-to-four-times greater rate of harmful behavior, whereas smoking increases the lung cancer rate by 34 times. Therefore, it can be argued that smoking is a much more serious problem. On the other hand, it also can be argued that spanking is the more serious problem of the two because almost all parents spank, and spanking puts entire generations at risk of harm. There is no need to decide if spanking is worse than smoking. Both are harmful, both need to be eliminated, and both can be eliminated. In the case of spanking, even though it may increase the probability of harm "only" two to four times, it is an unnecessary risk because children are more likely to be well-behaved if parents do not spank.

11

Social Evolution and Corporal Punishment

T he main purpose of this chapter is to put corporal punishment in a broad historical and cross cultural framework in
order to uncover clues to the socio-historical changes that may
underlie the reduction in corporal punishment that has already
taken place and clues to what might happen in the future. But
before doing that, it is time to take an overview of the evidence
on the prevalence and side effects of corporal punishment. The
evidence shows that:

- Almost all American parents hit toddlers—usually repeatedly. This is
  almost unchanged from a generation ago.

- More than a third continue into the early teen years. This is about half
  as many as a generation ago.

- The more corporal punishment a person experienced, the more likely
  they are

   later in childhood to:

   - Hit other children

   - Act out aggressively in other ways, such as hitting their par-
     ents (see Chapter 12)

   - Experience less rapid cognitive development (see Chapter
     12)

and as an adult to:

- Be depressed or suicidal

- Physically abuse their child or spouse

- Engage in other violent crime

- Have a drinking problem (Straus and Kaufman Kantor, 1994)

- Be attracted to masochistic sex

- Be less likely to achieve a high occupation and income

How Solid is the Evidence?

Many people are likely to think that these conclusions are ridiculous, and people with scientific training will quickly point out a number of reasons for doubting their validity. I will identify some of the key questions about validity and also identify reasons for taking the findings in Part II seriously.

Cross-Sectional Data Does Not Provide Evidence of Cause and Effect.

The most important reason for doubting that the studies in Part II demonstrate that corporal punishment causes social and psychological problems is that all those studies used what researchers call a "cross-sectional" research design (also called a "correlational" study). This is a particularly severe problem in studies of corporal punishment because it can be assumed that parents hit children to correct undesirable behavior. Thus, the spankings may have been a response to the child's behavioral problems rather than a cause.

At the time the original version of this chapter was written all I could do was alert readers to this problem and point out two reasons for taking the results of those cross-sectional studies seriously. First, I argued that some of the chapters reported studies of hypothesized side effects that are unlikely to be the cause of hitting by parents; specifically, depression and masochistic sex. It is unlikely, but not impossible, that these problems caused the parents to use corporal punishment because depression and masochistic sex do not usually become obvious until adulthood.

Second, although the cross-sectional evidence in Part II cannot prove that corporal punishment causes the behavior problems studied, those studies could have shown that there is no relation between corporal punishment and social and psychological problems. Each of the studies described in Part II provided an opportunity to refute the theory that corporal punishment is harmful, yet that did not occur.

As pointed out in the new preface, the situation has changed dramatically since the first edition. There are now five "longitudinal" studies (also called "prospective" studies). Prospective studies provide a much more solid basis for inferring that corporal punishment does harm children because they can take into account the misbehavior that led the parents to use corporal punishment. These studies found that the more corporal punishment parents used, the more likely it was, a year or more later, the child would:

- Engage in antisocial behavior

- Hit a parent

- Hit a dating partner

- Fall behind in cognitive development relative to other children

Each of these studies is described in the new postscript chapter. Although the new longitudinal studies are a great improvement, the cross-sectional studies in Part II remain important because they cover issues that have not yet been addressed by longitudinal research. Consequently, it remains necessary to consider their limitations and why those studies are nonetheless important.

Recall Data By Adults

Most of the evidence in Part II is based on recall of corporal punishment by adults and refers to corporal punishment as an adolescent. It is possible that the links between corporal punishment and problem behaviors are an artifact of a tendency for people who experienced these behavior problems to be more likely to recall having been hit by their parents. However, the fact that over

90 percent of adults recall corporal punishment (Bryan and Freed, 1982; Graziano and Namaste, 1990), including almost two out of three who recalled being hit as an adolescent (see Chapter 3) makes this unlikely. Moreover, the fact that corporal punishment as an adolescent was the typical experience of Americans of that generation makes the findings broadly applicable to that generation.

Inadequate Controls For Other Variables

The real cause of the link between corporal punishment and child behavior problems might be other family and parent characteristics that lead to both corporal punishment and child behavior problems. For example, parents who physically attack each other are more likely to also hit their children. To deal with this problem, the studies in Part II and other cross-sectional studies controlled for many variables that could be the "real cause" of the problems linked to corporal punishment, including:

Social Characteristics of the Parents and Family

Educational level of parents

Income, including very low income

Racial/ethnic group

Single parent versus two parent families

Number of children in the family

Sex of the parent

Age of the parent

Parental Role Behaviors

Adequacy of parent's supervision of children

Parental warmth and support

Whether parents established clear rules and expectations

Use of other disciplinary strategies such as time out

Parental consistency in discipline

Parental use of reasoning

Parental involvement and cognitive stimulation

Child Characteristics

Child's birth-weight

Sex of the child

Age of the child

Child's delinquency or antisocial behavior at Time 1

Child's cognitive ability at Time 1

Child-to-parent bond

Psycho-social Problems

Conflict between the parents

Violence between the parents

Violence in family in which the parents grew up

Parental alcohol abuse

Parent attitudes approving violence

Whether the parent also engaged in more severe violence ("physical abuse")

Depression of parents

No single study controlled for all of these alternative explanations. However, it is a well recognized scientific principle (sometimes called "triangulation" [Webb, Campbell, Schwartz, Sechrest, and Belew Grove, 1981]) that valid conclusions are possible on the basis of evidence from studies which, taken one by one, are not definitive. This is because the weak point of one study may be dealt with in another study. I think we have reached the point of triangulation concerning corporal punishment. There have been more than 80 studies examining the effects of corporal punishment, and with rare exception, they have found harmful long-term effects (Thompson, in press).

Overlap of Corporal Punishment and Physical Abuse

Corporal punishment and physical abuse overlap because almost every parent who kicks or punches a child also engages in legal forms of hitting children such as spanking and slapping. Consequently, what shows up as an effect of corporal punishment might really be due to unknowingly including children in the sample who were physically abused. However, there are studies in Part II that avoided that problem by removing physically abused children from the sample (Chapter 7, Chart 7–5; Chapter 8; also MacMillan, Boyle, Wong, Duku, Fleming, and Walsh, 1999; Straus and Yodanis, 1996; Vissing, Straus, Gelles, and Harrop, 1991). These studies, which did not include parents who exceeded ordinary corporal punishment, nonetheless found harmful side effects for corporal punishment.

Never Spanked Children Were Not Studied

Most of the research which shows a link between corporal punishment and aggression was carried out by comparing children whose parents hit them frequently and those whose parents hit less often. It can be argued that this shows that it is *frequent* hitting of children that gives rise to later aggressiveness. This is consistent with the belief that "moderate corporal punishment," i.e., hitting a child only once in a while, is harmless. The studies in Part II which compare those who reported never having been hit with those hit just once, twice, etc are based on recall by adults, and few if any adults can remember what happened at ages 2 and 3, the ages when spanking is most likely to have occurred. So, not having been hit as an adolescent does not mean never having been hit by parents.

Fortunately, three studies described in the postscript chapter avoid this memory problem because the corporal punishment data were obtained by asking mothers about spanking in the past week. That does not entirely solve the problem because mothers who did not spank in the past week might have spanked in some previous week. However, interviews with mothers in a study of a thousand children identified 189 who, at least according to the mothers, had never been spanked (Straus and Mouradian, 1998). These children had the lowest average antisocial behavior scores and were the least impulsive, even compared to children who were very rarely spanked (only once in the past six months).

If All Parents Spank, There Is No Way to Prove That Spanking Is Harmful

This is a valid statistical principle, but it does not apply to corporal punishment because, the phrases "almost all parents" and "almost universal" are not the same as "all." With a large enough sample, even the 6 percent who did not spank provides enough cases to determine if it makes a difference. As indicated in the previous paragraph, we found that never-spanked children are, on average, the best behaved. This finding, of course, contradicts "common sense" and the belief that never-spanked children will be "kids running wild." That reasoning and those beliefs have no basis in logic or science. The logical problem is a classic false dichotomy. It assumes that no-spanking means "permissiveness" in the sense of no rules and no-discipline. As for kids running wild, that is an American cultural myth, akin to the pro-natalist myth that only-children will be spoiled brats. The available scientific evidence is the opposite for both spanking and only-children. Of course, one can cite cases of children running wild, but that is also true of children whose parents use CP. Conversely, I know a family in which one spanking forever clouded the relationship between the mother and her daughter. However, such cases are rare, and I know of many more in which repeated spankings did not adversely affect the relationship between parents and children. But that does not make spanking not harmful, just as the fact that two-thirds of heavy smokers will not die from a smoking related disease does not make smoking not harmful.

What about just one spank? The Straus and Mouradian study and other evidence suggest that even a single spanking carries a risk of harmful side effects, although only a small risk. As a society, spanking is so taken for granted that we forget it is a euphemism for hitting. The degree to which our judgment about the harmful side effects of a single instance is based on cultural norms permitting and expecting that parents will hit children for repeated misbehavior can perhaps be seen better if we think of a husband slapping his wife "just once." The risk of harmful psychological effects from a single incident may be low for both errant children and errant wives, but our culture makes us perceive it as zero for children and high for wives.

Conclusion

The first Surgeon General's report on smoking had to rely on studies that, individually, were not definitive. Although none of the many studies they reviewed were definitive, the defects of one study were not applicable to other studies, which in turn had still other defects, but also other strong points. The triangulation of findings from different studies led to the conclusion that smoking does increase the risk of lung cancer, even though no single study was definitive.

The amount of research on corporal punishment is not nearly as large as the research on which the Surgeon General's report on smoking was based. However, the accumulated evidence, and especially the new longitudinal studies summarized in the postscript chapter, supports the conclusion that corporal punishment increases the risk of a wide variety of social and psychological problems. These studies consistently show that corporal punishment is associated with an increased risk of social and psychological problems, especially physical aggression and delinquency. There is enough evidence from well-controlled or longitudinal studies to conclude that the risk of harmful side effects occurs:

- Regardless of the presence or absence of other forms of violence such as verbal aggression and physical violence between the parents

- Regardless of whether the data are based on reports by parents of punishment carried out recently, or on recall by adults of punishment as an adolescent

- Even after removing from the sample children whose parents kicked or punched, or did other acts of severe violence

- Regardless of the age or gender of the child, gender of the parent, or the socioeconomic status of the family

- Regardless of whether the parents were otherwise good parents or poor parents as measured by whether they did such things as show warmth and affection, monitor the child's behavior, explained and reasoned with the child, or were consistent in their expectations and discipline

- Regardless of whether the child was hit frequently or very rarely (although victims of frequent corporal punishment were more likely to suffer side effects)

- Regardless of social class, and in about half the studies which examined this issue, regardless of ethnic group

These summary statements oversimplify a very complex process. As Ross Parke, one of America's most distinguished child psychologists, notes (1977), "The effectiveness [and side effect] of punishment is dependent on a variety of factors, including the timing and intensity of punishment, the nature of the relationship [between the parent and the child], the consistency with which punishment is administered, and the amount and type of verbal explanation that accompanies the punishment." Even that list is far from complete. For example, Parke's experiments show that the effectiveness of punishment is also influenced by the balance between reward and punishment, and later in the article just quoted, Parke discussed the impact of the child's style of interacting. He could also have mentioned the parent's ability to understand things from the child's perspective and to use that information. Despite the many other things that enter the equation, Parke concludes that "...physical punishment is generally unjustified and alternative techniques are both more humane and more effective" (p. 71).

That statement was made in 1977. Since then, there have been five editions of Parke's comprehensive child development text-book, but up to and including the most recent edition (Hetherington and Parke, 1999), the crucially important conclusion that "alternative techniques are both more humane and more effective" is nowhere to be found. Why it is nowhere to be found is an important question that I tried to answer in the preface to this edition and in Chapters 1 and 12. At this point, in the context of this discussion of the validity of the evidence concerning the harmful effects of corporal punishment, I will consider the possibility that textbook authors avoid recommending no-spanking because the currently available evidence makes that premature or even unethical.

Is It Premature To Advise Parents To Never Spank?

Some defenders of corporal punishment such as Larzelere et al. (1998) believe that an unconditional anti-spanking stance is unethical and irresponsible because even the evidence from the prospective studies summarized in Chapter 12 is not truly conclusive. However, there are circumstances when it is ethical and responsible to base advice on research that is less than conclusive. One example is research indicating, even though not conclusively, that a certain drug might have serious side effects. Advice based on that non-definitive evidence would be appropriate if there are equally effective drugs available that do not have those side effects. The abundance of evidence in Part II and the postscript chapter showing that corporal punishment may have harmful side effects, even though it is not definitive, requires advising parents to not spank. This is an ethical requirement because the research evidence, including experimental studies, clearly indicates that non-corporal disciplinary strategies are just as effective in the immediate situation (Larzelere et al., 1998; Larzelere, Schneider, Larson, and Pike, 1996; Roberts, 1988; Roberts and Powers, 1990), and more effective in the long run (Straus, Sugarman, and Giles-Sims, 1997). Using non-violent modes of discipline avoids the increased risk of the many harmful side effects of corporal punishment documented in Part II and Chapter 12 without giving up a necessary mode of discipline.

Corporal Punishment in Historical Perspective

There are some isolated tribal hunting and gathering societies in which parents almost never hit children (Montague, 1978), but these non-violent societies are the exceptions. They are important, however, because they are also societies where relationships between adults tend to be non-violent (Montague, 1978; Levinson, 1989). Adult members of most non-literate tribal societies, like people in almost all literate societies, hit children and are also prone to violence among themselves. Societies in which children are hit have cultural norms and beliefs that label corporal punishment as different from violence between adults. But in reality, the basic elements are almost identical. In fact, the only important way they are different is that the culture defines one as legitimate and the other as criminal.

Adult violence is similar to corporal punishment because most violent acts by adults are carried out for what the attacker thinks at the time is a morally correct purpose or a sense of personal violation. Take, for example, a confrontation between two men over a $50 loan made three months ago that was to be paid back in a week. They get into a fight, and one is killed. Violence that the aggressor thinks is morally necessary can be seen on television daily. The classic scene is the Western movie barroom fight over cheating in a poker game, but there are hundreds of others. Corporal punishment by American parents is also similar to adult violence because it is usually impulsive and carried out in anger.

Cultural norms that make violence by parents legitimate have been the predominant pattern of humanity. Still, change is occurring. Within the Western world, corporal punishment by parents, and others who are responsible for children has clearly decreased since the seventeenth century (DeMause, 1984; Radbill, 1987; Newell, 1989). The major decrease has been in the most extreme types of violence—physical abuse—but for the less extreme violence known as corporal punishment, the pace of change has been glacial. Nevertheless, glaciers do move and when they do, have tremendous impact.

A Moral Passage

A social problem exists when people come to believe that some state of affairs is morally indefensible and needs to be changed (Spector and Kitsuse, 1977). The situation may have existed for hundreds or thousands of years, but since it was not defined as a social problem people did not consider it wrong. Corporal punishment illustrates this principle. Children have been hit since the dawn of history and it has not been considered a social problem. Even today, chapters 1 and 2 show that hitting children continues to be defined as necessary, correct, and moral, not as a social problem to be condemned and changed. But we are now starting to experience what Gusfield (1963, 1981) calls a "moral passage." Although the pace of change has been slow and there are some counter trends, spanking and other legal forms of corporal punishment are being redefined more and more as a social problem. There are a number of signs that moral evaluation of hitting children is changing.

The most dramatic change occurred in 1979, when Sweden became the first country to make spanking children illegal. The movement has since spread to the rest of Scandinavia, with Finland following in 1984, Denmark in 1986, and Norway in 1987. Austria followed in 1989. In 1985, the Council of Europe recommended that its member nations limit or prohibit corporal punishment by parents.

In the United States, a series of less dramatic, but still important events has been taking place. In 1989, Adrienne Haeuser, a professor of social work who studied the Swedish law (Haeuser, 1990), organized a conference with support from the Johnson Foundation. The purpose was to develop a strategy to end corporal punishment by parents. That conference brought together a distinguished group of psychologists, pediatricians, educators, social workers, and sociologists, who adopted a position statement opposing corporal punishment by parents. Following this conference, several major organizations adopted position statements opposing corporal punishment by parents, including Parents Anonymous, the National Committee to Prevent Child Abuse, the National Foster Parent Association, the National Association of School Psychologists, and the National Association of Social Workers.

In 1991, Philip Greven's book, *Spare the Child: The The Religious Roots of Punishment and the Psychological Impact of Physical Abuse*, was praised in *the New York Times* book review section and other reviews. If this book had been published a decade or two earlier, the *New York Times* might not have reviewed it at all, much less reviewed it favorably. That same year also saw the establishment of EPOCH-USA, with a distinguished advisory board. EPOCH (End Physical Punishment Of Children) began in England in 1989 and has become a multinational federation of similar-thinking organizations.[1]

In 1992, Division 37 of the American Psychological Association established a task force charged with encouraging research on corporal punishment and with drafting a resolution that, would put the association on record as opposing corporal punishment by parents. The American Academy of Pediatrics created a similar task force in 1991. Both groups, however, have had difficulty reaching a consensus.

In 1992, the national Kiwanis organization purchased copies of a videoo tape called "Spanking—What To Do Instead" (Bavolek, 1992) and encouraged local chapters to show it. This indicates that idea of bringing up children without hitting is starting to take hold outside of academic life.

One of the great ironies of the campaign against child abuse is that the leading federal agency on child abuse—the National Center on Child Abuse And Neglect—still does not discourage corporal punishment in any of its major publications. In fact, as noted in Chapter 6, one of their most recent and widely circulated publications implicitly endorses corporal punishment. As for other child abuse prevention organizations, despite the position statements they adopted in 1989, none has made ending corporal punishment by parents a major part of its approach. But they are creeping up on it.

The National Committee to Prevent Child Abuse has been the leading private organization focused on preventing child abuse since the mid-1970s. It ignored corporal punishment until 1983, and in 1992 started distributing pamphlets on how to discipline a child without spanking. That is an important step, even though none of the committee's pamphlets or posters on physical abuse explicitly links spanking with physical abuse and says that a child should never be slapped or spanked.

The National Advisory Committee on Child Abuse and Neglect, established by Congress in 1988, has come out against corporal punishment by everyone *except* parents. But the fact that the committee has addressed the issue of corporal punishment at all is encouraging.

Although no national child-abuse prevention organization has made corporal punishment by parents a major focus, the issue has finally made its way to their agendas, however tenuously. This may signal the end of the policy of ignoring corporal punishment documented in chapters 1 and 6.

Another sign of progress, even if not yet a turning point, was a bill introduced into the 1992 Wisconsin legislature to ban corporal punishment by parents. This is probably the first bill of its type to come before an American state legislature, and that is more important than the fact that the bill did not progress beyond a committee hearing.

There is at least one other important sign of change—the ending of corporal punishment in public schools. In 1979, only four of the 50 U.S. states prohibited corporal punishment in the schools. In 1987 the National Coalition to Abolish Corporal Punishment in Schools was founded. By 1989, the number of states prohibiting corporal punishment in schools had grown to 19, and by 1993 to 25. The National Education Association (NEA), the nation's largest organization of teachers, finally dropped its opposition to ending corporal punishment by teachers (although state NEAs continue to be among the most important opponents of such legislation). The number of states considering a ban on hitting children in schools is growing, and it is likely that many state laws will be passed despite opposition by state teachers' organizations and Protestant fundamentalists.

Except for the trend to prohibit hitting children in schools, none the changes just listed is by itself momentous. I suggest that together they mark the beginning of a major social trend—a moral passage in which behavior that previously was expected of parents will become reprehensible. If such a moral passage is in progress, the question is why it is occurring at this point in history. What are the underlying historical and social forces? Are these forces likely continue and, if so, what does that suggest for the future?

Social Changes Underlying the Moral Passage

Why is the late twentieth century a time when the slow pace of change in corporal punishment seems to be speeding up? Many influences are at work, three of which will be briefly discussed. They are the expansion of human rights and humanitarian values, the development of a post-industrial economic system, and the growth of social scientific knowledge and the idea that social policies and services should be based on that knowledge.[2]

Expansion of Human Rights

Human rights and humanitarian values are expanding to include groups that were previously denied equal rights and protection. Slavery was abolished more than a century ago. The remnants of slavery in the form of official racial segregation ended a generation ago in .the United States and recently in South Africa. Women achieved the right to vote early in this century, and the remaining legal discrimination is just about gone. Equality in non-legal matters between men and women is still to be achieved (Hochschild, 1989; Martin, 1993; Sugarman and Straus, 1988; Straus, 1994b), but the movement is clearly in that direction.

Children are next on the agenda, including the right of a child to be free from the risk of physical assault by parents. The basis of this change is not evidence that corporal punishment harms children, just as the abolition of slavery was not fundamentally based on evidence that slavery hurt the economy, although in both cases there is an underlying connection. Instead, the change is in moral principles or beliefs. More and more people believe it is immoral to hit children, just as they have come to believe that it is immoral to own slaves or to "physically chastise an errant wife" (the old common-law right of husbands).

An expansion of human rights and humanitarian principles is only one of the causes of the change in corporal punishment.

Another that I believe is extremely important is the development of a post-industrial economy and social system.

Transition to a Post-Industrial Economy

Over the broad sweep of human history, the basic activities needed to sustain life—the subsistence patterns—have changed dramatically. There are three broad types of subsistence patterns: hunting and gathering, agricultural, and industrial. Within the final pattern, post-industrial societies (Bell, 1954), or advanced industrial societies (Janowitz, 1978), are distinguished from other industrial societies.

As the economic basis of human life evolved from hunting and gathering to a post-industrial economy, new social institutions developed and existing institutions adapted to the changes (Harris, 1977).[3] Over the long run, fundamental changes in the economic system tend to produce fundamental changes in the family and visa versa (Lee, 1982, Skolnick, 1992; Straus, 1977). The application of that principle to corporal punishment is summarized in Table 11–1.

Levinson's analysis of Human Relations Area Files data and his review of other studies (1989) show that corporal punishment tends to be least prevalent in hunting and gathering societies and most prevalent in agricultural and industrial societies. Why is this so? On the surface, agricultural and industrial societies seem to have little in common, and post-industrial societies even less in com-

TABLE 11-1. Links between the type of society and techniques for correcting and controlling children.

Type of Society	Predominant Characteristics of Major Adult Roles, Especially Occupational	Correctional an Control Strategies that Serve as Anticipatory Socialization
Agricultural, Industrial	Obedience Conformity Loyalty	Corporal punishment Absolute rules Unquestioned obedience
Hunt/Gather, Post-Industrial	Individuality Autonomy Cooperativeness	Reward Explanation Negotiation

mon with hunting and gathering societies. However, cross-cultural research on corporal punishment by Petersen et al. (1982) and Ellis and Petersen (1992) has identified an important common element.

In hunting and gathering societies, adults are frequently away by themselves foraging or hunting, or hunting in small groups. Survival depends on being independent and self-directed as well as being able to be a team player. In that type of society, it is important that parents bring up children who can be self-directed and independent, yet who can cooperate with one another as equals.

By contrast, Peterson et al. suggest that in agricultural and other complex societies, adults are primarily supervised by other people and must follow directions. Farms, businesses, and factories are owned privately, not collectively by the workers. The wealth and power derived from these individually owned enterprises is the property of wealthy and powerful people who use their wealth or influence to secure leadership positions in political and religious organizations. This further increases the hierarchical nature of the society. The inheritance system concentrates wealth and moves society still further away from equality. Industrial societies also need a disciplined labor force whose members can follow orders and tend machines.

Every society develops methods of bringing up children that will equip them to fulfill the roles they will play as adults. Agricultural and traditional industrial societies need members who can be obedient members of hierarchical groups, such as the male-dominated farm family or church, or the assembly-line factory. It is no accident that the only adult institutions in Western society that continued corporal punishment until the twentieth century were the most hierarchical of all institutions—the armed forces. Families also have remained very hierarchical, with many parents continuing to value unquestioning obedience, both for its own sake and as preparation for life. If unquestioning obedience is required of their children, those parents believe that corporal punishment can help equip children to take their place in that type of society (Kohn, 1977; Pearlin, 1971). Evidence from studies using the Human Relations Area Files shows that "the more conformity is valued relative to self-reliance, the more physical punishment is used in child rearing" (Ellis and Petersen, 1992, p. 47).

The same line of reasoning can be applied to the emerging post-industrial type of society. A post-industrial society requires that a larger proportion of the population be self-directed, independent, and creative, with the skills to cooperate, explain, and negotiate. When parents hit their children, they are teaching almost the opposite of the behaviors and skills their children will need. As noted in Chapter 9, relatively few jobs in a post-industrial society require a strong back and a weak mind. Instead, occupations are predominantly in management, services, the professions, and sciences. Services and management require skills in human relationships and in negotiating, among other things. These are not traits that are fostered by corporal punishment. Most high-level occupations also require the ability to be self-directed and independent, but also cooperative. There is a hierarchy of management today, but at each level, team management is becoming more prevalent. The same trend is occurring among blue-collar workers as more jobs require flexibility and decision making rather than the strength and perseverance required to maintain the pace of a typical assembly line. This is illustrated by Blauner's study of oil-refinery workers (1964). Where the assembly line survives, it is also being transformed. The line is now being organized by teams of workers who have mutual responsibility for production and quality control of a product or a major component of a product. It is reasonable to compare this new subsistence pattern with small groups of mutually dependent hunters.

For the reasons just presented, we seem to be on the threshold of a moral passage that will transform Western culture from one in which almost all children are socialized by corporal punishment to one in which this occurs for only a small minority of the population.

Although theoretically the growth in certain occupations has caused the shift away from corporal punishment, broad historical changes are always complex. For example, Chapter 9 showed that corporal punishment is linked with occupational and economic achievement. This is consistent with the idea that the tiny but growing number of children whose parents deviated from the social norm by using little or no corporal punishment contributed disproportionately to the growth of the new industrial and social technology that is creating our post-industrial society.

Over time, even small changes in corporal punishment will accumulate because children who were not spanked tend to be nonspankers themselves (see Chapter 4, and Straus, Gelles, and Steinmetz, 1980, p. 107). They learn from their own experience that children do not "need" to be spanked. Graziano and Namaste

(1990), for example, found that 72 percent of young adults who were spanked believed that spanking is effective, compared to only 28 percent of those who were not spanked. In addition, 47 percent of those who were spanked believed that "children need to be spanked to teach discipline," compared to 17 percent of those who were not spanked. Similar results were found by a 1981 Swedish study (cited in Newell, 1989, p. 16). It found that 41 percent of those who were physically punished believed that spanking was necessary in bringing up children, compared to only 11 percent of those who had not been hit by their parents.

Legitimating Role of Social Science

The steadily increasing quantity and quality of social science research on what it takes to bring up healthy non-delinquent children is a third development that makes a contribution to the emerging moral passage. At present, this is a minor contribution because it is indirect. The research shows the powerful role of parental warmth. Also important is setting standards and being an example of those standards, monitoring the child, and consistently enforcing standards. By implication, if a parent does these things, corporal punishment will not be necessary. Consequently, books for parents based on that research indirectly say that corporal punishment is not necessary. As chapters 1 and 10 noted, however, social scientists and authors of parental-advice books usually avoid saying that a child should never be spanked. Even psychologists such as Ross Parke, who are opposed to corporal punishment, phrase their opposition to imply that there are situations in which corporal punishment is appropriate. Parke (1982, p. 71), for example, says "... physical punishment is generally unjustified and alternative techniques are both more humane and more effective."

Earlier in this chapter we showed that more organizations and authors are starting to pay attention to corporal punishment. Authors of books and articles are starting to say unambiguously that a child should never be hit. An article in the June, 1993 *Redbook* magazine "The Ten Worst Discipline Mistakes" (Eberlin, 1993) illustrates the change. Spanking is not among the ten. However, there is one brief paragraph that says:

> Though spanking or slapping may halt misbehavior temporarily, over the long term physical punishment will backfire. A kid who's smacked

doesn't learn self-control; he learns fear—and that it's OK for a bigger person to hit a smaller one.

Even five years earlier, that paragraph would probably not have been in a mass-circulation magazine. If it had been written, it might have been deleted by a nervous editor who was afraid of alienating readers. Or, it might have been changed to say that parents should avoid spanking "if possible." It is a milestone when a paragraph that says unambiguously to never spank appears in a mass circulation magazine. In another five years, magazines of this type are likely to be carrying entire articles that say to never hit a child. They might even use the word *hit* rather than the euphemism *spank*. The Spring, 1992 issue of *Mothering* led the way among widely circulated magazines. It published an article by Adrienne Haeuser called "Swedish Parents Don't Spank," and featured it on the cover with the headline "Giving up Spanking." There are many other such signs of a change in our culture, as well. Ann Landers, the columnist who previously approved of and occasionally recommended corporal punishment, now says, no hitting.

As the idea of never hitting a child starts to become as uncontroversial as the idea of never hitting a spouse, there is likely to be a flowering of research on corporal punishment, just as there has been on wife beating (Straus, 1992a). This, coupled with the increasing acceptance of the idea that social science should guide our society, is likely to give that research even more clout.

Research on corporal punishment is not the only research that has been ignored: most social science research is ignored.[4] One of the main reasons is because there is no "buyer" who can see a way to profit from corporal punishment research. In the case of social science research, the buyer is usually an interest group or social science movement that can use the theoretical approach and the research to legitimize a cause. The connections between activists and researchers actually flow in both directions. Social science research is much more likely on topics that are also the focus of a social movement (Straus, 1992a). So, the research on corporal punishment since the turn of the century has been sporadic and largely ignored (see chapters 1 and 7). But, as sentiment against corporal punishment grows and interest groups such as EPOCH-USA are formed, the old research is being dug up, and an increasing amount of new research eventually will be published and publicized.

The primary use of the research is likely to be what Pelz (1978), and Weiss and Bucuvalas (1980) identify as "conceptual" and "legitimative." The conceptual use provides intellectual justification in the form of a theory. In other words, social science theories make the new moral beliefs scientifically rational. Social science research can provide evidence that new moral beliefs result in social and psychological conditions that are better than what prevailed under the old moral order. In our situation it is the belief that children will be better behaved and better off if parents do not hit them. Research in this area and research showing that the majority of adolescents are still being hit by their parents can help what has been called "claims making" in the struggle to focus public attention and resources on ending corporal punishment (Aronson, 1984; Best 1987; Gusfield, 1989).

Lessons from the Swedish No-Spanking Law

Sweden led the way in forbidding corporal punishment by parents; and more information is available on what happened in Sweden than in other countries that have passed similar laws. That information could help guide the movement against spanking in other countries, as it has in Norway, Finland, Denmark, Cyprus, Latvia, Croatia, Italy, and Austria. For one thing, the Swedish experience illustrates the way a small protest group can define a social problem and bring about change. At first, the abolition of corporal punishment in Sweden was greeted by derisive cartoons and editorials. Had it been up to the public at large, the change might not have occurred. In passing the law, the Swedish parliament evidently responded to the "claims makers" (Spector and Kitsuse, 1977) who were concerned about what seemed to be a dramatic increase in child abuse. They sought to redefine what was then legal and morally correct behavior carried out by most parents as a social problem that needed to be remedied. The objections and ridicule were gradually replaced by acceptance and an appreciation of the law. Today, 71 percent of Swedes favor managing children without corporal punishment. There are a number of reasons for the change in public opinion.

One is that the public has come to accept and welcome the no-spanking law because it is part of the civil code, not the criminal code. There are no criminal penalties for punishing parents who spank. The fear was that thousands of parents could be hauled into court, but obviously that never occurred. Rather than dole out punishment, the Swedish law was intended to establish a new national standard, to educate, and to help parents and children. After the law was passed, for example, the government sent all parents of children under age three a booklet on discipline without corporal punishment.

The help for parents provided by the no-spanking law is another reason for the change in public opinion. Parents who use corporal punishment are not labeled and defined as mean or cruel under the Swedish law. The law assumes that all parents occasionally have trouble managing their children and need help in this difficult task. Many kinds of assistance are available to help parents learn how to manage their children without hitting. Since most parents can use help at one time or another, the law has come to be appreciated rather than resented.

The law also aims to educate children as well as parents. Children are told in school and through the mass media that parents are not allowed to hit them. That probably sounds underhanded or even sinister to most Americans because of the depth of the American commitment to corporal punishment. It does not sound sinister or underhanded to Americans when children are told that everyone should wear a car seat belt, that no one should smoke, and that adults are not allowed to touch children's genitals. Americans enthusiastically support the idea that children should tell someone if a parent or other adult tries to have sex with them, but they are shocked by the idea that children should do the same if a parent physically assaults them. The difference is a matter of what society defines as wrong. Sex with children is defined as wrong (as it should be); hitting children is not, but also should be.

Why isn't hitting children also defined as wrong? One of the reasons is that hitting children to correct and train them reflects a deep but rarely perceived cultural approval of violence to correct many types of wrongs. It shows up in both subtle and obvious ways. For example, 75 percent of Americans endorsed the idea that it is good for boys to get into fist fights when they are growing up (Stark and McEvoy, 1970). Most Americans believe that murderers should be killed, and most Americans supported the Panama Invasion of 1989 and the Gulf War of 1991, both of which were examples of gunboat diplomacy. Given this deep-seated commitment to violence as a means of correcting wrongs, passing a law outlawing corporal punishment in the U.S. is not likely to have the same effect as in Sweden. American culture also needs to change in some fundamental ways.

Finally, the experience with Sweden's law gives us hints about the long-term effects of banning corporal punishment. There are no data on the extent to which the actual hitting of children has decreased since the law was passed in 1979. Swedish public opinion has changed drastically, however, and it is likely that this reflects at least some change in the behavior of the public. If change in attitudes is an important step in changing behavior, the Swedes have taken that step.

The history of other radical humanitarian social changes is similar. There is strong opposition at first, sometimes even war, as in the case of slavery in the United States. Sometimes there is just derision and foot dragging, as in the case of voting rights for women. The civil rights gains of the 1960s and the gains in women's rights in the 1970s depended on a mobilized minority. Had these issues been put to a popular vote at the time, like the Swedish law on corporal punishment, they might not have passed. If fact, the Equal Rights Amendment to the U.S. Constitution did not pass. Today, although there is lingering opposition, the overwhelming majority of Americans favor equal rights for women as well as for African-Americans and other minorities. Corporal punishment of children is as deeply ingrained an aspect of American society as was the idea that African-Americans and women are inferior human beings. It will take the determined efforts of a mobilized minority to end this ancient evil.

Obstacles to Ending Corporal Punishment

Even assuming that the moral passage towards a no-spanking standard has begun and that there are well-organized and well-funded advocacy groups pushing that change (there are not), the outlook is not good for a no-spanking law in the near future in the United States. Just mentioning a law to make hitting children illegal is almost universally regarded as off the wall. Even among professionals concerned with child abuse, only a tiny minority favors such a law. But social change is notoriously difficult to predict and, as we have seen, there are some favorable signs.

Most of the opposition or worry about abolishing the right of parents to hit their children takes the form of the cultural myths about corporal punishment described in the previous chapter.

However, there are also other obstacles, some even more deeply embedded. These obstacles reflect some deep-seated aspects of American culture and the American psyche. Among these are the approval of violence, extreme individualism, fear of government intervention in the family, and attitudes toward punishment. There also is the opposition of Protestant fundamentalists.

Individualism, Punitiveness, and Fear

American individualism reflects itself in many ways, both good and bad (Lipset, 1963). It is the basis for civil liberties, a source of economic strength, and a source of economic weaknesses. It underlies our fear of government interference in the economy and the family. The punitive nature of American culture and the American psyche also is related to our individualism.

When a law forbidding parents to hit children is mentioned, almost everyone believes it will result in the expensive and humiliating arrest and prosecution of parents, including parents who are struggling to do their best for their children, even if it is in misguided ways. If a non-spanking law has a policy of informing children and parents that spanking is prohibited, the specter arises of children informing on their parents. There is also a fear that welfare authorities will take children from their parents.

The Scandinavian experience provides no basis for such fears. Sweden, for example, is sometimes depicted as a very interventionist society, but it has much *lower* rate of children in foster homes or institutions than the United States. Furthermore, during the decade following the passage of Sweden's no-spanking law, the rate of moving children into foster homes and institutions did not increase, it decreased (Newell, 1989). The fact that children are so rarely placed under state supervision in Sweden and are so frequently in the United States reflects different political and social policies. The United States is committed to minimum government interference in family life. But, although that is not the intent, this commitment denies help to many families who need it. The ironic result is more drastic intervention in the long run, such as removing the child to a foster home. Sweden is committed to looking after the health and well-being of all children. All new parents are visited by a public health nurse, there is a compulsory medical examination at age four, family leave is extensive and paid, and so on. The long-term effect of this government "interference" is, not surprisingly, that things rarely get so bad that a child has to be removed from his or her home.

As for prosecutions under the no-spanking laws, Newell (1989) notes that in Sweden "...there has been no rush by children to drag their parents through the courts. It appears that there has been only one prosecution in 10 years ..." There have been none at all in Finland. The single prosecution in Sweden was not under the no-spanking law—it was under the criminal law on assault. The purpose of Sweden's no-spanking law is to set a national standard, to educate parents about that standard, and to help them bring up their children in accordance with the humane principles of that standard. The studies of Durrant (1999), Haeuser (1990), Newell (1989), Peltonini (1983), Ziegert (1983), and Solheim (1982) show that this is happening.

Fundamentalist Opposition

"Spare the rod and spoil the child" may be the single best-known "Biblical quotation." In fact, it is not from the Bible at all. That makes little difference, though, because there are numerous genuine Biblical passages that support corporal punishment or can be interpreted as supporting corporal punishment. Fundamentalist Protestants are a large segment of American society—about 28 percent (Ellison and Sherkat, 1993)—and they are increasing, while more mainstream denominations are decreasing. However, those who leave mainstream denominations have not necessarily become fundamentalists. Many have just become more secularized, and they may be part of what is fueling the move away from corporal punishment.

Assuming that fundamentalists will be the group that most resists ending corporal punishment (Ellison and Sherkat, 1993; Grasmick et al., 1991; Greven, 1991), it makes sense to focus on the majority of the population whose belief in corporal punishment is mainly secular. That is a sufficiently challenging goal. When the rest of the population has changed its attitude, the difference in the national climate will make it easier for the fundamentalists to change. In that context, they could well change on their own accord, just as almost all Catholics now use contraceptives. It may in fact be easier because although the core of fundamentalism is said to be a literal interpretation of the Bible, that really means "selective literalism." Not many fundamentalists have given all their worldly possessions to the poor, for example.

Cultural Rights and Family Privacy

Many African-Americans and some others (for example, Robert Larzelere, 1993) argue that an effort to end spanking amounts to imposing the unproven beliefs of one segment of society on others. Respect for minority rights is extremely important. But, valid and important principles often contradict other valid and important principles. One such principle is that children should be treated in ways that do not injure them. Unfortunately, the traditional culture of many societies does include injurious practices. Robert Edgerton's book, *Sick Societies: Challenging: the Myth of Primitive Harmony* (1992), gives many examples of injurious practices that are part of traditional cultures, and have been for centuries. Some of these apply to the whole society, such as the Dugum Dani, where warfare was valued and frequently practiced. Some apply to powerless segments of the society, such as footbinding of women in China or genital mutilation of girls in much of Northeast Africa. Mutilation of female genitals is an important example because, like spanking, it is defended most by its victims. It also is defended by Muslims who claim it is part of the Koran. Even if genital mutilation were in the Koran, it would still be a culturally approved form of abuse that kills many children and mars the life of those who survive the operation.

The injury from corporal punishment, like the injury from heavy smoking, is in the form of harmful side effects that, fortunately, most people escape. But the risk of side effects is there. Just as smokers have no way of seeing the harm they are doing to their bodies, parents have no way of seeing the harm they are unknowingly doing to their children. As this book shows, the injuries are not trivial. The principles of respecting traditional cultures and protecting family privacy conflict with the principle that children should be disciplined in ways that do not increase their risk of physical and mental problems. The choice is between principles. There is less of a quandary in the case of corporal punishment because there are ways of teaching and correcting misbehavior that are just as effective or more effective. It also is possible to make an accommodation between a commitment to the well-being of children and individual freedom, parental rights, and respect for cultural diversity. In Sweden there is no criminal penalty for spanking; instead, the law assumes that when parents spank, it is because they are having trouble controlling a child. The Swedes try to help such parents achieve the kind of control that helps children grow into decent human beings. When parents have that ability, they don't "need" to spank. Ending or reducing spanking in this way does not infringe on people's values because even parents who approve of spanking on religious or cultural grounds usually prefer that it were not necessary.

Cultural rights are only one reason for caution in using the law to end hitting children. It also may be a tactical mistake. It may be best to think of an anti-spanking law as a step that will help complete, rather than begin, the moral passage to a society in which children are not hit. In the meantime, government can do many things. It can sponsor research that may provide definitive evidence on the benefits of not spanking children. Government also can educate, as it has done on smoking and the use of seat belts. Part of that education can be in the form of warning labels on birth certificates and baby food, and in posters in the offices of pediatricians. These educational campaigns can draw on parents' obviously strong desire for their children to be happy and successful, just as the anti-smoking campaign drew on the obviously strong desire of people to avoid dying of lung cancer. As that campaign gained strength and the no-smoking cause was taken up by the elite, it became fashionable to not smoke rather than to smoke. Gradually the ground was prepared for the no-smoking laws that are being passed in many states and cities. The same scenario is likely for no hitting, but how long it will take is anyone's guess.

A Society Without Corporal Punishment

Research over the past 40 years been remarkably consistent in showing that hitting children increases the chances of a child becoming physically aggressive, delinquent, or both. The research in this book leads me to conclude that corporal punishment leaves invisible scars that affect many other aspects of life.

The results of those studies come at a point when the economic order is changing society in ways as fundamental as the changes accompanying the agricultural revolution thousands of years ago and the industrial revolution 200 years ago. The new social roles and psychological perspectives are inconsistent with corporal punishment. The change in world view being created by this massive change in society and the new information about the serious harm resulting from hitting children may together accelerate the transition to a new moral order. This moral passage will transform hitting children from something that loving parents are expected to do "when necessary" to an unacceptable evil. Regardless of whether ending corporal punishment reduces the rate of psychological and social problems among adults, ending the nearly universal practice of hitting children, in itself, makes society more humane. In addition, to the extent that hitting children is one of the causes of social and psychological problems, ending the time-honored practice of hitting children will affect all aspects of life. It will accelerate changes in the social order and have profound implications for creating a more humane society.

Hitting children is so common, so taken for granted, that the idea that ending the practice will have profound benefits for individuals and society is ridiculous to most people. They may be right. Although I do not think they are right, I do agree that there are three major grounds for skepticism.

First, as noted earlier, the links between corporal punishment and social and psychological problems may be false. Second, eliminating corporal punishment does not necessarily mean that the new state of affairs would be better. The effects of social change are notoriously difficult to predict, although it is fairly certain that perfection is not something humanity is likely to achieve. What is perfect for most children may be excruciatingly painful for others. The use of "social evolution" in the title of this chapter does not mean that society tends to get better and better. I do not believe that there can ever be a perfect society—unless you consider an ant-hill society as perfect! Every social arrangement suits some better than others, so there are always casualties of society. Some social arrangements produce more casualties (Edgerton, 1992), however. An example of this is violent child rearing.

Third, although this book shows that hitting children is related to many serious social and psychological problems, most of which have not been considered consequences of corporal punishment, the statistics in Appendix C also show that corporal punishment is only a small part of the explanation for these problems. So, even if all parents stopped hitting their children, it would not mean the end of violence, crime, depression, masochistic sex, and so on.

Let us assume that ending corporal punishment will result in a 10 percent reduction in these problems. Is that a "profound" change? It clearly is for the 10 percent who are spared these problems. There are also indirect victims, however. A much larger percentage will be spared the pain of being victimized by the crimes of this 10 percent. An even larger number will be spared the trauma of having a family member succumb to mental illness. Others will be spared the economic costs of the mental health problems of the 10 percent. While it is impossible to know the percentages and difficult to be sure that some new evil will not replace hitting children, the research reported in this book suggests that:

- Bringing up children without hitting will reduce the stress and trauma of being a parent and being a child. Parents will be able to bring up their children with less hassle. Young children, on the average, will be better behaved, and among older children, there will be less delinquency.

- When these children are adults and parents themselves, they will be less likely to physically abuse their spouses and children.

- Family relationships will be more rewarding because there will be a closer bond between parents and children.

- A society with little or no hitting of children is likely to result in fewer people who are alienated, depressed, or suicidal, and in fewer violent marriages.

- The potential benefits for the society as a whole are equally great. These include lower crime rates, especially for violent crimes; increased economic productivity; and less money spent on controlling or treating crime and mental illness.

A society that brings up children by caring, humane, and nonviolent methods is likely to be less violent, healthier, wealthier, and wiser. This will occur partly as a direct effect of not hitting children, but also because caring, humane, and non-violent child rearing can only predominate in a society that nurtures those characteristics. This book may be appearing at a point in history that is about to experience a social change that may seem minor to most people—the elimination of corporal punishment—but which will have profound and far reaching benefits for humanity.

12

The Benefits of Never Spanking: New and More Definitive Evidence

V irtually a revolution has occurred in the state of scientific knowledge about the long-term effects of corporal punishment in just the six years since *Beating The Devil Out Of Them* was published. The main purpose of this chapter is to summarize the results of that new research and to explain why the new research shows, more clearly than ever before, the benefits of avoiding corporal punishment.

Somewhat ironically, at the same time as this evidence was appearing, voices arose in state legislatures, the mass media, and in social science journals to defend corporal punishment. Consequently, a second purpose is to put these recent defenses of corporal punishment in perspective.

This is followed by a section explaining a paradox concerning trends in corporal punishment. Public belief in the necessity of corporal punishment and the percentage of parents who hit teenagers is about half of what it was only 30 years ago. Despite these dramatic changes, the percent of parents who spanked toddlers was about the same in 1995 as it was in 1975.

The chapter concludes with an estimate of the benefits to children, to parents, and to society as a whole that could occur if corporal punishment were to cease.

Defenders of corporal punishment say or imply that no-corporal punishment is the same as no-discipline or "permissiveness" (see for example Baumrind, 1996). Consequently, before discussing the new research, it is important to reemphasize the point made in Chapter 10 about this myth: that no-corporal punishment does not mean no-discipline. Writers and organizations leading the movement away from corporal punishment believe that rules and discipline are necessary, but that they will be more effective without corporal punishment. Their goal is to inform parents about these more effective disciplinary strategies, as exemplified in the very name of one such organization—the Center For Effective Discipline (see their web site: http://www.stophitting.com; see also the web site of Positive Parenting program http://parenting.umn.edu).

The Chicken and Egg Problem with Previous Research on Corporal Punishment

In order to grasp the importance of the new research, the limitations of the previous 45 years of research need to be understood. These 45 years saw the publication of more than 80 studies linking corporal punishment to child behavior problems such as physical violence. A meta-analysis of these studies by Thompson (in press) found that almost all showed that the more corporal punishment a child had experienced, the worse the behavior of the child. Thompson's review reveals a consistency of findings that is rare in social science research. Thompson concluded that "Although...corporal punishment does secure children's immediate compliance, it also increases the likelihood of eleven [types of] negative outcomes [such as increased physical aggression by the child and depression later in life]. Moreover, as pointed out in the new preface, experiments and other studies conducted by defenders of corporal punishment show that, even when the criterion is immediate compliance, non-corporal discipline strategies work just as well as corporal punishment (Larzelere et al., 1998; Larzelere, Schneider, Larson and Pike, 1996; Roberts, 1988; Roberts and Powers, 1990).

The chapters in Part II are examples of the type of negative outcome reviewed by Thompson. To take a specific example, Chart 7–2 (page 104) shows that the more corporal punishment experienced, the greater the probability of hitting a wife or husband later in life. Another example is a study of kindergarten children by Strassberg et al. (1994). The data on corporal punishment for this study was obtained by interviews with the mothers of the children. Six months later, the children were observed in school and instances of physical aggression were tallied for each child. The

CHART 12–1. Physical attacks on other children in kindergarten are twice as frequent if the mother used corporal punishment six months earlier

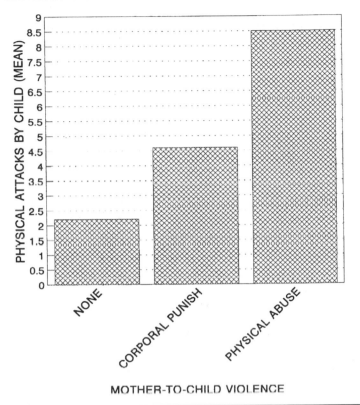

MOTHER-TO-CHILD VIOLENCE

From Straussberg, Dodge, Petit, & Bates, 1994, p. 452

second bar of Chart 12–1 shows that the children of mothers who used corporal punishment attacked other children twice as often as the children whose mothers did not. The third bar in Chart 12–1 also shows that the children of mothers who went beyond ordinary corporal punishment had four times the rate of attacking other children. This illustrates another principle: that the psychologically harmful effects of corporal punishment are parallel to the harmful effects of physical abuse, except that the magnitude of the effect is less.

Despite the unusually high constancy in the findings of research on corporal punishment, there is a serious problem with all the previous research. As pointed out in Chapter 11, the problem is that these studies do not indicate which is cause and which is effect. That is, they do not take into account the fact that aggression and other behavior problems of the child lead parents to spank. The chart in chapter 7 showing that the more corporal punishment, the greater the probability of hitting a spouse later in life could simply indicate that the parents were responding to a high level of aggression by the child at Time 1. For example, they might have spanked because the child repeatedly grabbed toys from or hit a brother or sister. Since aggression is a relatively stable trait (Berkowitz, 1993), it is not surprising that the most aggressive children at Time 1 are still the most aggressive at Time 2 and are now hitting their wives or husbands. To deal with that problem, the research needs to take into account the child's aggression or other antisocial behavior at Time 1 (the time of the spanking). Studies using that design can examine whether, in the months or years following, the behavior of children who were spanked improves (as most people in the USA think will be the case) or gets worse. There are finally new studies that use this design and provide information on long term *change* in the child's behavior.

Five New Landmark Studies

In the three-year period 1997–1999 five studies became available that can be considered "landmark" studies because they overcame this serious defect in 45 years of previous research on the long-term effects of corporal punishment. All five of the new studies took into account the child's behavior at Time 1, and all five were based on large and nationally representative samples of American children. None of them depended on adults recalling what happened when they were children.

Study 1: Corporal Punishment and Subsequent Antisocial Behavior

This research studied over 3,000 children in the National Longitudinal Survey of Youth (Straus, Sugarman, and Giles-Sims, 1997). The children were in three age groups: 3 to 5, 6 to 9, and 10 to 14. The mothers of all three groups of children were interviewed at the start of the study in 1988, and then again in 1990 and 1992. The findings were very similar for all three age groups and for change after two years and four years. To avoid excess detail only the results for the 6 to 9 year old children and for the change in antisocial behavior two years after the first interview will be described here.

Measure of corporal punishment. To measure corporal punishment, the mothers were told "Sometimes kids mind pretty well and sometimes they don't," and asked "About how many times, if any, have you had to spank your child in the past week?"

Measure of Antisocial Behavior. To measure antisocial behavior the mothers were asked whether, in the past three months, the child frequently "cheats or tells lies", "bullies or is cruel/mean to others", "does not feel sorry after misbehaving", "breaks things deliberately", "is disobedient at school", "has trouble getting along with teachers." This was used to create a measure of the number of antisocial behaviors frequently engaged in by the child.

Other Variables. We also took into account several other variables that could affect antisocial behavior by the child. These include the sex of child, cognitive stimulation provided by the parents, emotional support by the mother, ethnic group of the mother, and socioeconomic status of the family.

Findings. Chart 12–2 shows that the more corporal punishment used during the first year of the study, the greater the tendency for antisocial behavior to increase subsequent to the corporal punishment. It also shows that this effect applied to both Euro American children and children of other ethnic groups. Of course, other things also influence Antisocial Behavior. For example, girls have lower rates of Antisocial Behavior than boys, and children whose mothers are warm and supportive are less likely to behave in antisocial ways. Although these other variables do lessen the effect of corporal punishment, we found that the tendency for corporal punishment to make things worse over the long run applies regardless of race, socioeconomic status, gender of the child, and regardless of the extent to which the mother provides cognitive stimulation and emotional support.

Study 2: A Second Study of Corporal Punishment and Antisocial Behavior

Sample and Measures. Gunnoe and Mariner (1997a) analyzed data from another large and representative sample of American children—the National Survey of Families and Households. They studied 1,112 children in two age groups: 4 to 7 and 8 to 11. In half of the cases the mother was interviewed and in the other half the

CHART 12–2. The more spanking was used to correct misbehavior, the worse the behaviour 2 years later, for both Euro-American and minority children.

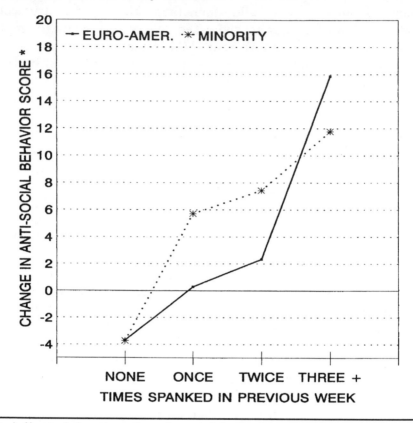

* Adjusted for time-1 anti-social behaviour, congnitive stimulation, parental emotional support, child gender, and ses.

father provided the information. The parents were first interviewed in 1987–1988, and then 5 years later. Gunnoe and Mariner's measure of corporal punishment was the same as in the Straus et al. study just described; that is, how often the parent spanked in the previous week.

Gunnoe and Mariner examined the effect of corporal punishment on two aspects of the child's behavior: fighting at school and antisocial behavior. Their antisocial ehavior measure was also the same as in the Straus et al. study.

Findings on Fighting. Gunnoe and Mariner found that the more corporal punishment in 1987–1988, the greater the amount of fighting at school five years later. This is consistent with the theory that in the long run corporal punishment is counter-productive. However, for toddlers and for African-American children, they found the opposite, i.e. that corporal punishment is associated with less fighting 5 years later. Gunnoe and Mariner suggest that this occurs because younger children and African-American children tend to regard corporal punishment as a legitimate parental behavior rather than as an aggressive act. However, corporal punishment by parents of young children and by African-American parents is so nearly universal that it suggests an alternative explanation: that no-corporal punishment means no-discipline. If that is the case, it is no wonder that children whose parents exercise no-discipline are less well behaved. Corporal punishment may not be good for children, but failure to properly supervise and control is even worse.

Findings on Antisocial Behavior. The findings on the relation of corporal punishment to antisocial behavior show that the more corporal punishment experienced by the children in Year 1, the higher the level of antisocial behavior five years later. Moreover, they found that the harmful effect of corporal punishment applies to all the categories of children they studied—that is, to children in each age group, to all races, and to both boys and girls. Thus, both of these major long term prospective studies resulted in evidence that, although corporal punishment may work in the short run, in the long run it tends to boomerang and increase the probability of antisocial behavior.

An important sidelight of the Gunnoe and Mariner study is that it illustrates the way inconvenient findings can be ignored to give a desired "spin." The findings section includes one brief sentence acknowledging that their study "replicates the Straus et al. findings." This crucial finding is never discussed in detail. The extensive discussion and conclusion sections omit mentioning the results of their research showing that corporal punishment at Time 1 was associated with more antisocial behavior subsequently for children of all ages and all ethnic groups. Marjorie Gunnoe told me that she is opposed to spanking and has never spanked her own children. So the spin she put on the findings is not a reflection of personal values or behavior. Perhaps it reflects teaching at a college affiliated with a church which teaches that God expects parents to spank.

Study 3: Corporal Punishment and Child-to-Parent Violence

Brezina (1999) analyzed data on a nationally representative sample of 1,519 adolescent boys who participated in the Youth in Transition study. This is a three-wave panel study that was begun in 1966. Although the data refer to a previous generation of high school students, there is no reason to think that the relationship between corporal punishment and children hitting parents is different now that it was then, except that the rate may have decreased because fewer parents now slap teen-agers.

Measure of Corporal Punishment. Corporal punishment was measured by asking the boys "How often do your parents actually slap you?" The response categories ranged from 1 (never) to 5 (always). Twenty eight percent of the boys reported being slapped by their parents during the year of the first wave of the study when their average age was 15, and 19 percent were slapped during the wave 2 year (a year and half later).

Measure of Child Aggression. The boys were asked similar questions about how often they hit their father and their mother. Eleven percent reported hitting a parent the first year, and 7 percent reported hitting a parent at Time 2 of the study.

Findings. Brezina found that corporal punishment at Time 1 was associated with an increased probability of a child assaulting the parent a year and a half later. Thus, while it is true that corporal punishment teaches the child a lesson, it is certainly not the lesson intended by the parents.

As with the other four studies, the data analysis took into account some of the many other factors that affect the probability of child-to-parent violence. These include the socioeconomic status and race of the family, the age of the parents, the child's attachment to the parent, child's attitude toward aggression, and child's physical size.

Study 4: Corporal Punishment and Dating Violence

Simons, Lin, & Gordon (1998) tested the theory that corporal punishment by the parents increases the probability of later hitting a partner in a dating relationship. They studied 113 boys in a rural area of the state of Iowa, beginning when they were in the seventh grade or about age 13.

Measure of Corporal Punishment. The mothers and the fathers of these boys were asked how often they spanked or slapped the child when he did something wrong, and how often they used a belt or paddle for corporal punishment. These questions were repeated in waves 2 and 3 of this 5-year study. The scores for the mother and the father for each of the three years were combined to create an overall measure of corporal punishment. More than half of the boys experienced corporal punishment during those years. Consequently, the findings about corporal punishment apply to the majority of boys in that community, not just to the children of a small group of violent parents.

Measure of Dating Violence. The information on dating violence came from the boys, so it is not influenced by whether the parents viewed the boy as aggressive. The boys were asked whether, in the last year, "When you had a disagreement with your girlfriend, how often did you hit, push, shove her?"

Measure of Delinquency at Time 1. As explained earlier, it is critical to take into account the misbehavior that leads parents to use corporal punishment. In this study, that was done by asking the boys at Time 1 how often they had engaged in each of 24 delinquent acts such as skipping school, stealing, and physically attacking someone with a weapon; and also how often they had used drugs and alcohol.

Parental Involvement and Support. Finally the study also took into account the extent to which the parents showed warmth and affection, were consistent in their discipline, monitored and supervised the child, and explained rules and expectations. In addition, it also controlled for witnessing parental violence.

Findings. Simons and his colleagues found that the more corporal punishment experienced by these boys, the greater the probability of their physically assaulting a girlfriend. Moreover, like the other prospective studies, the analysis took into account the misbehavior that led parents to use corporal punishment, and also for the quality of parenting. This means that the relation of corporal punishment to violence against a girlfriend is very unlikely to be due to poor parenting. Rather, it is another study showing that the long run effect of corporal punishment is to engender more rather than less misbehavior. In short, spanking boomerangs.

Study 5: Corporal Punishment and Child's Cognitive Development

The last of these five studies (Straus and Paschall, 1999) was prompted by studies showing that talking to children (including pre-speech infants) is associated with an increase in neural connections in the brain and in cognitive performance (Blakeslee, 1995). Those findings led us to theorize that if parents avoid corporal punishment, they are more likely to engage in verbal methods of behavior control such as explaining to the child, and that the increased verbal interaction with the child will in turn enhance the child's cognitive ability.

This theory was tested on 806 children of mothers in the National Longitudinal Study of Youth who were age 2 to 4 in the first year of our analysis, and the tests were repeated for an additional 704 children who were age 5 to 9 in the first year. Corporal punishment was measured by whether the mother was observed hitting the child during the interview and by a question on frequency of spanking in the past week. A corporal punishment scale was created by adding the number of times the parent spanked in two sample weeks. Cognitive ability was measured in Year 1 and two years later by tests appropriate for the age of the child at the time of testing such as the Peabody Picture Vocabulary Test.

The study took into account the mother's age and education, whether the father was present in the household, number of children in the family, mother's supportiveness and cognitive stimulation, ethnic group, and the child's age, gender, and child's birth weight.

Chart 12–3 shows what we found. However, to understand this chart, a number of technical aspects need to be explained. One of them is that these cognitive ability scores follow the convention of making 100 the average for children of each age. Consequently, a decrease of, for example 1.5 points ("–1.5" in Figure 12–3) does not indicate that, after two years, the children in that group had less cognitive ability than at the start of the study. On the contrary, the children in a group with an average of –1.5, like all normal children, increased their cognitive skills tremendously in those two years. What a change of –1.5 points means is that the children in that group lagged behind the average rate of cognitive development by 1.5 points.

Children Age 2 to 4. The upper line in of Chart 12–3 is for children age 2 to 4 at the start of the study. (1) At the right side of the upper line are the children who were hit three or more times in the two sample weeks. This was the typical experience for children this age (48 percent). Since they are the typical children, it should not be surprising that they followed the typical pattern of cognitive development, as shown by the mean change of zero,

CHART 12–3. Children who were not spanked had faster than average mental development, and children who were spanked a lot fell behind the average.

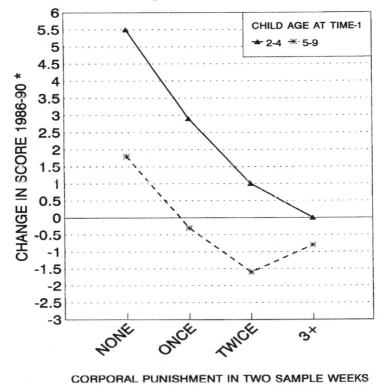

CORPORAL PUNISHMENT IN TWO SAMPLE WEEKS

---

* Adjusted for cognitive stimultion and emotional support by mother, mother's age and education, child's race, age and sex, number of children, birthweight, and father in household.

i.e. they did not either gain or fall behind other children in their cohort. (2) The children in the next group to the left are those who were hit less often during the two sample weeks (2 times) and their mean of +1 indicates slightly above average cognitive development. (3) The children who were hit only once during those two weeks gained considerably more (an average of 3 points) during the two years covered by the study. (4) Finally, at the upper left are the rare children (only 10 percent) who were not spanked in either of the two sample weeks. They gained an average of 5.5 points relative to the average cognitive ability of children their age. In summary, the upper line of Figure 13 shows that the less corporal punishment parents use on toddlers, the greater the probability that the child will have an above average growth.

Children Age 5-9. The lower line of Chart 12–3 is for children age 5 to 9. (1) The plot point at the left for the children who were not spanked in the two sample weeks shows that they experienced above average cognitive growth during the two years of this study. However, the benefit is not as great as for toddlers (just under 2 points compared to 5.5 points for toddlers), perhaps because at age 5 to 9, not spanking is not as exceptional. (2) Children who were spanked once during the two sample weeks (the typical experience for this age) also experienced the typical pattern of cognitive development. However, those who were spanked two or three times during the two sample weeks, i.e., spanked more than average, fell behind the average cognitive development.

The greater benefit of avoiding corporal punishment for the younger children is consistent with the research showing the most rapid growth of neural connections takes place in the brain at early ages. It is also consistent with the theory that what the child learns as an infant and toddler is crucial because it provides the necessary basis for subsequent cognitive development (Johnson, 1999). The greater adverse effect on cognitive development for toddlers has an extremely important practical implication because the defenders of corporal punishment have now retreated to limiting their approval to toddlers (Friedman and Schonberg, 1996). Their recommendation is not based on empirical evidence. The evidence from this study suggests that, at least in so far as cognitive development is concerned, supporters of corporal punishment have unwittingly advised parents to use corporal punishment at the ages when it will have the most adverse effect on cognitive development.

The Message of the Five Studies: "Don't Spank"

Each of the five studies I summarized is far from perfect. They can be picked apart one by one, as can just about every epidemiological study. This is what the tobacco industry did for many years. The Surgeon General's committee on smoking did the opposite. Their review of the research acknowledged the limitations of the studies when taken one-by-one. But they concluded that despite the defects of the individual studies, the cumulative evidence indicated that smoking does cause lung cancer and other diseases, and they called for an end to smoking. In respect to spanking, I believe that the cumulative weight of the evidence, and especially the five prospective studies provides sufficient evidence for a new Surgeon General's warning. A start in that direction was made by the American Academy of Pediatrics, which published "Guidelines for Effective Discipline" that advises parents to avoid spanking (American Academy of Pediatrics, 1998).

Is There a Backlash?

It is ironic that during the same period as the new and more definitive research was appearing, there were hostile or ridiculing articles in newspapers and magazines on the idea of never spanking a child (e.g., Lemonick and Park, 1997; Rosellini, 1998). In 1999, Arizona and Arkansas passed laws to remind parents and teachers that they have the right to use corporal punishment and to urge them to do so. There has also been a contentious debate in scientific journals on the appropriateness of corporal punishment. These developments made some advocates for children concerned that there is a backlash against the idea of no-spanking. However, there are several reasons for doubting the existence of a backlash in the sense of a reversal in the trend of decreasing public support for corporal punishment, or in the sense of non-spanking parents reverting to using corporal punishment.

The Trend Away From Corporal Punishment Continues

One reason for doubting the existence of a backlash is that, each year, a larger and larger proportion of the American population opposes corporal punishment. Chart 12–4 (updated from a chart in Straus and Mathur, 1996) shows that in 1968, which was only a generation ago, almost everyone (94 percent) believed that corporal punishment is sometimes necessary. But in the last 30 years, Chart 12–4 shows that public support for corporal punishment has been decreasing. By 1999, almost half of US adults rejected the idea that spanking is necessary.

The Advocates Are Long-Time Supporters

In 1968, those who favored corporal punishment did not need to speak out to defend their view because, as just indicated, almost everyone believed it was necessary. The dramatic decrease in support

CHART 12–4. The percent agreeing that a "good hard spanking is sometimes necessary" dropped from near unanimity to 55 percent in one generation.

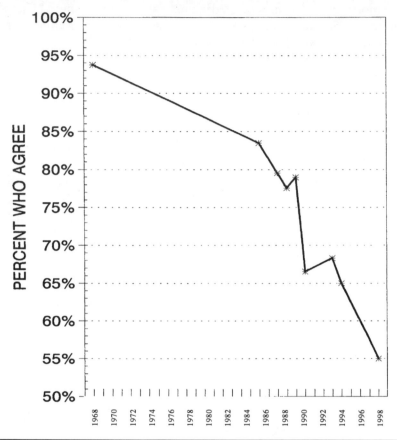

Updated for 1995 and 1999 from Straus & Mathur, 1996.

for corporal punishment shown in Chart 12–4 means that long time advocates of corporal punishment such as Dobson (1992), Ezzo (1995), Larzelere (1994), and Rosemond (1994), now have reason to be worried and they are speaking out. These authors have always favored corporal punishment. Consequently, their recent publications do not indicate a backlash in the sense of a change from being opposed to corporal punishment to favoring it. I suggest that it is more like dying gasps of support for an ancient mode of bringing up children that is heading towards extinction.

Fear about the Increase in Crime by Youth

The efforts of those who favor corporal punishment have also been spurred on by the increase in crime in many countries. The rise in youth crime, although recently reversed, is a very disturbing trend, and it has prompted a search for causes and corrective steps. It should be no surprise that people who have always believed in use of corporal punishment believe that a return to their favored mode of bringing up children will help cure the crime problem. They argue that children need "discipline," which is correct. However, they equate discipline with corporal punishment, which is not correct. As noted in the introduction to this chapter, no-corporal punishment does not mean no-discipline. Delinquency prevention does require, among other things, discipline in the sense of clear rules and standards for behavior and parental supervision, monitoring and enforcement (Empey, 1982). To the extent that part of the explanation for crime, especially crime by youth, is the lack of discipline, the appropriate step is not a return to corporal punishment but parental standards, monitoring, and enforcement by non-violent methods. In fact, as the studies just reviewed indicate, if discipline takes the form of more corporal punishment, the problem will be exacerbated because, while corporal punishment does work with some children, more typically it boomerangs and increases the level of juvenile delinquency and other behavior problems.

The Normal Questioning Mode of Science

The criticism in scientific journals of research on corporal punishment is also not a backlash. It has to be viewed in the light of the norms of science. A standard aspect of science is to examine research critically, to raise questions, and to suggest alternative interpretations of findings. This results in a somewhat paradoxical tendency for criticism to increase as the amount of research goes up. There has recently been an increase in research showing long-term harmful effects of corporal punishment. Given the critical ethos of science, it is only to be expected that the increased research has elicited more commentary and criticism, especially on the part of those who believed in corporal punishment in the first place.

Most Parent Education Inadvertently
Perpetuates Corporal Punishment

Three paradoxical aspects of the movement away from corporal punishment will be highlighted in this section. The first is that, although approval of corporal punishment had declined precipitously in the last generation, almost all parents continue to spank toddlers. The second paradox is that professionals advising parents, including those who are opposed to spanking, generally fail to tell parents not to spank. They call this avoiding a "negative approach." Finally, and most paradoxically of all, focusing almost exclusively on a so-called "positive approach," unwittingly contributes to perpetuating corporal punishment and helps explain the first paradox.

Paradox 1: Contradictory Trends

Some aspects of corporal punishment have changed in major ways. A smaller and smaller percent of the public favors spanking. Fewer parents now use belts, hairbrushes, and paddles. The percent of parents who hit adolescents has dropped by half since 1975. Nevertheless, other aspects of corporal punishment continue to be prevalent, chronic, and severe. The 1995 Gallup national survey of parents (Straus and Stewart, 1999) found that:

- Almost all parents of toddlers (94 percent) used corporal punishment that year

- Parents who spanked a toddler, did it an average of about three times a week

- 28 percent of parents of children age 5–12 used an object such as a belt or hairbrush

- Over a third of parents of 13-year-old children hit them that year

The myths about corporal punishment in Chapter 10 provide important clues to understanding why parents who "don't believe in spanking" continue to do so. These myths also undermine the ability of professionals who advise parents to do what is needed to end corporal punishment.

Paradox 2: Being Opposed to Spanking but Failing to Say Never Spank or Even Don't Spank

Many pediatricians, developmental psychologists, and parent educators are now opposed to corporal punishment, at least in principle. But, like the Director of Child Protection at Boston Children's Hospital, quoted in Chapter 1, and the director of an organization devoted to ending corporal punishment in schools, cited in the new Preface, most also continue to believe that there may be a situation where spanking by parents is necessary or acceptable. This is based on the cultural myths that spanking works when other things do not (see Chapter 10, Myth 1) and that "mild" corporal punishment is harmless (Myth 3). All but a small minority of parents and professionals continue to believe these myths despite the experimental and other evidence showing that other disciplinary strategies work just as well as spanking, even in the short run (Larzelere et al., 1998; Larzelere, Schneider, Larson, and Pike, 1996; Roberts, 1988; Roberts and Powers, 1990), and are more effective in the long run as shown by the first four of the studies described earlier in this chapter. Consequently, when I suggest to pediatricians, parent educators, or social scientists that it is essential to tell parents that they should never spank or use any other type of corporal punishment, that idea has been rejected with rare exception. Some, like one of America's leading developmental psychologists, object because of the unproven belief that it would turn off parents. Some object on the false belief that it could be harmful because parents don't know what else to do (see Myths 5, 9, and 10). They argue for a "positive approach" by which they mean teaching parents alternative disciplinary strategies, as compared to what they call the "negative approach" of advising to never spank. As a result, the typical pattern is to say nothing about spanking. Fortunately, that is slowly changing. Although they are still the exception, an increasing number of books for parents, parent education programs, and guidelines for professionals advise no-spanking.

Both the movement away from spanking and an important limitation of that movement are illustrated by Publication of the "Guidelines for Effective Discipline" of the American Academy of Pediatrics (American Academy of Pediatrics, 1998). This was an important step forward, but it also reflects the same problem. It recommends that parents avoid corporal punishment. However, it also carefully avoids saying that parents should never spank. This may seem like splitting hairs, but because of the typical sequence of parent-child interaction that eventuates in corporal punishment described in the next section, it is a major obstacle to ending corporal punishment. Omitting a never-spank message is a serious obstacle because, in the absence of a commitment to never-spank, even parents who are against spanking continue to spank. It is important to understand what underlies the paradox of parents who are opposed to spanking, nonetheless spanking.

Paradox 3: Why Failing to Be Explicit about Never Spanking Results in Everyone Spanking

This paradoxical situation reflects a combination of needing to cope with the typical behavior of toddlers and perceiving those behaviors through the lens of the myth that spanking works when other things do not.

When a toddler is corrected for a misbehavior (such as hitting another child or disobeying), the "recidivism" rate is about 80 percent within the same day and about 50 percent within two hours. For some children, it is within two minutes (Larzelere et al., 1998; Larzelere, Schneider, Larson, and Pike, 1996). Moreover, Larzelere (who is a defender of corporal punishment) found that these "time to failure" rates apply equally to corporal punishment and to other disciplinary strategies. Consequently, on any given day, a parent is almost certain to find that so-called alternative disciplinary strategies such as explaining, deprivation of privileges, and time out, "do not work." When that happens, they turn to spanking. So, as pointed out previously, just about everyone (at least 94 percent) spanks toddlers.

The difference between spanking and other disciplinary strategies is that, when spanking does not work, parents do not question its effectiveness. The idea that spanking works when other methods do not is so ingrained in American culture that, when the child repeats the misbehavior an hour or two later (or sometimes a few minutes later) parents fail to perceive that spanking has the same high failure rate as other modes of discipline. So they spank again, and for as many times as it takes to ultimately secure compliance. That is the correct strategy because, with consistency and perseverance, the child will eventually learn. What so many parents miss is that it is also the correct strategy for non-spanking methods. Thus, unless there is an absolute prohibition on spanking, parents will "see with their own eyes" that alternatives do not work and continue to find it is necessary to spank.

"Never-Spank" Must Be the Message

Because of the typical behavior of toddlers and the almost inevitable information processing errors just described, teaching alternative disciplinary techniques by itself is not sufficient. There must also be an unambiguous "never-spank" message to increase the chances that parents who disapprove of spanking will act on their beliefs. Consequently, it is essential for pediatricians and others who advise parents to abandon their reluctance to say "never-spank." To achieve this, parent-educators must themselves be educated. They need to understand why, what they now consider a "negative approach," is such an important part of ending use of corporal punishment. Moreover, because they believe that a "negative approach" does not work, they also need to know about the experience of Sweden. The Swedish experience shows that, contrary to the currently prevailing opinion, a never-spank approach has worked (Durrant, 1999).

In short, the first priority step to end or reduce spanking may be to educate professionals who advise parents. Once professionals are ready to move, the key steps are relatively easy to implement and inexpensive.

- Parent-education programs, such as STEP, which are now silent on spanking, can be revised to include the evidence that spanking does *not* work better than other disciplinary tactics, even in the short run; and to specifically say "never spank."

- The Public Health Service can follow the Swedish model and sponsor no-spanking public service announcements on TV and on milk cartons.

- There can be a "No-Spanking" poster and pamphlets in every pediatrician's office and every maternity ward.

- There can be a notice on birth certificates such as:

WARNING: SPANKING HAS BEEN DETERMINED TO BE DANGEROUS TO THE HEALTH AND WELL BEING OF YOUR CHILD—

DO NOT EVER, UNDER ANY CIRCUMSTANCES, SPANK OR HIT
YOUR CHILD

Until professionals who advise parents start advising parents to
never spank, the paradox of parents becoming less and less favorable to spanking while at the same time continuing to spank
toddlers will continue. Fortunately, that is starting to happen.

Benefits to Children and Society of Ending
Corporal Punishment

The benefits of avoiding corporal punishment are many, but they
are virtually impossible for parents to perceive by observing their
children. The situation with spanking is parallel to that of smoking. Smokers could perceive the short run satisfaction from a ciga-
rette, but had no way to see the adverse health consequences down
the road. Similarly, parents can perceive the beneficial effects of a
slap (and, for the reasons explained in the previous section, fail to
see the equal effectiveness of alternatives), they have no way of
looking a year or more into the future to see if there is a harmful
side effect of having hit their child to correct misbehavior. The
only way parents can know this would be if there were a public
policy to publicize the results of research such as the studies summarized in this chapter.

Another reason the benefits of avoiding spanking are difficult
to see is that they are not dramatic in any one case. This is illustrated by the average increase of 2 to 5 points in mental ability
associated with no-corporal punishment. An increase of that size
would hardly be noticed in an individual case. However, it is a
well established principle in public health and epidemiology that
a widely prevalent risk factor with small effect size, for example
spanking, can have a much greater impact on public health than a
risk factor with a large effect size, but low prevalence, for example, physical abuse (Cohen, 1996; Rose, 1985; Rosenthal,
1984). For example, assume that: (1) 50 million US children experienced corporal punishment and 1 million experienced physical abuse. (2) The probability of being depressed as an adult is
increased by 2 percent for children who experienced corporal
punishment and by 25 percent for children who experienced physical abuse. Given these assumptions, the additional cases of depression caused by corporal punishment is 1.02 times 50 million,

or 1 million. The additional cases of depression caused by physical abuse are 1.25 times 1 million, or 250,000. Thus corporal punishment is associated with a four times greater increase in depression than is physical abuse.

Another example of a major benefit resulting from reducing a risk factor that has a small effect, but for a large proportion of the population, may be the increase in scores on intelligence tests that has been occurring worldwide (Neisser, 1997). Corporal punishment has also been decreasing worldwide. The decrease in use of corporal punishment and the increase in scores on IQ tests could be just a coincidence. However, the results of the study described earlier in this chapter which showed that less spanking is associated with faster cognitive development suggest that the trend away from corporal punishment may be one of a number of social changes (especially, better educated parents) that explain the increase in IQ scores in so many nations.

The other four prospective studies reviewed in this chapter, together with the studies in Part II, show that ending corporal punishment is likely to also reduce juvenile violence, wife-beating, and masochistic sex, and increase the probability of completing higher education (Straus and Mathur, 1995), holding a high income job, and lower rates of depression and alcohol abuse (see Chapter 5 and Straus and Kaufman Kantor, 1994). Those are not only humanitarian benefits, they can also result in huge monetary savings in public and private costs for dealing with mental health problems, school problems, marital and family problems, and crime.

Chart 12–5 estimates how much could be gained if corporal punishment were ended. However, the reduction in social and psychological problem behaviors would not be as large as those in Chart 12–5. One reason is that Chart 12–5 compares the experience of no-corporal punishment with the experience of a high frequency of corporal punishment. These extremes are a large group in absolute numbers but, because they are a relatively small part of the total population, the degree to which problems are reduced will be less for those who experienced more typical amounts of corporal punishment. Consequently, after averaging in those smaller reductions, the overall decrease in human problems will be less than suggested by Chart 12–5, but would still represent an important reduction in human suffering and in problems for society.

CHART 12–5. How much could ending corporal punishment decrease psychologocal and social problems?

	CORPORAL PUNISHMENT		
	HIGH	NONE	CHANGE

A. CHILD BEHAVIOR PROBLEMS

	HIGH	NONE	CHANGE
REPEATEDLY AND SEVERELY ATTACKED A SIBLING IN PREVIOUS 12 MONTHS (p.102)	40%	18%	55% LESS
NUMBER OF TIMES HIT OTHER CHILDREN IN SCHOOL IN TWO WEEK PERIOD (MEAN) (Strassberg et al. 1994)	4.3	2.1	51 % LESS
LESS RAPID GROWTH IN MENTAL ABILITY IN 4 YEARS			
CHILDREN AGE 2-4 IN YEAR 1	0.0	+5.5	5.5% LESS
CHILDREN AGE 5-9 IN YEAR 1	-0.8	+1.8	2.6% LESS
(p. 203)			
JUVENILE DELINQUENCY IN PAST 12 MONTHS (p. 108; see also Straus et al., 1997)	15%	3%	80% LESS
SYMPTOMS OF PSYCHOLOGICAL DISTRESS (MEAN) (Turner& Finkelhor, 1994)	.99	.65	34% LESS

B. ADULT PROBLEMS

	HIGH	NONE	CHANGE
GRADUATE FROM COLLEGE (Straus & Mathur, 1 995)	15%	22%	47% MORE
SERIOUSLY DEPRESSED (90TH PERCENTILE) (p.74; see also Durant, 1995)	13%	7%	46% LESS
HIT SPOUSE IN PREVIOUS 12 MONTHS (p.104; see also Simons et al., 1998)	25%	8%	68% LESS
PHYSICALLY ABUSED OWN CHILD IN PAST 12 MONTHS (i.e. went beyond legal corporal punishment) (p.94)	24%	8%	67% LESS

NOTE: Page references are to this book unless a different author is indicated.

The final words of the original concluding chapter (Chapter 11) were that ending corporal punishment by parents "portends profound and far reaching benefits for humanity." The new research summarized in this chapter now makes those words even more appropriate. We can look forward to the day when children in almost all countries have the benefit of being brought up without being hit by their parents; and just as important, to the day when many nations have the benefit of the healthier, wealthier, and wiser citizens who were brought up free from the violence that is now a part of their earliest and most influential life experiences.

Appendix A
A Theoretical Model

Little progress can be made in research without a theoretical framework to stimulate and guide it and to aid in interpreting its findings. Indeed, the absence of a theoretical framework focused specifically on corporal punishment may be part of the reason why so few social scientists have found it an interesting problem to investigate. This appendix presents such a framework in the form of a causal model, diagramed in Chart A–1. The model identifies some of the most important causes and consequences of corporal punishment, thus laying out a minimal agenda for empirical and theoretical research.

Chart A–1 is labeled a "system model" because it assumes that corporal punishment and its effects are a function of other characteristics of the society and that corporal punishment, in turn, influences the society. It illustrates the idea that corporal punishment can be adequately understood only as part of the dynamic interplay between the characteristics of the parents, the child, the family unit, aspects of parent-child interaction other than corporal punishment, the socio-cultural environment, and the place of the family in that social context. The dashed lines in Chart A–1 indicate one aspect of these dynamics—the effects of corporal punishment on the characteristics of the society, which in turn influences the probability of the future use of corporal punishment.[1]

There also should be arrows between the elements *within* each block of Chart A–1 but, except for block II at the center of the

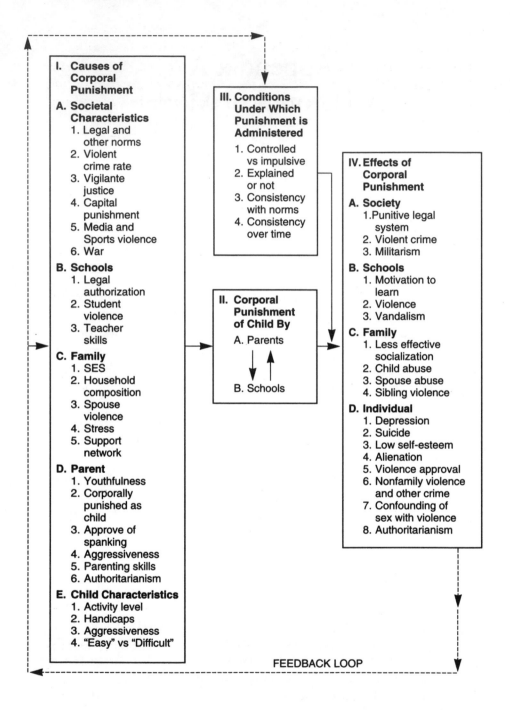

I. **Causes of Corporal Punishment**

A. **Societal Characteristics**
1. Legal and other norms
2. Violent crime rate
3. Vigilante justice
4. Capital punishment
5. Media and Sports violence
6. War

B. **Schools**
1. Legal authorization
2. Student violence
3. Teacher skills

C. **Family**
1. SES
2. Household composition
3. Spouse violence
4. Stress
5. Support network

D. **Parent**
1. Youthfulness
2. Corporally punished as child
3. Approve of spanking
4. Aggressiveness
5. Parenting skills
6. Authoritarianism

E. **Child Characteristics**
1. Activity level
2. Handicaps
3. Aggressiveness
4. "Easy" vs "Difficult"

III. **Conditions Under Which Punishment is Administered**
1. Controlled vs impulsive
2. Explained or not
3. Consistency with norms
4. Consistency over time

II. **Corporal Punishment of Child By**
A. Parents
B. Schools

IV. **Effects of Corporal Punishment**

A. **Society**
1. Punitive legal system
2. Violent crime
3. Militarism

B. **Schools**
1. Motivation to learn
2. Violence
3. Vandalism

C. **Family**
1. Less effective socialization
2. Child abuse
3. Spouse abuse
4. Sibling violence

D. **Individual**
1. Depression
2. Suicide
3. Low self-esteem
4. Alienation
5. Violence approval
6. Nonfamily violence and other crime
7. Confounding of sex with violence
8. Authoritarianism

FEEDBACK LOOP

model, they are omitted to avoid a confusing welter of arrows. The arrows within box II suggest a mutually reinforcing relationship between corporal punishment in the schools and by parents. It seems highly plausible that in a society that approves of parents hitting children, more parents (but not all parents) will tend to approve of teachers doing the same. Conversely, corporal punishment in the schools encourages parents to also hit children. This type of relationship is illustrated by Lambert, Triandis, and Wolf's (1959) study of nonliterate societies, which found that societies that rely on corporal punishment also tend to have a religious system in which deities are punitive. In the United States, most state laws grant permission to use corporal punishment to both parents and teachers in the same statute (Chapter 1). When a society changes and eliminates corporal punishment, the change seems to come first in schools and only later in homes (Graziano and Namaste, 1990; see also the concluding chapter).

For the most part, Chart A–1 shows only direct paths between hypothesized causes and effects; thus, the path between having been physically punished as a child (box I, section D2) and using corporal punishment on your own children. This is a vast oversimplification. To start with, it ignores all the other variables in box I, each of which influences the extent to which those who were spanked will also spank. Second, many important aspects of the process leading to hitting a child are not included in Chart A–1. Including everything that potentially influences this process would result in an unmanageable diagram. It would be a classic case of "more is less" because almost no one would be able to read it. As I said earlier, Chart A–1 is a minimal model intended only to provide an overview. More specific models are given in each of the chapters in Part II.

The choice of what to include in Chart A–1 no doubt was influenced by the fact that I am a sociologist. Consequently, social characteristics are more completely covered than are psychological variables, but even the social characteristics are intended to be only illustrative. Nothing at all concerning biologically based predispositions to violence is included despite its importance (Gelles and Lancaster, 1987). From a psychological perspective, much more study is needed on the personality of parents and children, their cognitive styles, and styles of interacting with their children (Maccoby and

Martin, 1983). As Holden (1989) shows, although corporal punishment may seem to happen instantly and automatically, a complex information-processing and decision-making process is involved. Just to show those contingencies would require an additional box of variables to intersect each of the paths between boxes I and II. The model in Chapter 7 (Chart 7–10) makes a start at specifying some of the many contingencies that intervene between corporal punishment and outcome variables such as aggression and crime.

Links to Other Theories

Although Chart A–1 identifies some key relationships, much greater theoretical depth is needed, including integration with other relevant theories. The need to examine corporal punishment from a variety of theoretical perspectives is being addressed in a book I am editing with Michael Donnelly, *Corporal Punishment in Theoretical Perspective*. This appendix only briefly illustrates the possibilities.

Social and Cultural Support Theories

Chapter 7 used *cultural spillover theory* (Baron and Straus, 1988) as the main framework for interpreting its findings. Cultural spillover theory overlaps with what Farrell and Swigert (1988:295) identify as "social and cultural support" theories of crime. These include differential association theory, delinquent subculture theory, and social learning theory. Each of these theories seeks to show that crime is not just a reflection of individual deviance (as in psychopathology theories of crime) or the absence of social control (as in social disorganization theory). Rather, they hold that crime is also engendered by integration of a potential criminal into a group with norms and values that support behavior the rest of society considers to be criminal. Thus, one of the processes that produce criminal behavior are structurally parallel to the processes that produce conforming behavior, but the cultural content differs.

Social Learning and Differential Association Theory

The bulk of research on the links between corporal punishment and aggressiveness of the child has used a social learning framework (Bandura, 1973; Berkowitz, 1962; Eron, *et al.*, 1971; Mc-Cord, 1988). At the macrosociological level, an analogous process is the "brutalization" theory developed by Bowers (1984) to investigate the effects of capital punishment. The evidence summarized by Hawkins (1989) provides considerable support for the proposition that executions provide a model of violence and lead to an elevated homicide rate. As Hawkins also shows, however, both the brutalization theory and the closely rated cultural spillover theory are primitive theories that need to be further developed. One direction for increasing the scope of these theories is to integrate them with other related theories. One that comes to mind is differential association theory as formulated by Sutherland (1947). In some respects differential association theory is parallel to social learning theory explanations of crime (Akers *et al.*, 1979). However, differential association goes beyond social learning theory in specifying the social structures, such as neighborhoods and gangs, that organize the learning process. Membership in these groups not only provides the models of behavior and values to be learned, but also the social ties and "differential identification" (Glaser, 1956) that maximizes the learning process. Farrell and Swigert (1988:294–99) suggest ways in which these theories are interrelated.

Personality Mediated Theories

Suppose there were longitudinal data showing that children who have been physically punished have higher rates of violence as adults than do children who committed the same infractions but were not physically punished. This would not prove the cultural spillover theory because it does not demonstrate that the reason for the greater violence is legitimization of violence through corporal punishment. There are many other mediating factors in life that could produce that result. As suggested in Chapter 9, for example, corporal punishment might cause changes in personality, such as lowered self-esteem or increased powerlessness and alienation. These personality variables can, by themselves, serve as risk factors for violence. A "competing theories" research design and triangulation using several different types of research are required to reach dependable conclusions.

Control Theory

One of the most important explanations of juvenile crime is what Hirschi (1969) calls *control theory*. Corporal punishment does not seem to have been investigated by researchers working with that theory. Such studies are likely to be fruitful, however, because it is plausible to assume that corporal punishment by parents and teachers tends to undermine their bond with the child. To the extent that the parent-child and the school-child bond is undermined, so also is commitment to conventional law-abiding behavior. The problem tends to worsen over time because weakened bonds make it more difficult for parents and teachers to use nonpunitive modes of influencing behavior. These methods tend to depend heavily on the closeness of the attachment between parent and child (Hirschi, 1969; Lytton-Hugh, 1979).

Labeling Theory

Corporal punishment may have an important labeling effect, including both self-labeling and labeling by others. Other children in the family and in the classroom observe the child being hit by the teacher. If they are shown a picture or read a story about a child being hit and then are asked to explain what is going on, children almost always say that the child was doing something wrong; that is, they attribute being hit to the child's bad behavior. It also seems plausible that some children will internalize an image of themselves as bad, stupid, no-good or whatever term the parent or teacher tends to favor when using corporal punishment. This can result in a "deviance amplifying" process in which the child gradually comes to act out the role implied by the label (Scheff, 1984; Straus, 1973).

Empirical Tests

Using empirical research to test the model in Chart A–1 is extremely difficult. First, such a test is a huge undertaking. It is not something that can be accomplished by one investigator or even one team of investigators. The empirical research carried out for this book investigated only parts of the model. Even the parts that were investigated used cross-sectional survey data, which cannot establish the causal directions or be used to investigate the feedback loops in Chart A–1.

Most of the data in this book, as well as most other research on corporal punishment, was obtained by interviewing or observing parents or children. These studies may show that physically punished children have higher rates of delinquency and other psychosocial problems. However, they cannot rule out the possibility that the findings just reflect the fact that parents tend to hit misbehaving children. A parent might slap a toddler because the child is over-active and aggressive. Ten years later that child still may be aggressive, not because the parent used corporal punishment but because of a biologically based predisposition to aggression.

In principle, longitudinal research can establish which comes first—the corporal punishment or the misbehavior. However, the fact that parents hit a two- or three-year-old for misbehavior does not necessarily mean that the misbehavior comes first. This is because up to half of all children are hit when they are infants. A rather broad view of misbehavior is required to say that a mother is punishing misbehavior by slapping an infant's hand for putting something dirty in her mouth; that is part of the natural behavior of infants. So a longitudinal study would have to start observing parent and child almost from birth on. Unfortunately, longitudinal research is not much better than cross-sectional research in disentangling the effects of corporal punishment from the effects of other aversive behavior that usually goes with corporal punishment, such as verbal attacks on the child, the lack of warmth or support, and the failure to set clear standards.

For these and other reasons, previous comprehensive reviews (Kandel, 1991; Maurer, 1974; Steinmetz, 1979), the review conducted for this book, and its findings do not prove that corporal punishment has adverse long-run effects. Despite its limitations, however, nonexperimental research is by no means a futile exercise. Nonexperimental studies may not be able to prove the theory but they *can* falsify the theory. This would occur if the studies tended to find no support for the relationships deduced from the theory. Instead, the opposite has happened. Research that could have falsified the theory, did not. With very few exceptions, the findings show that the more corporal punishment, the higher the rate of undesirable behaviors or thoughts later in life, such as delinquency, approval of violence, alienation, depression, and lowered earnings. These findings greatly strengthen the theory that corporal punishment is one of the causes of these undesirable behaviors. This is an extremely important point because the prevailing belief is that corporal punishment, when administered in moderation and for just cause, is not associated with undesirable behavior. This belief is so strong that even more preliminary evidence is needed to support the theory. I say this on the basis of the opposition I encountered in 1992 and 1993 from two national committees of distinguished social scientists when I urged giving priority to research on corporal punishment. Until there is a sizable body of evidence to challenge the belief that corporal punishment is not associated with undesirable behavior, it will be difficult to obtain support to do the kind of research needed for more definitive tests of the model.

In the center of Chart A–1, the arrows from boxes II and III lead to the adverse effects of corporal punishment on children listed in box IV. These paths probably represent the greatest practical implications for the well-being of children and, therefore, of society as a whole. They are also the most controversial aspects of the model and the most difficult research issues.

The optimum research design is an experiment. The classic experiment is rarely possible, however, because only experimenters who are convinced that corporal punishment is truly helpful to children are willing to assign a random half of a sample of parents to a spanking treatment and the other half to a no-spanking treatment. Both groups of parents might object strenuously, perhaps with those in the no-spanking treatment the most outraged. However, such studies have been done. Day and Roberts (1983) randomly assigned the use of corporal punishment to some mothers and not to others when a child violated time out. Social scientists like me, who are convinced that corporal punishment is harmful, would not be willing to randomly assign parents to spank. Other types of experimental studies are possible however. These include laboratory analog studies (Holden, 1989) and certain types of field experiments or quasi-experiments. I am currently engaged in an experiment in which one of two small cities is fielding a community-wide education project to become a "no-hitter community." The program is designed to reach parents directly (though parent-education programs, Head Start, Sunday schools, and so on) and also to change attitudes in the community as a whole. The experiment is based on the idea that parents need support from their network of kin and friends to change their attitudes. Corporal punishment is so embedded in the culture that the effects of parent education programs will be undone unless steps are taken to change these attitudes and values in the community as a whole.

Appendix B
Samples and Measures of
Corporal Punishment

Measures of Corporal Punishment

One of the most fundamental problems in conducting empirical research on corporal punishment is how to measure the extent to which parents hit children. The best way would be actual observation in the home or laboratory. Short of that, it is possible to use interview data, but this depends on the respondent being willing to confide in the interviewer and being able to recall instances of having used corporal punishment. Since spanking children is something that almost everyone thinks is sometimes necessary and is morally correct, willingness to disclose this information is probably not an important problem. In any case, more than 90 percent of parents of toddlers did tell the interviewer about instances in which they had used corporal punishment. However, memory is a problem, a fact that is discussed in this appendix.

Two ways of measuring corporal punishment were used for this book. The results of these two measures will be called *adult recall* data and *contemporary* data. Chapter 3 compares the two methods. The adult recall data was used for chapters 5, 6, 7, 8, and 9. Contemporary data was used for chapters 2, 3, 4, 7, and 8.

Adult Recall Measure

These data were obtained by asking respondents, "Thinking about when you yourself were a teenager, about how often would you say your mother or stepmother used corporal punishment, like slapping or hitting you? Think about the year in which this happened the most. Never, Once, Twice, 3–5 times, 6–10 times, 11–20 times, More than 20 times." This was followed by a parallel question asking about the corporal punishment the respondent experienced at the hands of his or her father. Previous analyses found that the peak years for hitting adolescents are ages 13 and 14 (Wauchope and Straus, 1990). Since respondents were asked how much corporal punishment occurred in the year it happened the most, the adult recall data probably refers to ages 13 and 14. The N for the adult recall data is 5,452.

The referent period for the adult recall questions was set at ". . . when you yourself were a teenager" and ". . . the year this happened the most" on the assumption that memory of events before age 13 would be too incomplete. In retrospect, setting a specific age, such as "when you were 13," might have been better because "the year it happened the most" makes the specific year unknown. For purposes of the data analysis in Chapter 3, we assumed it was ages 13 and 14 because the prevalence rate drops off sharply after 14.

LIMITATIONS OF THE ADULT DATA

Although data provided by victims are at least as important as data provided by parents, there are several limitations.

First, almost no one can recall events that took place as a toddler. Memory of events increases thereafter, and there is some evidence that events that happened between the ages of 15 and 25 are recalled fairly accurately by older adults (Hyland and Ackerman, 1988). Nevertheless, accuracy may be compromised when people are asked to recall what happened 25 years earlier.

Another problem is the possibility of selective recall. This would occur if current psychological difficulties or problems lead some adults to remember more of the bad things about their childhoods, including corporal punishment. On the other hand, perhaps corporal punishment is so traumatic for some children that they may repress memories of these incidents.

Contemporary Measure

The "minor violence" scale of the Conflict Tactics Scales, or CTS, (Straus, 1979b; 1990a) was used to obtain information on corporal punishment by the respondents during the 12 months up to the interview. The items in the minor violence scale, such as slapping and spanking, were used as the measure of corporal punishment because all the acts in that index are legal in every state of the U.S. The CTS is described in more detail in the following sections, and complete information is in the CTS manual (Straus (1990d).

LIMITATIONS OF THE CONTEMPORARY DATA

A random half of the participants in the National Family Violence surveys were fathers and the other half were mothers. The contemporary data in this book refer to corporal punishment by the parent who was interviewed. The parent who was interviewed could have been asked about corporal punishment administered by the other parent; in fact, there would have been advantages in obtaining such data. Despite this, we decided to focus only on the parent who was interviewed because of doubts about the validity of the data. The interviewed parent might not know about the extent and frequency of the other parent's use of corporal punishment and the other parent behaviors measured by the Conflict Tactics Scales (Reasoning and Verbal Aggression). In light of this problem and the need to restrict the length of the interview, it seemed better to devote the time that an additional CTS administration would take to other information that was needed about the family. Consequently, a limitation of this data is that the "no punishment" group inevitably includes some children who did experience corporal punishment, but by the parent who was not interviewed. The contemporary data also do not permit classification and comparison of families in which both parents hit adolescents, versus those that are "father only" and "mother only."

The contemporary data also underestimate the prevalence of corporal punishment because it refers to the 12 months immediately preceding the interview. A particular 14-year-old child may have not been corporally punished that year but may have experienced a great deal of corporal punishment when he or she was 13. Third, the contemporary data may underestimate prevalence if hitting adolescents is less socially acceptable than hitting toddlers. If so, parents may be especially reluctant to tell an interviewer about corporal punishment of an adolescent.

Another limitation of the contemporary data is that only a relatively small proportion of the sample had an adolescent living at home. This reduces the sample size and, therefore, the reliability of the data.

The availability of both adult recall and contemporary data provided an important opportunity to examine the consistency between research based on these two sources of information. The results in Chapter 3 show a remarkable degree of correspondence.

The Conflict Tactics Scales (CTS)

STRUCTURE OF THE CTS

The CTS was designed to measure three tactics used in interpersonal conflict within the family: reasoning, verbal aggression, and physical aggression or violence. The CTS is constructed on the principle of a cross tabulation or factorial design experiment by crossing the three conflict tactics just listed with family role relationships, such as parent-child, child-parent, husband-wife, and wife-husband.

The page of the CTS in this appendix is the part used to obtain information on the tactics used by the interviewed parent on the child who was the focus of the interview. The pages for husband-wife and other role relationships are similar except for the introductory statement and the pronouns, as shown in the CTS manual (Straus, 1990d).

Spanish translations of the Conflict Tactics Scales are included in the *Manual for the CTS*, obtainable from the Family Research Laboratory, University of New Hampshire, Durham, NH 03824.

CORPORAL PUNISHMENT AND PHYSICAL-ABUSE MEASURES

Corporal punishment was measured by items K, L, and M. Items N through S are the indicators of severe violence or physical abuse because they carry a greater risk of injury. For purposes of studying legal forms of corporal punishment, the physical abuse items were used only to partial out physical abuse in a statistical analysis or to remove abused children from the sample in order to avoid confounding corporal punishment with physical abuse.

In previous publications, what is called corporal punishment in this book was called the "minor violence" index. If the parent carried out one or more of the three minor acts of violence, the child was categorized as having been corporally punished.

TABLE B–1. The Conflict Tactics Scales, Child Form R*

Murray A. Straus
Family Research Laboratory, University of New Hampshire, Durham, NH 03824

Ask Q24 & 25 in pairs: for each item answered "NEVER" or "DON'T KNOW" on Q24, ask Q25.

Parents and children use many different ways of trying to settle differences between them. I am going to read a list of things that you might have done WHEN YOU HAD A PROBLEM WITH (*referent child*). I would like you to tell me how often you did each of these things in the past year: once, twice, 3–5 times, 6–10 times, 11–20 times, or more than 20 times). READ ITEM A.

	Q24. In Past Year 1—Once 2—Twice 4—4–5 Times 8—6–10 Times 15—11–20 Times 25—More than 20 0—Never (don't read)							If NEVER on Q25: Has it Ever happened? 1—Yes 0—No	
A. Discussed an issue calmly with (*child's name*)	1	2	4	8	15	25	0	1	0
B. Got information to back up your side of things	1	2	4	8	15	25	0	1	0
C. Brought in, or tried to bring in someone to help settle things	1	2	4	8	15	25	0	1	0
D. Insulted or swore at him/her	1	2	4	8	15	25	0	1	0
E. Sulked or refused to talk about an issue	1	2	4	8	15	25	0	1	0
F. Stomped out of the room, house, or yard	1	2	4	0	15	25	0	1	0
G. Cried**	1	2	4	8	15	25	0	1	0
H. Did or said something to spite him/her	1	2	4	8	15	25	0	1	0
I. Threatened to hit or throw something at him/her	1	2	4	8	15	25	0	1	0
J. Threw, smashed, hit, or kicked something	1	2	4	8	15	25	0	1	0
K. Threw something *at* him/her	1	2	4	8	15	25	0	1	0
L. Pushed, grabbed, or shoved him/her	1	2	4	8	15	25	0	1	0
M. Slapped or spanked him/her	1	2	4	8	15	25	0	1	0
N. Kicked, bit, or hit him/her with a fist	1	2	4	8	15	25	0	1	0
O. Hit or tried to hit him/her with something	1	2	4	8	15	25	0	1	0
P. Beat up him/her	1	2	4	8	15	25	0	1	0
Q. Burned or scalded him/her	1	2	4	8	15	25	0	1	0
R. Threatened him/her with a knife or gun	1	2	4	8	15	25	0	1	0
S. Used a knife or fired a gun	1	2	4	8	15	25	0	1	0

*There are now revised versions of the CTS. See Straus et al (1996, 1998). This page is from the 1985 National Family Violence Survey (see appendix to Gelles and Straus, 1988). The full CTS replicates the questions on this page for each of the family-role relationships that are relevant for the user, such as husband-to-wife, wife-to-husband, sibling-to-sibling, etc. This page assumes that the respondent is the parent or other caretaker. It is also possible to ask the respondent about the behavior of her/his spouse toward the child by adding columns of response categories headed "Spouse/Partner." This has the advantage of providing a more complete indication of the abuse that a child might have experienced. However, since one spouse is unlikely to be fully informed about the behavior of the other toward the child, the data will still be an underestimate.

**This item is not used to score any CTS index.

Prevalence and Frequency Measures

The corporal punishment and physical abuse indexes of the CTS can be used in several ways. For this book they were used to estimate one-year prevalence rates and the frequency, or chronicity, with which the parent used corporal punishment or engaged in abusive acts that year.

PREVALENCE RATES

The CTS asks parents about events in the preceding 12 months (although it can be modified for any period). A parent was classified as having used corporal punishment if he or she engaged in one or more of the three corporal punishment acts. Similarly, a parent was classified as having abused the child if he or she used any one or more of the six severe violence items. Since the resulting data refer to events in the preceding 12 months, they are annual prevalence rates.

FREQUENCY

The prevalence rates disregard how often each act occurred. It is important to know how often parents who physically attacked the child did so. This is measured by adding the code for the response categories indicating the number of times the parent reported doing each of the acts in the index. Since there are three items and the response category scores range from 1 to 25, the frequency scores for the corporal punishment index can range between 1 and 75 (see the CTS manual). The same procedure was used to measure the frequency of physical abuse. Since there are six physical abuse items, the theoretical score range is 1 to 150. Although the maximum possible physical abuse score is double the theoretical maximum corporal punishment score, in practice the highest frequency of abuse is much lower because the acts in the abuse scale, fortunately, occur relatively infrequently.

Validity and Reliability

The Conflict Tactics Scales were developed in the early 1970s and have been used and refined in numerous studies since then. They have provided the data for five books and more than 200 papers.

RELIABILITY AND VALIDITY

Information on many studies of the reliability and validity of the CTS is summarized in Straus (1990a). Readers interested in using the CTS in their own research will need the more detailed information given in the CTS manual (Straus, 1990d).

Factor analyses by six investigators have independently established that the CTS measures three separate dimensions: reasoning, verbal aggression, and physical aggression or violence (Straus, 1990a).

Reliability assessments by seven investigators found alpha coefficients of reliability ranging from .41 to .96. The main source of these differences in reliability is the number of items in the scale. The corporal punishment index has only three items, and the reliability is correspondingly low (.55 for the 1975 survey and .41 for 1985.

Validity is more difficult to establish than factor structure or reliability. It can be assumed that the CTS produces "lower bound" estimates of the prevalence and frequency of corporal punishment and physical abuse.

More than 200 articles have been published that involve research using the CTS. The results of much of that research can be interpreted as evidence of construct validity (see Straus, 1990a, and the bibliography in Straus, 1990d). In addition, some studies show that scores on the CTS are not heavily influenced by social-desirability response sets. The evidence on construct validity and on social desirability is summarized in a paper on the validity of the CTS (Straus, 1990).

A Note on Terminology

Previous publications on the CTS used the terms *minor violence index* and *severe violence index* to refer to what in this book are called the corporal punishment and physical abuse indexes.

SYNONYMS

Several terms will be used for corporal punishment, most often *spanked* and *hit* but occasionally also *physically attacked* or *assaulted*. In a technical sense, "spanked" and "hit" are not really synonyms for corporal punishment as measured by the CTS. An explanation of why they are not literal synonyms for corporal punishment will also help make clear just what is measured by the corporal punishment index.

The technical problem with using "spanked" as a synonym for corporal punishment as measured by the CTS is that spanking is only one of the of several modes of causing the child to feel physical pain that are included in the CTS corporal punishment index. Specifically, the index also includes slapping, pushing, grabbing, shoving, and throwing something at the child. Therefore, the CTS is more inclusive.

The problem with "hit" is that there is no item in the CTS that uses that exact word. So, in a literal sense, "hit" cannot be used as a synonym for what the corporal punishment index measures.

The main justification for using the words *spanking* and *hitting* is that the public and books of child-rearing advice tend to use *spank* and *hit* as synonyms for corporal punishment in general. This was illustrated during an interview with the mother of a four-year-old. The child repeatedly interrupted the mother despite her pleas. Finally, she slapped the child on the shoulder. Then, somewhat embarrassed, she explained, "There are times when nothing except *spanking* will get a child to mind" (italics added). A recent book for parents says that at about 18 to 24 months, spanking means ". . . a brief swat on the fingers or leg at the instant of infraction" (Guarendi and Eich, 1990:217). On the other hand, some people restrict "spank" to the more specific sense of hitting on the buttocks (see also the discussion of the biased terminology in Chapter 1).

Corporal Punishment and Physical Abuse

The boundary between legitimate corporal punishment and physical abuse is controversial. One of the unresolved issues in research on physical abuse is whether the child needs to be injured to be classified as abused. For reasons explained in Chapter 1 and in greater detail elsewhere (Straus, 1990), the CTS operationalizes physical abuse on the basis of whether the child was attacked in ways that have a greater risk of an injury (such as being kicked) than the acts in the corporal punishment index (such as being slapped). The CTS classifies a child who was kicked as abused regardless of whether the kick results in an injury.

There is also controversy about whether certain items in the CTS should be part of the physical abuse or the corporal punishment scale. "Hit or tried to hit with an object" is used for the physical abuse scale because of the relatively high risk of injury. Instead of using risk of injury as the basis for classifying "hit with an object," however, the classification could be based on social norms concerning what is not abuse. The normative approach suggests that hitting a child with an object is not necessarily abuse. There are traditionally acceptable objects for hitting children, such as paddles, belts, and hair brushes. Many people, perhaps the majority of Americans, consider hitting with these objects to be strong discipline but not abuse. A 1992 decision of the New Hampshire Supreme Court reflects that view. The case involved a child whose mother hit him with a belt. The welts were visible four days later. The mother's attorney introduced medical evidence that the marks were visible for this long because the child "bruised easily," and the court ruled that it was not physical abuse.

The results analyses in Chapter 2 and in Wauchope and Straus (1990) are also consistent with the view that hitting with an object belongs in the corporal punishment scale rather than the physical abuse scale. They found that the "hit with object" item followed a pattern that was more similar to the three "minor violence" items than to the "severe violence" or "abuse" items. Graziano and Namaste (1990) found that objects such as belts were used by 57 percent of the parents of the students they studied. Thus, there is some justification for including "hitting with an object" as part of the corporal punishment scale. But there also is justification for considering attacks with belts, hair brushes, rulers, and so on as physical abuse. In the end, I decided to continue the original CTS scoring procedure that uses hitting a child with an object as an indicator of abuse. Chapter 2 gives separate data on "hit with an object" so that readers can decide for themselves how to interpret those statistics.

There also is controversy about whether "throwing things" and "shoving, pushing, and grabbing" belong in the corporal punishment index. Just as certain types of objects are traditionally legitimate for hitting a child, there also are types of objects that can be thrown. For example, implicit cultural norms seem to permit a parent to throw a bucket of water at a child without it being considered abuse, but not a pot of hot water. In general, it is permissible to throw objects that carry a small risk of injury, and that is generally what is thrown. The CTS uses this concept as an indicator of corporal punishment rather than physical abuse.

Pushing, shoving, and grabbing are included in the index because they are among the most frequently used methods of inflicting corporal punishment. Parents who grab and shove do not often realize that they are using corporal punishment because usually it is done while getting a child to go somewhere or come from somewhere. Consider a child who will not get out of the car despite repeated requests and pleading. The parent gets angry and jerks the child out with far more force than is necessary. The rough handling part of grabbing and removing the child is a type of corporal punishment because it is "an act carried out with the intention of causing physical pain, but not injury, for purposes of correction and control," but few parents realize that this is the case. The data presented in Chapter 2 also show that this is an extremely frequent mode of corporal punishment.

Confounding of Corporal Punishment with Physical Abuse

Almost everyone who engages in severely abusive violence against a child, such as kicking or punching, also uses socially acceptable modes of hitting, such as spanking or slapping. Consequently, to simply compare all children who were corporally punished with those who were not stacks the cards in favor of finding harmful effects of corporal punishment because the corporally punished group contains some children who were victims of much more severe violence. To prevent that happening, where possible, children were excluded from the analysis if their parents reported an instance of severe violence. This was done to test hypotheses in chapter 3, 7, and 8. However, it could not be done for the other chapters because information on physical abuse was not available.

Samples

Most of the data for this book come from the 1975 and 1985 National Family Violence surveys. Certain chapters also use data from three other samples. The National Family Violence surveys are described here because they are the basis for several chapters. The other samples are described in Appendix C.

The National Family Violence Surveys

The sample design and interviewing for the 1975 survey was done by Response Analysis Corporation of Princeton, New Jersey. Interviews with 2,143 respondents were completed. The sample design and interviewing for the 1985 survey was done by Louis Harris Associates of New York, which completed interviews with 6,002 respondents. However, the number of cases used for each statistical analysis is always smaller. When the analysis uses adult recall data on corporal punishment, the reductions in sample size depend on how many variables were used in the analysis. Since there are always some respondents for whom a particular question does not apply or some respondents who decline to answer a question, the number of cases depends on which variables are used for an analysis.

DATA TAPES

The data tapes and code books for both surveys are available from the Inter-University Consortium for Political and Social Research at the University of Michgan (ICPSR study numbers 7733 and 9211). The two surveys are also available on CD-ROM and are much easier to use in that form. Contact Sociometics Corporation, 170 State Street, Suite 260, Los Altos, CA 94022.

RESPONDENTS INTERVIEWED

In both 1975 and 1985, the respondent was the wife or female partner for a random half of the sample. For the other half, the husband or male partner was interviewed. This design gives firsthand reports of corporal punishment by fathers as well as mothers, but the problem is that corporal punishment by only one of the child's parents is recorded.

REFERENT CHILD

In both the 1975 and 1985 surveys, the questions on corporal punishment and physical abuse were asked in relation to only one child. When more than one child under the age of 18 was in the household, a random procedure was used to select the "referent child" as the focus of these questions. The 1975 survey excluded children under age three and children of single parents; the 1985 survey included both children under three and single parents.

INTERVIEW SCHEDULES

The full schedule of questions used for the 1985 study is given in Gelles and Straus (1988). The interview schedule for the 1975 study, including a Spanish translation, is available from the ICPSR, which also can provide data files for the two surveys. These data files (and full documentation, including interview schedules) also are available as part of the American Family Data Archive, of the Sociometrics Corporation.

The 1975 Survey

Data for the 1975 National Family Violence Survey were gathered in face-to-face interviews of a national probability sample of 2,143 currently married or cohabiting persons aged 18 through 70. Participating households were drawn from a sample of interviewing locations that had been stratified by geographic region, type of community, and other population characteristics. Information on the sampling design is in Straus (1990b) and in greater detail in the methodological report prepared by Response Analysis Corporation (Weisbrod, 1976). (Write to Response Analysis Corporation, Research Park, Route 206, Princeton, NJ 08540).

If the household included a child or children between the ages of 3 and 17, a "referent child" was selected using a random procedure. The restriction to children aged 3 through 17 was made because we were uncertain of the appropriateness of using the Conflict Tactics Scales for children younger than three. In addition, one aim of the study was to obtain meaningful data on sibling violence, and we erroneously believed that the data on children aged one or two would not be meaningful for this purpose. Interviews lasted approximately one hour. The completion rate of the entire sample was 65 percent.

The 1985 Survey

Data for the 1985 resurvey were obtained by telephone interviews of a national probability sample of 4,032 U.S. households and additional over-samples described in the following section. Telephone numbers were selected using random-digit dialing that stratified the United States into four regions (East, South, Midwest, and West) and three community types (urban areas with populations greater than 100,000; suburban areas with populations of less than 100,000; and rural areas with populations of less than 2,500). This cross-sectional national sample was augmented by three over-samples. First, 958 households were randomly selected from 25 states in order to assure that the total sample included at least 100 completed interviews from 36 of the 50 states. Second, over-samples of 508 black and 516 Hispanic households were added to the total sample to assure enough black and Hispanic families to provide reliable data on these two groups. The data from this total sample of 6,002 households were than weighted to adjust for the state, black, and hispanic over-samples, making the total weighted sample representative of the U.S. population. However, comparisons with the 1975 study use only the comparable age and marital status parts of the 1985 sample.

To be included, a household had to include a person 18 years of age or older who was: 1) married, or 2) living as a male-female couple, or 3) either divorced or separated within the last two years, or 4) a single parent living with a child under the age of 18. When more than one eligible adult was in the household, a random procedure was used to select the gender and marital status of the respondent. Interviews lasted an average of 35 minutes. The response rate, calculated as "completes as a proportion of eligibles," was 84 percent. A detailed report on the methodology of the study is available from the author for the cost of reproduction.

Methodological Differences Between the Two Surveys

Data collection for the two surveys differs in two important respects. First, data for the 1975 survey were collected by in-person interviews, while the 1985 survey was conducted over the telephone. Research has shown no major differences between the results from telephone and face-to-face interviews (Groves and Kahn, 1979; Marcus and Crane, 1986), and the telephone is now the most widely used method of interviewing. The telephone survey offers a greater sense of anonymity for the respondent, and trained telephone interviewers have been able to increase response rate by converting many would-be refusals into completed interviews. The 1985 survey had an 85 percent completion rate, compared to the 65 percent completion rate of the 1975–76 survey. The second major difference in the data collection methods of the two surveys is that the 1975 survey was limited to married and cohabiting couples, while the 1985 survey also included separated or divorced individuals and single parents. This inclusion, combined with the higher completion rate, presumably means that the 1985 survey is a more representative national sample. The anonymity of the telephone interviews may have lead to more truthful responses to sensitive questions.

Another methodological difference is that in the 1975–76 survey, each respondents was handed a card listing the response categories for the Conflict Tactics Scales. All possible answers, including "never," were on the card. For the 1985 telephone interviews, interviewers read the response categories, beginning with "once" and continuing to "more than 20 times." Respondents had to volunteer "never" or "don't know" responses. Experience has shown that rates of reported sensitive or deviant behavior are higher if the subject has to volunteer the "no" or "never" response (see, for example, Kinsey *et al.*, 1948).

Strengths and limitations of the Two Surveys

While questionnaires and interviews obtain data rapidly from a large number of people, the amount of information per case is small compared to data derived from clinical studies of intimate violence. The 1975 survey took 60 minutes for each respondent and included about 200 questions. The 1985 telephone survey included about 125 questions and lasted, on the average, 35 minutes (the outer limit of time a respondent can be expected to remain on the telephone).

Large national surveys can help develop a portrait of behavior that can be generalized to families throughout the United States. But such a portrait is little more than a snapshot of families at a particular point in time. Obtaining more data requires additional interview sessions, which raises the cost of such research into the millions of dollars.

A second limitation is that we learn only what people are willing to reveal. Survey research provides information on what people say about their behavior. The most bizarre and humiliating events experienced by the most victimized individuals are typically not accessible in surveys. For this type of information, clinical studies or in-depth interviews with a limited number of individuals offer the most detailed and useful data.

Finally, there are biases of inclusion and exclusion in surveys. In the 1975 survey, the face-to-face interviewers had the most difficulty obtaining interviews in the most dangerous and the most affluent neighborhoods. The 1985 telephone survey excluded people without telephones. Fortunately, there is no evidence that the 1985 survey is any more or less biased in this respect than the 1975 survey.

Ninety-three percent of the households in the United States have telephones. Therefore, a telephone survey will theoretically cover a less representative sample than an in-person survey. Since homes without telephones are more likely to be low-income or minority households, telephone sampling is systematically biased. However, this problem also applies to in-person interviews. Anyone who has attempted to interview low-income inner-city residents knows that the completion rate for face-to-face interviews is low. Our colleagues at survey-research organizations inform us that, practically speaking sampling coverage is the same with in-person and telephone interviewing. This occurs because in-person interviewers are frequently unable to secure complete interviews from the lower-income and minority households that do not have telephones. As a result, there is little practical evidence that the sampling frames in the two surveys were different. The category of households excluded from the second survey were in all likelihood not reached in the first survey either—even though they were theoretically available in the sampling frame.

Direct evidence of equality of coverage in the two surveys is presented in Straus and Gelles (1990, Appendix A). It shows a high degree of consistency between the two surveys. Both produced samples with almost the same average age of respondent and average length of marriage. The unemployment rate for men in the 1985 study, however, was lower than in 1975. Rather than being evidence of sampling bias, the lower rate is consistent with the lower national unemployment rate in 1985. There is little difference in the average education of the two samples. The racial composition of the sample shows changes that are consistent with the growth of the Black and Hispanic populations during this decade. Taken as a whole, the data is consistent with the methodological research on telephone versus in-person interviews in that it shows no important difference between the results obtained by the two methods (Groves and Kahn, 1979; Marcus and Crane, 1986; and Smith, 1986).

TABLE B–2. Sample Sizes for 1975 and 1985 National Family Violence Surveys

	1975	1985C	1985T
All respondents	2,143	2,212	6,002
Males	960	902	2,337
Females	1,183	1,310	3,665
Households with a child under 18 at home			
Male respondent	528	902	1,218
Female respondent	626	1,310	2,144
Male referent child	587	1,132	1,684
Female referent child	552	1,080	1,675
Male respondent and male child	269	469	626
Male respondent and female child	251	433	591
Female respondent and female child	318	663	1,058
Female respondent and female child	301	647	1,084
Number of children of each age			
Under 1	—	—	344
1	—	—	298
2	—	—	390
3	101	282	385
4	148	284	246
5	158	303	409
6	152	282	353
7	141	302	384
8	147	262	345
9	124	270	349
10	154	276	365
11	162	256	329
12	165	288	350
13	154	292	374
14	152	286	356
15	144	279	363
16	157	284	363
17	128	238	324

1985C refers to the part of the sample that is comparable to the 1975 sample: that is, it omits families with children under age three and those from single-parent families because these groups were not studied in 1975.

1985T refers to the entire sample, including oversamples of Black and Hispanic households. Statistics in this book using the total sample are weighted to adjust for the oversampling and achieve estimates of the U.S. population.

For both surveys, there is a close correspondence between the demographic characteristics of the samples and census data on American families. As noted however, the fact that a sample is representative of the U.S. population says little about whether the information it provides is accurate. This issue is particularly important for the data on corporal punishment and physical abuse as measured by the Conflict Tactics Scales (CTS). The CTS produces "lower bound" estimates of prevalence and frequency. Nevertheless, studies of the validity and reliability of this instrument found coefficients that meet or exceed those typical for measures of social psychological variables (Straus, 1990).

Sample Sizes and Comparability

Although the overall samples for these two studies numbered 2,143 and 6,002 cases, a smaller number of cases are used for any specific analysis. There are several reasons for this. The largest reduction in sample size occurs in analyses that use data on whether and how often the respondent hit the referent child during the 12 months preceding the interview. This is because about half of all American couples do not have a minor child living at home. Either they have not had a child or their children have grown up and left.

In principle, the entire sample can be used when the data on corporal punishment was obtained by asking respondents about the extent to which they had been corporally punished when they were in their teens. However, there always are some respondents for whom a question does not apply or who do not answer because they can't remember, or just prefer not to answer. If only two questions are involved in a statistical analysis, the loss of cases usually is very small. Let us assume that there is no data for 30 people on Question X and no data for 30 others on Question Y. That would make the effective sample size 60 fewer than the oveall sample size, which is only 2.6 percent less than the original 6,002 cases. But if the data from 20 questions were analyzed in one statistical analysis, the reduction would be 600. Consequently, the effective sample size is often considerably less than 2,143 and 6,002 for other reasons. Table B–2 gives the starting sample sizes for analyses involving various subgroups of the overal samples.

For analyses in which the issue is whether the rate of corporal punishment changed between 1975 and 1985, certain cases were dropped from the 1985 sample to make it comparable to the 1975 sample. This is because the 1975 sample was restricted to families with children aged 3 through 17 living with two parents. Consequently, when the rates obtained in 1985 are compared with those from the 1975 study, children under age three and children from single-parent households are dropped from the 1985 sample.

Table B–3 presents demographic information on each of the samples and sub-samples that help identify some imporant characteristics of families in the two National Family Violence surveys.

TABLE B–3. Characteristics of the 1975 and 1985 Samples[1]

	1975	1985C	1985T
Median age of respondent	39	—	38
with child at home	37	36	35
Median number of children at home	2	2	1
Two-Parent households with child at home	100%	100%	81.3%
Median years of education—husbands	12	—	12
with child at home	12	12	12
Median years of education—wives	12	—	12
with child at home	12	12	12
Percent with paid employment—husbands	84.4%	—	78.9%
with child at home	89.9%	90.5%	91.1%
Percent with paid employment—wives	43.8%	—	54.2%
with child at home	40.8%	58.4%	59.9%
Median family income	$13,500	—	$27,500
with child at home	$17,500	$27,500	$27,500
Percent with income below poverty level	7.6%	—	12.9%
with child at home	7.2%	11.5%	17.0%
Percent minority race/ethnic group	9.1%	—	31.5%
with child at home	9.7%	32.3%	36.9%
Percent living in a metropolitan area (SMSA)	34.9%	—	26.0%
with child at home	34.9%	27.0%	26.0%
Years married/living with current partner	15	—	14
with child at home	13	13	11
Percent previously married—husband	14.6%	*	*
with child at home	13.4%	*	*
Percent previously married—wife	15.2%	*	*
with child at home	14.6%	*	*

1. All 1985 statistics are for the sample before weighting to compensate for over-samples of minority groups and states with small populations.
—Not applicable because the column refers to those with children at home.
*Data not available.

Appendix C

Statistical Methods and Measures

The first part of this appendix is for readers who are not trained in statistics and who want a brief explanation of what is meant by statistical controls and spurious findings. The second section of the appendix is for readers with training in statistics. The second section explains one of the less widely known statistical procedures we used—logistic regression, or logit.

The third and largest part of the appendix documents the measurement procedures and statistical tests used to obtain the findings reported in chapters 2 through 9.

Statistical Controls

Although the research in this book has some limitations, we were able to control for many possible sources of spurious findings. A spurious finding would occur if the relationship between corporal punishment and a presumed consequence were really the effect of a third characteristic that overlapped both corporal punishment and the effect being studied. A silly example can make this more clear. If we wanted to test the hypothesis that the larger the shoe size the better the child's reading ability, the findings undoubtedly would support that hypothesis. This is not because having big feet is an intellectual advantage, however. It is because older children have bigger feet and also read better. To see if this is the case, the statistical analysis would control, or standardize, the age of the child. It would show that for children of the same age, shoe size has no effect on reading ability. A third characteristic—age—explains both. Thus, the relationship between shoe size and reading ability is spurious, that is, it is caused by a third characteristic. When the overlap between age and shoe size is removed by statistically controlling, or standardizing, for the child's age, the relationship between shoe size and reading ability disappears. Another example is the relationship between ice cream consumption and the amount of crime. Unless we are willing to believe that eating ice cream causes criminal behavior, we have to look to a third characteristic for the explanation. The real explanation for this relationship probably relates to the time of year. As the outdoor temperature rises, so does ice cream consumption. Street crimes also increase during the summer months, when days are longer and people spend more time outdoors. If temperature is controlled, the relationship between ice cream and street crime vanishes.

In research on corporal punishment, certain characteristics are associated with both corporal punishment and its outcomes. For example, the age of the child is associated with both the prevalence and the frequency of spanking, as well as with many of the consequences of corporal punishment. If age is not controlled and a large relationship is found between corporal punishment and one of its purported consequences (for examples, aggression), it may be that age is really responsible. Young children are hit more than older children and also have poorer control of aggression. So if age were the underlying cause of both spanking and aggression, an analysis that related spanking to aggression and controlled for age would show no relationship between spanking and a child's aggression. To find out if that is the case, we could compute the correlation between spanking and aggression separately for children who are two years old, three years old, and so on. That method is cumbersome, however, and also has other disadvantages. Instead, the method used to control for the age of the children includes age as part of the equation used to test the theory. The resulting statistics on the relationship between spanking and aggression tell us what the relationship is after subtracting out the overlap between age and spanking. As Chapter 7 shows, after doing this to control for the fact that age affects the rate of spanking, there is still a strong tendency for aggression to increase as the amount of corporal punishment increases.

The statistics reported in this book are based on controlling for a number of such overlapping characteristics. These include the age and sex of the child, the sex of the parent, the socioeconomic status of the family, whether there was violence between the parents, whether the parent interviewed had a drinking problem, the extent to which the parent explained things and reasoned with the child, and so on. The tables in this appendix list the characteristics that were controlled when doing the research for each chapter.

Tests of Statistical Significance

All findings reported or graphed are statistically significant, at least at the .05 level. The specific values for F, t, and so on are given in the sections of this appendix for each chapter.

Causal Inferences and Terminology

In many fields of science, especially the social sciences, it is not possible to carry out experiments to prove or disprove a theory. That certainly is the case with research on the harmful side effects of corporal punishment. It would be unethical to do an experiment in which one group of parents is instructed to spank for misbehavior and another group is prohibited from spanking. In fields of science where experiments to test a theory are not possible or ethical, theories tend to be confirmed or disproven by a long series of studies, none of which by itself is definitive, but whose cumulative effect gradually leads to the validation or invalidation of the theory.

When a researcher reports findings based on multiple regression (as in this book), it is customary to refer to the research as *testing* a model and to use such terms as *effect* and *explain* to describe the results. However, readers need to understand that the findings do not prove a cause-effect relationship. A statistically significant relationship consistent with a theoretical model means only that the data fit the model. Such findings do not prove or disprove the causal theory that underlies the model because there are almost always plausible rival interpretations of the findings. Rather, findings from testing causal models, such as those in this book, should be interpreted as either supporting the theory if the findings are consistent with the model, or failing to support the theory if they are not.

Logistic Regression

Chapter 4 and all the chapters in Part II use logistic regression, or logit (Aldrich and Nelson, 1984; Hamilton, 1992). Logistic regression is a form of multiple regression that is used when the dependent variable is categorical, usually dichotomous. The variable is coded as 0 if it is absent and 1 if it is present. Logistic regression can be used to estimate the probability of the characteristic being present for each unit of the independent variable. For this book, the predicted probabilities were plotted using the statistical program STATA and the conditional plotting technique in Hamilton (1990, 1992).

It should be noted that the graphs show the regression line (in the form of the predicted probability of the dependent variable), not the observations. In chapters 4 through 9, these predicted probabilities are often described as a certain percent chance of hitting a child, thinking about suicide, and so on. Strictly speaking it is not appropriate to express the predicted probabilities in this way. We do so, however, to make the book more easily understandable. Readers who are not trained in statistics are more likely to understand the findings when they are expressed as percentages.

Each graph plots these predicted probabilities contingent on specified values of the other independent variables in the model. Unless otherwise indicted, the mean of the variable was the value specified.

Logistic regression also was used in some chapters to estimate the odds ratio for each unit increase in the independent variable.

T tests in the tables in the appendix indicate the significance level of each logit coefficient in the model tested. The Chi-squares in the tables indicate if the model is better at predicting the dependent variable than chance. If the *p* of the Chi-square is less than .05, the hypothesis that the model is no better than chance is rejected, and we conclude that the model supports the theory on which it is based.

Note on the Charts

Two main types of graphs are used in this book. First, are plots of the predicted probability of the dependent variable for each category of corporal punishment, based on logistic regression. They are the equivalent of the regression line in OLS regression. Second, are plots of the mean for a dependent variable for each category of corporal punishment, based on an analysis of covariance. These two graphing techniques complement each other, and some chapters use both.

Both types of graphs show computed data points rather than observed data points, either means or predicted probabilities. Consequently, neither shows the variance around the plot points. In most cases, the variance around the plot lines is large, that is, the residual, or unexplained, variance is large. This is to be expected because most of the dependent variables are influenced by many things in addition to corporal punishment. Indeed, for some dependent variables, corporal punishment is a less important determinant than some of the other variables in the model tested. That does not undermine the findings presented because the issue is not whether corporal punishment is *the* cause, or even whether it is the most important cause. Rather, the issue for this book is whether corporal punishment is one of the possible causes.

It would have been possible to create graphs showing the standard error for each plot point. That would have made the graphs completely indecipherable by readers who are not trained in statistics, however.

It also should be noted that the graphs show predicted probabilities and means that have been adjusted for covariates. As a result, the predicted probabilities do not coincide with the observed prevalence of the dependent variable. For example, Chart 4–5 shows the results of testing the hypothesis that marital violence is associated with an increased probability of hitting children. The findings support that hypothesis because the predicted probability of hitting a 16-year-old child goes up from .48 for mothers whose husbands were not violent, to .71 for mothers who were physically attacked by their partners. However, the predicted probability of .48, which can be thought of as the equivalent of a prevalence rate of 48 percent is much higher than the prevalence rate of about 32 percent for 16-year-old children in Chart 2–1. The predicted probability is higher than the observed percentage because the control variables were set at values that provided the most stringent test of the hypothesis that marital violence increases the probability of hitting a child. In this case, the plot was done for male children, for relatively young parents, and for parents who were themselves hit as teenagers (see Table C–3) because each of these specifications is associated with an increased probability of corporal punishment. Thus, Chart 4–6 shows that marital violence is associated with an increased probability of hitting a child and that this is in addition to the effect of these three variables known to be associated with the use of corporal punishment. However, these specifications also mean that the .48 predicted probability of hitting a child by mothers who were not victims of violence by their partners, does not apply to all such mothers. It applies to mothers who are at greater risk of hitting their child because the child is a boy, because they are relatively young, and because they were themselves hit as teenagers.

Samples, Measures, and Statistical Analyses Used in Each Chapter

To avoid cluttering the main text, information about the samples and descriptions of the measures used in each chapter are given in Appendix B and in this appendix. Appendix B describes the National Family Violence Survey, which is the data source used for most of this book, and the Conflict Tactics Scales, the method of measuring corporal punishment and physical abuse used in most of this book. The following sections describe the sample used for each chapter (if it was not the National Family Violence Survey) and the measures used for that chapter. This appendix also includes tables showing regression coefficients and tests of significance for the findings mentioned in the text or graphed in the charts.

The statistical analyses for all chapters were done using the program SPSS/PC, with the exception of the logistic regressions, which were done using STATA.

Chapter 1

The empirical basis used in previous research for including corporal punishment as one item in a multi-item index of harsh parenting is the statistical technique called *factor analysis*. Use of factor analysis has typically shown that the parent behaviors tend to cluster into factors such as nurturance, control, and harsh discipline. Corporal punishment is one component of the harsh-discipline factor. The theoretical basis for that approach is the idea that the real meaning of corporal punishment is not the act of hitting the child, but that act as part of a more general pattern of punitive and arbitrary behavior by parents. For this reason, a factor score rather than corporal punishment per se became the focus of research. For many purposes this is a sound procedure. However, when this approach is used, it prevents the researcher from learning about corporal punishment per se because it is impossible to study the effect of corporal punishment when the parents are not otherwise punitive and arbitrary, which is true of a great many parents. It prevents investigating the effects of corporal punishment committed by parents who explain things and are otherwise warm and loving. According to the defenders of corporal punishment, those are precisely the circumstances under which it should be used. The effects of corporal punishment under those specific circumstances must be studied as well.

In statistical terms, the problem is that a large percentage of variance of the corporal punishment item is *not* explained by the factor score. There may be only a 10 or 20 percent overlap, so that 80 or 90 percent of the variation in corporal punishment is not reflected in the index. Thus, the spanking component of the factor can operate quite differently than the factor itself. Corporal punishment could have effects that are different than the overall index. Since most of the studies that have obtained data on corporal punishment use that data as part of a harsh parenting factor, they have made it impossible to conclude anything about corporal punishment in and of itself.

This is not to say that the factor analysis approach is wrong. The mistake was in relying exclusively on overall factors and not investigating specific components of the factor such as corporal punishment. The advantage of analyzing a factor score rather than each of the behaviors making up that score lies in the assumption that the essence of corporal punishment is best captured in the context of other related parent behaviors, and that what matters for the child is the overall pattern. This is a plausible hypothesis. However, those who use factor scores do not treat it as a hypothesis. They take it as a self-evident assumption. To the best of my knowledge that assumption has never been investigated empirically.

This raises the question of what led those who investigated parent behaviors to such an exclusive reliance on factor scores. There were probably several causes. First, computers became widely available in the 1950s and '60s. They enabled the ordinary researcher to use techniques at the cutting edge of research technology. When the new technology combined with the fascination of scientists with new analytical techniques and with pressure from peers to use those techniques, factor analysis became almost irresistible to researchers. Factor analysis was the "in thing" in developmental psychology. Anyone who investigated parent behaviors and did not apply factor analysis to those data would find it difficult to have the report published in a scientific journal.

Other areas of social science research also took advantage of this new and powerful technique of factor analysis, but they did not make the mistake of almost exclusive reliance on factor scores. For example, factor analysis is widely used in research on socioeconomic status. The difference is that specialists in social stratification insisted from the beginning on the importance of also analyzing each of the specific components of a socioeconomic status index. Being in a high- or low-status occupation may have different effects than high or low income even though both are "highly loaded" on an overall socioeconomic status factor, just as corporal punishment is highly loaded on an overall harsh-parenting factor.

This reliance on harsh-parenting scores also probably occurred because of a deep and unconscious acceptance of corporal punishment. Like the general public, sociologists and child psychologists accept the legitimacy and value of corporal punishment in moderation. They do not question the use of corporal punishment, only excessive use, hitting children without explanation, or in the context of cold or harsh treatment of the child. As was noted in Chapter 1, there has been an implicit consensus that there is no need to study moderate corporal punishment. Social scientists are part of American society and share the common background assumptions of our culture about corporal punishment.

Chapter 2

With one exception, the data in this chapter are based on analyses of the 1975 and 1985 National Family Violence surveys, described in Appendix B.

National Longitudinal Study of Youth (NLYS). The statistics on corporal punishment that occurred during the interview and in the previous week were computed from the 1988 data for the mother and child files. The questions on corporal punishment refer to hitting in the last week, so they are not comparable to the statistics on hitting in the last year from the National Family Violence surveys. Each referent period has advantages and disadvantages. The disadvantage of the "last year" is that most instances are forgotten. The disadvantage of the "last week" is that about half of parents who do spank, did not do so in the last week and, therefore, are misclassified as non-spanking parents.

Although neither study adequately describes how often parents actually hit children, both are useful as an ordinal measure that can be used to test hypotheses about whether corporal punishment is associated with an increase in social and psychological problems of children.

Significance Tests for Change in Prevalence Rates (Chart 2–2). The chi-square and p values for the difference between 1975 and 1985 are:

Corporal punishment index	0.5, $p < .82$
Slapped or spanked	1.5, $p < .22$
Pushed, shoved, grabbed	0.9, $p < .34$
Threw something at the child	6.5, $p < .01$
Hit or tried to hit with something	9.9, $p < .001$.

Significance Tests for Change in Frequency (Chart 2–3). Chi-square tests show that all differences between 1975 and 1985 are statistically significant. The chi-squares and p values are:

Corporal punishment index	15.6, $p < .001$
Slapped or spanked	17.7, $p < .001$
Pushed, shoved, grabbed	8.3, $p < .003$
Threw something at the child	3.9, $p < .041$
Hit or tried to hit with something	17.2, $p < .002$

Significance Tests for Chart 2–4. Differences between 1975 and 1985 are statistically significant.

Significance Tests for Difference in Prevalence by Gender of Child. This was tested by analysis of covariance, which resulted in $F = 3.88$, $p < .05$ in 1975, and $F = 6.58$, $p < .01$ in 1985.

TABLE C–1. Frequency of Corporal Punishment of Teens, by Gender of Parent and Child

Frequency	Adult Recall Data						Contemporary Data			
	By Mother		By Father		By Either		By Mothers		By Fathers	
	Daughters	Sons	Daughters	Sons	Daughters	Sons	Daughters	Sons	Daughters	Sons
A. Mean, Standard Deviation, and Median Number of Times										
Mean	5.62	6.45	4.55	5.36	6.57	8.06	5.56	5.75	4.44	8.55
SD	6.90	7.08	6.31	6.57	7.45	7.98	6.11	5.02	7.32	10.55
Median	2.00	4.00	2.00	2.00	4.00	4.00	4.00	4.00	2.00	4.00
B. Percentage Distribution										
Once	28.8	20.6	41.5	30.9	23.2	17.3	22.4	10.7	40.2	10.6
Twice	22.5	19.3	21.6	20.0	19.8	15.8	19.9	21.3	34.8	30.7
3–5 times	22.9	28.8	17.3	24.1	25.0	23.6	27.2	27.8	12.8	13.5
6–10 times	10.6	12.9	8.1	10.9	13.5	17.8	16.9	31.9	0.0	23.7
11–20 times	7.0	9.3	5.2	7.0	7.8	11.6	7.9	5.6	5.0	7.9
21+ times	8.3	9.1	6.3	7.1	10.8	13.8	5.8	2.7	7.2	13.6
n	1,200	1,025	884	1,035	1,416	1,298	52	55	21	43

Significance Tests for Difference in Chronicity by Gender of Child. Analysis of covariance resulted in $F = 3.67$, $p < .06$ for the 1975 survey and $F = 4.97$, $p < .03$ for 1985.

Validity of Chronicity Data. As indicated in Chapter 2, the findings on how often children were hit in the past year severely underestimate the true rate. On the other hand, we assume that on the average, parents who report many instances of corporal punishment do it more than parents who report few instances. To the extent that assumption is correct, it means that the data are useful as an ordinal measure for testing hypotheses concerning the correlates of corporal punishment.

Chapter 3

Sample. The data for this chapter come from the 1985 National Family Violence Survey (see Appendix B).

To make the contemporary data in this chapter as comparable as possible in age to the adult recall data, the contemporary analyses are based on the 380 children who were 13 or 14 at the time the parent was interviewed.

Table C–1 gives a detailed, comparison of the frequency of corporal punishment measured by adult recall and contemporary data.

The Socioeconomic Status (SES). The SES index used in this and other chapters reporting data on the 1985 National Family Violence Survey is a factor score created by using the principle components analysis option of SPSS/PC. The five SES indicators included in the factor analysis were: the education of the husband and wife, the Treiman occupational prestige score (1977) of the husband and wife, and family income. The analysis revealed one factor, which accounted for 62.1 percent percent of the variance. The five-item index has an Alpha reliability coefficient of .80. We transformed the factor score from a Z score to a ZP score (Straus, 1980) to produce an index with a range of 0 to 100, a mean of 50, and a standard deviation of 20.

Significance Test for Difference Between Sons and Daughters, (Adult Recal Data). An analysis of covariance resulted in the following: F (gender of child) $= 107.71$, $p < .001$.

Significance Tests For Chart 3–2. An analysis of covariance comparing sons and daughters result in an F of 1.50 for gender of child,

$p < .11$. The F for differences between fathers and mothers is 2.42, $p < .06$. There is no bar in Chart 3–2 for "By Either" because the contemporary data is based on interviews with only one of the parents and refers to what he or she did in the previous 12 months.

Significance Test for Chart 3–3. Chart 3–3 uses adult recall data because the contemporary data is available only for the parent who was interviewed. Chi-square for the relationship between child's gender and gender of the parent who punishes is $(df = 1, 2) = 78.68, p < .001$.

Charts 3–4 and 3–5. These graphs plot the moving averages. The observed means are given in Straus and Donnelly (1993).

It is remarkable that the relationship to SES using contemporary data tends to follow roughly the same pattern as was found using the adult recall data because the contemporary data is based on only one tenth as many cases, and the resulting small number of cases in each SES decile makes the results less reliable.

Chapter 4

Sample. The data are from the 1985 National Family Violence Resurvey, described in Appendix B.

Husband-to-Wife Violence. This variable was measured by the Conflict Tactics Scales (CTS) described in Appendix B.

Socioeconomic Status (SES). The SES index is described in the section of this appendix for Chapter 3.

Sex of respondent. Father = 0, Mother = 1

Ethnic Group. Minority = 1, Non-Hispanic White = 0

Approval of Corporal Punishment Index. This index is the sum of three "semantic differential" items (Osgood, Suci, and Tannenbaum, 1957). We asked respondents to rate the phrase "Slapping or spanking a 12-year-old." They were asked to make three ratings using a scale from 1 to 7:

> (1) Necessary . . . . . . .Unnecessary   (7)
> (1) Not normal . . . . . .Normal   (7)
> (7) Good . . . . .Bad   (1)

Parent Hit As A Teen. See the section on Adult Recall Data in Chapter 3 and in Appendix B.

Socioeconomic Status (SES) Index. The SES index described in the section of this appendix for Chapter 3 was originally included in the analyses for this chapter. However, since it was not significantly related, it was dropped in order to reduce the number of independent variables.

Logistic Regression. The correlations among the independent variables were examined to determine if any were large enough to pose a problem with multicollinearity. The only correlation suggesting a possible problem was between husband-to-wife and wife-to-husband violence (.59). This suggests that both should not be included in the same logit analysis. We decided to include husband-to-wife violence because we regard it as the more severe problem (Straus, 1990). The data on the extent to which the parents were themselves physically punished by their fathers and mothers also posed a multicollinearity problem. Consequently, these two variables were summed to form a single variable. The initial logit analysis included nine variables. Backward elimination was used to arrive at the final model.

The final logit equations are shown in Table C–2. Three logistic regressions were computed because of the need to introduce different specifications for certain analysis. The regression shown in Part A of Table C–1 is the basic model; the other two differ only by specifying limitations for the parent's age. The analysis shown in Part B of Table C–2 was restricted to respondents aged 62 and under because we were not confident of the accuracy of the data for the few cases in which there was a child aged 4 and a parent aged 63 and over. The same reasoning was used to restrict the analysis in Part C of Table C–2 to respondents older than 24 and younger than 63.

Specifications Used for Charts

The graphs showing the effect of each independent variable on the predicted probability of corporal punishment include separate plot lines for children aged 4 and 16. Age 4 was used because it is a peak age for corporal punishment (see Chapter 2). Age 16 was used because it is past the age when even advocates of corporal punish-

TABLE C–2. Logistic Regression Analyses of Parent's Level of Corporal Punishment (N = 2952)

Independent Variable	Coefficient	Standard Error	t	Prob	Mean
A. Parent's Use of Corporal Punishment					
Child's sex	-.375	.092	-4.053	0.000	.505
Child's age	-.095	.010	-8.775	0.000	8.229
Parent's sex	.235	.096	2.450	0.014	.553
Parent's age	-.027	.007	-3.873	0.000	35.710
Minority group	.463	.118	3.901	0.000	.818
Parent hit as teen	.012	.006	1.931	0.054	3.827
Husband violent	.749	.163	4.588	0.000	.115
Constant	1.687	.265	6.364	0.000	

Chi2(7) = 307.75 Prob > chi2 = 0.001
Log Likelihood = 1363.3549

B. Parent's Use of Corporal Punishment: 4-year-olds					
Child's sex	-.373	.093	-4.014	0.000	.506
Child's Age	-.095	.011	-8.619	0.000	8.203
Parent's sex	.240	.096	2.499	0.013	.554
Parent's age	-.027	.007	-3.576	0.000	35.493
Minority group	.465	.119	3.897	0.000	.819
Parent hit as teen	.012	.006	1.950	0.051	3.844
Husband violent	.758	.165	4.586	0.000	.115
Constant	1.668	.275	6.045	0.000	1

Chi2(7) = 300.81 Prob > chi2 = 0.001
Log Likelihood = 1353.3438

C. Parent's Use of Corporal Punishment: 16-year-olds					
Child's sex	-.390	.097	-3.997	0.000	.504
Child's age	-.104	.011	-9.090	0.000	8.623
Parent's sex	.248	.101	2.452	0.014	.549
Parent's age	-.036	.008	-4.342	0.000	36.438
Minority group	.439	.127	3.453	0.001	.826
Parent hit as teen	.019	.006	2.762	0.006	3.725
Husband violent	.845	.181	4.663	0.000	.106
Constant	2.110	.311	6.771	0.000	1

Chi2(7) = 324.86 Prob > chi2 = 0.001
Log Likelihood = 1233.3512

TABLE C–3. Specifications Used to Plot Predicted Probability of Parents Using Corporal Punishment

Variable	Specification	Reason
Gender of child	Male	boys are more often recipients of physical punishment.
Gender of parent	Female	Mothers spend more hours in child care and therefore, do more disciplining, including physical punishment.
Age of child	4 and 16	Age 4 is the peak year; age 16 is when the rate has dropped substantially.
Age of parent	31 for parents of child aged 4 42 for parents of child aged 16	These are the median ages of parents of 4- and 16-year-old children.
Whether parent was hit as an adolescent	Yes	The majority of Americans were hit by parents during adolescence.
Husband-to-wife violence	None	Most couples did not have a violent incident during the referent year.
Race	White	Whites make up most of the sample.
Socioeconomic status	Median	

ment feel it is appropriate but, nonetheless, an age at which about a third are still being hit by their parents.

The predicted probabilities were computed using the specifications listed in Table C–3 (unless the variable is used for the X axis of the graph, in which case the full range of scores is shown). The rationale for these specifications is shown on the right side of Table C–2.

Chapter 5

Sample. This chapter is based on corporal punishment experienced as an adolescent by the adults interviewed for the 1985 National Family Violence Survey. This sample is described in Appendix B. The method of measuring corporal punishment is described and evaluated in the sections on Adult Recall Measures in Chapter

3 and Appendix B. The possible problems with using corporal punishment of adolescents as the independent variable are discussed in the following sections.

Does Corporal Punishment of Adolescents Have Unique Effects? It is possible that findings based on corporal punishment during adolescence may not apply to corporal punishment experienced as a toddler or young child. Concern over this potential source of error is somewhat mitigated by the results of previous research associating corporal punishment of even very young children with increased rates of such problem behaviors, including physical aggressiveness, limited development of an internalized conscience (Sears, Maccoby & Levin, 1957), and increased interpersonal problems with other children, delinquency, and aggression (see Chapter 7 and Vissing *et al.*, 1991).

Depressive Symptoms. Identifying who is depressed in a large cross-sectional sample of Americans is a difficult and controversial task. The method used in the 1985 National Family Violence Survey is based on the Psychiatric Epidemiological Research Instrument, or PERI (Dohrenwend, *et al.*, 1976). The PERI provides data on a number of different psychiatric problems and is too long to be included in the half-hour interviews we conducted. The measure of depression consists of the following four PERI items that Newman (1984) found to be most indicative of depression:

- Was bothered by feelings of sadness or depression
- Felt very bad and worthless
- Had times when he or she couldn't help wondering if anything was worthwhile anymore
- Felt completely hopeless about everything

Respondents were asked to indicate how often in the past year each of these things occurred using the following categories: Never = 0, Almost Never = 1, Sometimes = 2, Fairly Often = 3, Very Often = 4. These items were factor analyzed using the SPSS Principle Components program. The analysis found a single factor that accounted for 66 percent of the variance. The depressive symptoms index used for this study is the factor-weighted sum of these four items and has an Alpha coefficient of reliability of .82.

Suicidal Ideas. Suicidal thoughts often accompany depression, but they are a separate phenomenon. Consequently, we asked our respondents if they had thought about taking their own life in the previous 12 months. The response categories, Yes and No, were coded as 1 and 0.

Specification of the Model to Control for Confounding with Other Variables. Many risk factors, such as socioeconomic status and gender, have been linked to depression in addition to the hypothesized effect of corporal punishment. Unless such variables are controlled, the findings might be spurious. For example, it is important to control for SES because numerous studies show that low-SES persons have a higher rate of most types of psychological problems (Dohrenwend *et al.*, 1992), and Chapter 4 shows that SES is related to the chronicity of corporal punishment of adolescents. This could produce an association between corporal punishment and depression even if corporal punishment does not increase the probability of depression.

Covariates. In view of the preceding, the logistic regression and the analysis of covariance included specifications of four variables that are known to be confounded with corporal punishment, depression, or both: socioeconomic status (see the section of this appendix for Chapter 3), marital violence (see Appendix B for the measure), gender of respondent (coded men = 0, women = 1), witnessing violence between parents, and heavy drinking (see the following sections for the measures of these final two variables).

Heavy Drinking. This variable was measured by coding as heavy drinkers the "High" and "High Binge" categories of the "Drinking Types" described in Kaufman, Kantor, and Straus (1987).

Witnessing Violence Between Parents. The extent of husband-to-wife violence in the respondent's family of origin was measured by asking if and how often the respondent's father or stepfather hit or threw something at his or her mother during the respondent's teenage years, and a parallel question about the mother or stepmother.

Analysis of Covariance. Charts 5–1 and 5–2 are based on a 7 by 2 analysis of covariance. The seven-level variable is corporal punishment ranging from never to 20 or more times. The two-level variable is the gender of the subject. Four analyses were computed. The first used scores on the depressive symptoms index as the dependent variable and the frequency of being corporally punished by the father as the main independent variable. The second repeated this but

TABLE C–4. Symptoms Index by Corporal Punishment, Analysis of Covariance

| Source of Variance | DF | Corporal Punishment by | | | |
| | | Mother | | Father | |
		F	p <	F	p <
Main Effects					
Corporal punishment	6	10.54	.001	5.57	.001
Gender of respondent	1	108.81	.001	113.33	.001
Interaction Effect					
Corporal punishment by gender	6	1.05	.391	1.83	.089
Covariates					
Socioeconomic status	1	37.02	.001	38.37	.001
Husb-to-wife violence	1	167.66	.001	163.32	.001
Heavy drinking	1	0.02	.899	0.29	.594
Violence between respondent's parents	1	42.74	.001	40.55	.001

TABLE C–5. Suicidal Thoughts by Corporal Punishment, Analysis of Covariance

| Source of Variance | DF | Corporal Punishment by | | | |
| | | Mother | | Father | |
		F	p <	F	p <
Main Effects					
Corporal punishment	6	6.81	.001	4.84	.001
Gender of respondent	1	2.86	.091	6.06	.014
Interaction Effect					
Corporal punishment by gender	6	1.49	.178	0.34	.918
Covariates					
Socioeconomic status	1	0.67	.415	0.85	.357
Husb-to-wife violence	1	122.45	.001	112.62	.001
Heavy drinking	1	0.03	.862	0.46	.498
Violence between respondent's parents	1	31.48	.001	34.72	.001

with corporal punishment by the mother as the independent variable. The third and fourth analyses were identical except that the dependent variable was the percent who thought about committing suicide during the preceding 12 months.

Table C–4 gives the results of the analyses of covariance to test the hypothesis that the more corporal punishment, the higher the depressive symptoms index score. The parallel lines on the graphs in Chapter 5 suggest that the effects are very similar for sons and daughters. This is confirmed by the third row of Table C–4, which indicates that there is no significant interaction between the gender of the child and corporal punishment. It also is important to note that four other variables—socioeconomic status, the gender of the child, husband-to-wife violence, and witnessing violence between parents, are also related to depression. Despite this, the effect of corporal punishment remains significant after controlling for possible confounding with these four variables. It is remarkable that corporal punishment accounts for any of the variance in depression after subtracting out the effect of so many other significant variables.

The analyses just described were repeated separately for each of the four items making up the depression index. All four depressive symptoms were found to be significantly related to corporal punishment, but the relationships were not as regular or as strong as those based on the combined effect of all six indicators in the form of the depression index. This is probably because single indicator measures are generally less reliable and less valid measures of an underlying latent construct (Straus and Wauchope, 1992).

Suicidal Ideas. The test of the hypothesis that corporal punishment is associated with an increased probability of suicidal thoughts is given in Table C–5. The effects of corporal punishment on suicidal ideas are similar for men and women, and the third row of Table C–4 indicates that there is no significant interaction between the gender of the child and corporal punishment. Again, corporal punishment is significant, even when controlling for socioeconomic status, the child's gender, husband-to-wife violence, excessive drinking, and witnessing violence between parents.

Replication Using Logistic Regression. The hypotheses concerning depressive symptoms and suicidal ideas were retested using logistic regression for several reasons. The most general reason was

TABLE C–6. Logistic Regression Analyses of Depression and Suicidal Ideation on Corporal Punishment and Five Other Variables

Independent Variable	Odds Ratio	Standard Error	t	p <*
A. Depression				
Corporal punishment	1.116	.030	4.088	.001
Gender (1 = female)	1.869	.227	5.145	.001
Socioeconomic status	.978	.003	-7.493	.001
Husband-to-wife violence	3.077	.384	8.999	.001
Heavy drinking	1.295	.240	1.394	.082
Violence between parents	1.233	.181	1.429	.077
Chi-Square = 221.18, N = 4524, p < .001				
B. Suicidal Ideation				
Corporal punishment	1.118	.040	3.120	.001
Gender (1 = female)	1.358	.214	1.946	.003
Socioeconomic status	1.002	.004	.489	.310
Husband-to-wife violence	3.825	.605	8.476	.001
Heavy drinking	1.251	.300	.934	.176
Violence between parents	1.745	.314	3.096	.001
Chi-Square = 117.33, N = 4534, p < .001				

to examine the robustness of the findings across a different statistical analysis method. A more specific reason is that suicidal ideation was measured as a dichotomy. Analysis of covariance should not really be used with a dichotomous dependent variable, but logit can be. The opposite applies to using the depressive symptoms index as the dependent variable in logistic regression. Consequently, for logit analysis, the depressive symptoms index was dichotomized at the 90th percentile. Dichotomizing at the 9th percentile is also conceptually important because, as noted by Jacobson and Revenstorf (1988), the theoretically and clinically important issue is the occurrence of a high or chronic level of depressive symptoms. The results of these logistic regressions are in table C–6.

Table C–6 indicates that even when the covariates are controlled, corporal punishment significantly affects the probability of depression and suicidal ideation. The odds ratio of 1.12 shows that for each increase of one unit in the seven-interval corporal punishment index, there is an average increase of 12 percent in the probability of being high in depression. The odds ratio for corporal punishment in section B of Table C–5 shows a similar relation of corporal punishment to the probability of thinking about suicide.

Chapter 6

Sample. The analyses are based on 2,342 parents in the 1985 Family Violence Resurvey (see Appendix B) who resided with a child under age 18 at the time of the survey.

Physical Abuse Measure. Physical abuse was measured using the Conflict Tactics Scales, or CTS, described in Appendix B.

Corporal Punishment Measure. See the sections on Adult Recall Measure in Chapter 3 and Appendix B.

Depressive Symptoms. See the section of this appendix for Chapter 5.

Approval of Interpersonal Violence. This measure uses two questions from the survey conducted for the National Commission on the Causes and Prevention of Violence (as reported in Owens and Straus, 1975). Respondents were asked, "Are there situations that you can imagine in which you would approve of a husband slapping a wife's face?" The question was repeated for a wife slapping her husband's face. The responses were coded Yes = 1, No = 0, Not sure = missing. The answers to the two questions were combined to form a variable that has a range of 0 to 2.

Marital Violence. See the section on the Conflict Tactics Scales in Appendix B.

Witnessing Violence Between Parents. See the section of this appendix for Chapter 5.

Socioeconomic Status (SES). The SES index is described in the section of this appendix for Chapter 3.

Couple conflict. The extent of conflict between the respondent and his or her spouse was measured by questions on how often the respondent and the spouse or partner disagreed on managing the money, cooking, cleaning, or repairing the house, social activities and entertaining, affection and sex relations, and things about the children. This index has an alpha coefficient of reliability of .87. Additional information is in Straus, Gelles, and Steinmetz, 1980, Appendix C.

Sex of Respondent. Father = 0, Mother = 1

Minority Groups. Non-hispanic white = 0, Minority = 1

TABLE C–7. Comparison of Abuse and Control Cases on All Independent Variables

Independent Variables	Measure	All Cases[a]		Path Analy Cases[b]	
		Abuse	Control	Abuse	Control
CP of respondent	Mean	2.45	1.52	2.54	1.51
by parents	StDev	2.20	1.95	2.24	1.92
Depression	Mean	59.36	49.57	56.51	48.31
	StDev	18.94	18.38	18.58	17.72
Approval of violence	%	51.00	31.00	55.00	31.00
Couple violence	Mean	.88	.37	.85	.37
	StDev	1.26	.89	1.27	.89
Violence btwn resp. parents	%	30.00	15.00	29.00	14.00
Age of respondent	Mean	34.34	35.61	34.58	35.38
	StDev	8.13	8.70	7.96	8.39
Socioeconomic status	Mean	47.99	50.51	49.61	51.94
	StDev	18.32	19.41	18.52	19.23
Couple conflict	Mean	1.41	1.11	1.38	1.10
	StDev	.75	.69	.73	.68
Minority groups	%	48.00	35.00	42.00	29.00
Number of minor children	Mean	2.14	1.90	2.22	1.93
	StDev	1.15	1.00	1.16	1.00
Age of selected child	Mean	8.12	8.49	7.83	8.01
	StDev	4.54	5.43	4.50	5.41
Sex of respondent = female	%	67.00	63.00	59.00	58.00

[a]N's range from 306 to 395 abuse cases and 2,394 to 2,964 control cases
[b]N = 268 abuse cases and 2,074 control cases

TABLE C–8. Regression of Physical Abuse on All Variables

Independent Variable	Prob>|t|	Beta	Regress Coeff	Std Err	t
CP as a teen	0.003	.065	.031	.0108	2.951
Depression	0.000	.096	.005	.0012	4.340
Approval of violence	0.001	.068	.099	.0302	3.276
Marital violence	0.017	.052	.055	.0231	2.386
H-W viol of par	0.098	.035	.096	.0583	1.657
Age of respondent	0.538	.016	.001	.0032	0.615
SES	0.695	-.008	-.000	.0011	-0.392
Couple conflict	0.293	.022	.033	.0322	1.052
Minority groups	0.022	.047	.122	.0534	2.299
Number of children	0.006	.055	.056	.0208	2.732
Age of child	0.027	-.058	-.010	.0048	-2.211
Gender of resp	0.516	.013	.027	.0426	0.650

F (12,2329) = 9.90 p < .001 Adjusted R-square = .04

Number of Children. The number of children under 18 living in the household with the respondent at the time of interview.

Comparison of Abuse and Control Families. Table C–7 compares the abusive families in the survey with those who reported no act of severe violence against the referent child. The left side panel makes the comparison for All Cases and, at the right side of the table (Path Analysis Cases), for the part of the sample for which data was available for all the variables needed for the path analysis. Regardless of whether it is the total sample or the smaller number of cases used for the path analysis, Table C–7 shows findings that are consistent with the model.

Path Analysis. The model tested is in some ways more complete than the model in Chart 6–1, but in other ways less complete. It is more complete because the model tested specified the eight additional exogenous variables just listed as controls for confounding with corporal punishment experienced by parents.

The model tested is less complete than that shown in Chart 6–1 because it includes only the effects of corporal punishment experienced by parents when they were adolescents. Specifically, we hypothesized that the processes linking corporal punishment and physical abuse operate, at least partly, by increasing the approval of violence to correct misbehavior and by increasing the probability of marital violence and depression. Future research is needed to test the other parts of the model.

Direct Effects on Physical Abuse. Table C–8 presents the results of regressing the physical abuse index on all other variables in the model. The first row shows that there is a significant direct path from corporal punishment experienced by a parent to physical abuse of a child. The next three rows show that there are significant paths from each of the three hypothesized intervening variables (depression, approval of violence, and couple violence) to physical abuse. The remaining rows show that four of the control variables are also significantly related to physical abuse: violence between the respondent's parents, the number of minor children in the household, minority group, and the age of the referent child.

Indirect Effects on Physical Abuse. Table C–9 gives the results of regression analyses testing the hypothesized indirect effects, with controls for a number of other variables. The most important coefficients for the theory being tested are in the first row of each panel of Table C–8.

The path at the top of Chart 6–2 of .128 from corporal punishment to depression shows that, as hypothesized, there is a significant indirect path from corporal punishment to physical abuse through depression. This is consistent with the theory that corporal punishment increases the risk of depression, which in turn increases the risk of physical abuse.

Chart 6–2 also shows the hypothesized indirect paths from corporal punishment to physical abuse through approval of violence and through marital violence. That is, corporal punishment is associated with an increase in attitudes favorable to violence and an increase in the level of violence between the respondent and his or her spouse, which in turn are associated with an increased risk of physical abuse.

Other Indirect Effects. Each of the three panels in Table C–9 includes a number of other significant indirect effects. The panel showing paths to depression has five significant indirect paths to physical abuse through their relationship with depression: low socioeconomic status, a high number of children at home, female gender, conflict between the respondent's parents, and violence by the respondent's father to his or her mother.

TABLE C–9. Regression Analyses Testing Indirect Paths

Independent Variable	Prob>|t|	Beta	Regress Coeff	Std Err	t
	A. Paths Through Depression				
CP as a teen	0.000	.128	1.124	.1778	6.322
H-W viol of par	0.000	.071	3.508	.9694	3.619
Age of respondent	0.801	-.006	-.013	.0534	-0.252
SES	0.000	-.101	-.095	.0185	-5.153
Couple conflict	0.000	.293	7.724	.5032	15.351
Minority groups	0.344	-.018	-.841	.8903	-0.946
Number of children	0.008	.050	.922	.3466	2.661
Age of child	0.208	.030	.100	.0795	1.260
Gender of resp	0.000	.136	4.856	.6993	6.944
F (9,2378) = 48.84 *p* < .001 Adjusted R-square = .15					
	B. Paths Through Approval of Violence				
CP as a teen	0.000	.092	.031	.0073	4.245
H-W viol of par	0.021	.049	.092	.0399	2.312
Age of respondent	0.015	-.064	-.005	.0022	-2.437
SES	0.073	-.037	-.001	.0007	-1.796
Couple conflict	0.000	.081	.082	.0207	3.987
Minority groups	0.114	-.032	-.058	.0367	-1.580
Number of children	0.021	.046	.033	.0143	2.314
Age of child	0.268	.028	.003	.0033	1.109
Gender of resp	0.000	-.112	-.153	.0288	-5.328
F (9,2348) = 12.49 *p* < .001 Adjusted R-square = .04					
	C. Paths Through Marital Violence				
CP as a teen	0.000	.117	.053	.0095	5.663
H-W viol of par	0.000	.096	.248	.0519	4.779
Age of respondent	0.001	-.082	-.009	.0028	-3.240
SES	0.007	-.054	-.002	.0009	-2.711
Couple conflict	0.000	.220	.304	.0269	11.288
Minority groups	0.076	-.034	-.084	.0476	1.774
Number of children	0.705	.007	.007	.0185	0.378
Age of child	0.000	-.082	-.014	.0042	-3.316
Gender of resp	0.424	.016	.029	.0374	0.799

F (9,2374) = 36.90 *p* < .001 Adjusted R-square = .12

Six of the control variables have indirect effects on physical abuse through their relationship to approval of violence: violence between the respondent's parents, couple conflict, the number of children under the age of 18 in the household, and approval of violence.

Finally, there are also seven exogenous variables that have an in-

TABLE C–10. Physical Abuse by Corporal Punishment, Analysis of Covariance Controlling for Eleven Covariates

| BY | Q2930R8 | Corporal Punishment of Respondent |
| | SEXR | Gender of Respondent 0 = MALE 1 = FEMALE |

COVARIATES

	XQ3132R	Violence Between Respondent's Parents
	Q1	Age of Respondent
	SESFZP	Socioeconomic Status Index
	XQ34R	Couple Conflict Index: 90th Percentile
	F5R	Minority Group
	Q19X	Number of Minor Children In Household
	FAGE	Age Of Referent Child

Source of Variation	Sum of Squares	DF	Mean Square	F	Signif Signif of F
Main Effects	4.718	8	.590	6.168	.000
Q2930R8	4.715	7	.674	7.046	.000
SEXR	.131	1	.131	1.375	.241
Covariates	9.852	7	1.407	14.721	.000
XQ3132R	2.428	1	2.428	25.397	.000
Q1	0.21	1	.021	.224	.636
SESFZP	.024	1	.024	.250	.617
XQ34R	3.333	1	3.333	34.858	.000
F5R	.985	1	.985	10.306	.001
Q19X	1.487	1	1.487	15.557	.000
FAGE	.013	1	.013	.135	.714
2-way Interactions	.778	7	.111	1.163	.321
Q2930R8 SEXR	.778	7	.111	1.163	.321
Explained	15.348	22	.698	7.297	.000
Residual	226.495	2369	.096		
Total	241.842	2391	.101		

direct effect on physical abuse of children through their relationship to couple violence: violence between the respondents' parents, couple conflict, minority group status, youthfulness of the parents, young children, and low socioeconomic status. Each of these is associated with an increase in the rate of couple violence, and couple violence is in turn related to an increased rate of physical abuse.

Replication Using Analysis of Covariance. The hypothesized relationship between corporal punishment experienced by parents and physical abuse of their own children was re-tested using analysis of covariance. This technique has the advantage of showing the average amount of physical abuse for specific amounts of corporal punishment, after controlling for the eight exogenous variables listed in Table C–8. The main effect for corporal punishment was significant ($F = 6.17$, $df = 8, 2391$, $p < .001$) and there was no significant interaction with the gender of the parent. Chart C6–3 plots the cell means. The TOTAL-ADJ line shows that even one instance of corporal punishment is associated with an increase in physical abuse, and the rate continues upward monotonically.

Chapter 7

Chart 7–1. Chi-square for the 4 by 2 cross tabulation on which this chart is based = 204.97, < .001.

Chart 7–2 This chart is based on the analysis of covariance in Table C–11.

Chart 7–3. This chart is based on the analysis of covariance in Table C–12.

Chart 7–4. Chi-square for the 2 by 2 analyses of Hit Non-Family Member = 14.65 p < .001. Chi-square for the 2 by 2 analyses of Stole $50 Or More = 2.47, p < .11.

Socioeconomic Status (SES). The SES index is described in the section of this appendix for Chapter 3.

Chart 7–8. The homicide mortality rates for infants (children under one year) are from the World Health Statistics Annual. These data must be interpreted with caution because they might reflect differences in procedures for recording the cause of death.

The graph is a standardized partial plot (Noursis et al., 1988:B241) based on an OLS multiple regression with the following independent variables in addition to teacher attitudes: Gross National Product per capita, educational expenditures per capita, ratio of military expenditures to GNP, parents favor corporal punishment, and population per 100 physicians. Beta for teacher attitudes = .53, p < .02.

TABLE C–11. Assault on Spouse by Corporal Punishment, Analysis of Covariance Controlling For Eight Covariates

A. Assaults By Husbands On Wives

| BY | Q2930R8 | Corporal Punishment of Respondent |
| | SEXR | Gender of Respondent 0 = MALE 1 = FEMALE |

COVARIATES

	XQ3132R	Violence Between Respondent's Parents
	Q1	Age of Respondent
	SESFZP	Socioeconomic Status Index
	XQ34R	Couple Conflict Index: 90th Percentile
	F5R	Minority Group
	Q19X	Number of Minor Children In Household
	FAGE	Age Of Referent Child

Source of Variation	Sum of Squares	DF	Mean Square	F	Signif of F
Main effects	4.829	8	.604	6.379	.000
Q2930R8	4.826	7	.689	7.287	.000
SEXR	.128	1	.128	1.351	.245
2-way Interactions	2.033	7	.290	3.070	.003
SEXR Q2930R8	2.033	7	.290	3.070	.003
Covariates	61.081	8	7.635	80.693	.000
DEPRESZ9	7.439	1	7.439	78.616	.000
APPROVER	5.170	1	5.170	54.639	.000
XQ34R9	11.124	1	11.124	117.124	117.562
.000					
XQ3132R	6.045	1	6.045	63.885	.000
Q1	13.761	1	13.761	145.434	.000
SESZPM	.364	1	.364	3.848	.050
F5R2R	.381	1	.381	4.024	.045
Q19X	.501	1	.501	5.291.021	
Explained	67.943	23	2.954	31.220	.000
Residual	414.056	4376	.095		
Total	482.000	4399	.110		

B. Assaults By Wives On Husbands

Source of Variation	Sum of Squares	DF	Mean Square	F	Signif of F
Main effects	3.675	8	.459	4.558	.000
Q2930R8	3.618	7	.517	5.128	.000
SEXR	.002	1	.002	.022	.882
2-way Interactions	1.575	7	.225	2.232	.029
SEXR Q2930R8	1.575	7	.225	2.232	.029
Covariates	63.780	8	7.972	79.088	.000
DEPRESZ9	4.883	1	4.883	48.438	.000
APPROVER	6.094	1	6.094	60.452	.000
XQ34R9	10.365	1	10.365	102.822	.000
XQ3132R	6.932	1	6.932	68.768	.000
Q1	18.387	1	18.387	182.401	.000
SESZPM	.091	1	.091	.902	.342
F5R2R	.914	1	.914	9.067	.003
Q19X	2.138	1	2.138	21.212	.000
Explained	69.030	23	3.001	29.773	.000
Residual	441.124	4376			
Total	510.154	4399	.116		

TABLE C–12. Assault on Spouse by Corporal Punishment Used by Respondent, Analysis of Covariance Controlling for Five Covariates

		A. Assaults by Husbands
BY	XC6NR6	Corporal punishment by respondent
	QW7R	Gender 1 = female
COVARIATES		
	Q43	Number of children at home
	Q109	Respondent age
	Q112R	Minority group = 1
	SESFZP	Socioeconomic status index
	X2	Marital conflict index

Source of Variation	Sum of Squares	DF	Mean Square	F	Signif of F
Main Effects	11489.848	7	1641.407	2.049	.047
XC6NR6	11327.973	6	1887.995	2.357	.029
QW7R	261.425	1	261.425	.326	.568
Covariates	87139.140	5	17427.828	21.758	.000
Q43	.108	1	.108	.000	.991
Q109	15669.216	1	15669.216	19.563	.000
Q112R	140.116	1	140.116	.175	.676
SESFZP	2805.715	1	2805.715	3.503	.062
X2	64869.823	1	64869.823	80.989	.000
2-way Interactions	8348.020	6	1391.337	1.737	.109
XC6NR6 QW7R	8348.020	6	1391.337	1.737	.109
Explained	106977.008	18	5943.167	7.420	.000
Residual	675215.567	843	800.967		
Total	782192.575	861	908.470		
	B. Assaults by Wives				
2-way Interactions	2020.618	6	336.770	.457	.840
XC6NR6 QW7R	2020.618	6	336.770	.457	.840
Covariates	71753.702	5	14350.740	19.484	.000
Q43	354.840	1	354.840	.482	.488
Q109	23986.439	1	23986.439	32.567	.000
Q112R	427.514	1	427.514	.580	.446
SESFZP	3494.517	1	3494.517	4.745	.030
X2	39411.135	1	39411.135	53.510	.000
Main Effects	12136.816	7	1733.831	2.354	.022
XC6NR6	12135.646	6	2022.608	2.746	.012
QW7R	25.012	1	25.012	.034	.854
Explained	85911.137	18	4772.841	6.480	.000
Residual	623834.822	847	736.523		
Total	709745.958	865	820.516		

Chapter 8

Sample. The student sample is limited because college students are primarily from middle-class families and all but a few are in their late teens and early twenties. Consequently, a college-student sample is not a sound basis for estimating the prevalence of masochistic sex in the general population. However, if a study of people this young finds that the more spanking the higher the level of masochism, it is not far-fetched to think that this probably applies to other parts of the population as well.

The data were obtained by questionnaires distributed in classes. They were told that participation was entirely up to them. The students were asked to put their questionnaire in a box at the front of the room when they were done. If they did not want to participate, they could just put the uncompleted questionnaire in the box. They also were free to skip parts of the questionnaire that they did not wish to answer. Since the questionnaires did not ask for identification, no one could know who had turned in a blank questionnaire, providing anonymity for those who chose not to complete the questionnaire. Ninety-two percent of the students completed the questionnaires, for a total of 456. Each questionnaire was examined for indications of being completed carelessly and for derogatory comments or other signs that the subject might have give distorted responses. Fewer than 10 such cases were identified, and they were discarded from the sample.

This method of selecting the sample usually avoids the most important type of bias in research of this type—self-selection. If we had advertised in newspapers or other places for subjects for a study of sexual behavior, there is a strong possibility that it would result in a sample that included a disproportionate number with sexual or other problems. That is unlikely in this case because participation was so high.

Despite the 92 percent return, there still could be a self-selection bias because 29 percent of the 455 students failed to answer a number of the questions. The loss is minimal for any one question. For example each of the data points in Charts 8–1 and 8–2 are based on about 420 cases. However, the loss of cases is much larger when an analysis uses many different questions. Some of the eight independent variables used multi-indicator indexes. For example, the masochism index used nine indicators, the SES index used four, and the corporal punishment index used six. Consequently, the analyses needed for this chapter involved more than 30 variables. These indexes, and the logistic regression, were computed using listwise deletion. This eliminates a case from the entire analysis if even one question was not answered. As a result, the sample size for this part of the chapter was reduced to 207. This raises serious questions concerning how representative these 207 are of the 455 students in the overall sample.

Masochism Index. We measured masochistic sex by presenting a series of items on a range of sexual activities, including the following, which were judged to be masochistic:

- "Having a partner restrain me as part of sex play"
- "Having a partner spank me as part of sex play"
- "Engaging in playful fights and being physically rough with partner"

The subjects were asked to respond to each item twice, once for ". . . how many times you have become sexually aroused while *imagining*" each item on the list, and then for " . . . how many times you have become sexually aroused while *doing*" each of the activities. The answer categories were Never, Once, Twice, 3 to 5 times, 6 to 10 times, 11 to 20 times, and 20 or more times.

We used the answers to these six questions to identify those who have an interest in masochistic sex on the basis of having been sexually aroused by imagining or doing one or more of the three activities. More specifically, each of the six indicators was dichotomized by coding the respondent as 1 if he or she reported one or more instances, and 0 if he or she said they were never aroused by the activity. The alpha coefficient of reliability for the six-item scale was .72. It should be noted that all three activities are what might be called mild masochistic sex in the sense that they do not result in physical injury or death, as happens in cases of autoerotic asphyxia (the DSM-IIIR disorder hypoxyphilia) in which people masturbate to climax while limiting their oxygen intake by smothering, choking, or hanging themselves (Hazelwood, 1983).

Corporal Punishment Index. The index used to measure corporal punishment for this chapter is somewhat different than in the other chapters in Part II. It is based on the following six questions, asked first for the mother and then for the father: "the year when they most often spanked or hit," "when you were about 10," and "when you were about 17." We used the same "Never" to "More than 20 times" response categories used to measure masochistic sexual activities.

The corporal punishment index was created by a principal components analysis of the six indicators. The regression factor score for the first factor was saved. The alpha coefficient of reliability for the index is .79. The sample was divided into quintiles based on their score on this index. The highest-scoring fifth of the students were given a score of five, the next-highest fifth a score of four, and so on. The lowest-scoring fifth, that is, those who experienced the least corporal punishment, were assigned a score of 1.

Control Variables. The questionnaire used for this study included information on a broader range of parent behaviors than was available for the other chapters. This is important because it permits addressing the question of whether the relationship between corporal punishment and psychological and social problems is actually due to a general pattern of parental inadequacy, of which corporal punishment is only one manifestation. We included an item to measure four key aspects of parenting: warmth, reasoning, monitoring, and consistency. Since a small portion of parents who corporally punish are also physically abusive, we also included a control for the presence of physical abuse in the parent-child relationship. These measures are described in the following sections.

Parent-Behavior Indexes. The items measuring parental warmth, monitoring, consistency, and reasoning are taken from the Cornell Parent Behavior Inventory (Bronfenbrenner and Devereaux, 1970; Siegelman, 1965). Each index is based on eight items. Respondents were asked to indicate how many times each parent behaved in certain ways when they were 10 and when they were 17.

The warmth index used the following items and has a standardized alpha item reliability of .91:

- "I could talk with him or her about everything."
- "Comforted me and helped me when I had troubles."

The monitoring index included the following items and has a standardized alpha item reliability of .86:

- "Insisted that I get permission first before going to a movie or some other entertainment."
- "Wanted to know exactly how I spent my money."

TABLE C–13. Logistic Regression Analysis of Masochistic Sexual Arousal* on Corporal Punishment and Eight Other Variables

Independent Variable	Odds Ratio	Standard Error	t	p <
Corporal punishment	1.334	.196	1.960	.051
Parental warmth	.514	.165	-2.060	.041
Parental monitoring	1.110	.258	0.449	.654
Parental consistency	1.199	.253	0.860	.391
Parental reasoning	1.205	.343	0.658	.511
Interaction: warm* spank	1.170	.145	1.271	.205
Socioeconomic status	1.207	.209	1.087	.278
Gender	.817	.267	-0.617	.538
Physical abuse	1.063	.212	0.307	.759

Chi-Square = 17.47, N = 207, p < .04
*Scored 1 = aroused by doing or imagining one or more of the three masochistic acts in the index.

The consistency index included the following items and has a standardized alpha item reliability of .94:

• "Applied rules inconsistently."
• "Applied punishment inconsistently.

The reasoning index included the following items and has a standardized alpha item reliability of .92:

• "When I had to do something, explained why."
• "When punishing me, explained why."

Abuse Measure. Respondents were coded as having been physically abused if they answered "yes" to the following question:

Now, thinking about your entire childhood, did your mother or father kick, punch, bite, choke you, attack you with a weapon, or beat you up?

Other Controls. Two other variables were included in the logistic regression analysis as controls since they are correlated with both spanking and masochism: gender and socioeconomic status (SES). The SES construct was measured by the following four indicators: mother's education and occupation, and father's education and occupation. These four indicators were factor analyzed using a principal components analysis. A single factor was found, which accounted for 58 percent of the variance. The Alpha coefficient of reliability for the SES index is .81.

Logistic Regression. Charts 8–3, 8–4 and 8–5 were computed from the coefficients shown in Table C–13. This table gives the results of testing the hypothesis that corporal punishment as a child was associated with masochistic sex as an adult, with controls for a number of other parent practices.

Chapter 9

Sample 1. The hypothesis that corporal punishment is associated with decreased occupational and economic achievement was tested using data from the 1975 National Family Violence Survey (see Appendix B). The 1985 survey could not be used because it obtained total family income rather than the income of each partner, which was necessary to test the hypothesis that a person's income is related to corporal punishment experienced as an adolescent.

Sample 2. The hypothesis that corporal punishment is associated with an increased probability of alienation was tested using data from a survey of 238 students in two New England colleges. The subjects were students in introductory sociology and anthropology classes in 1971, 1972, and 1973. The data were obtained by questionnaires filled out in these classes. Of the 583 questionnaires distributed, 95.2 percent, or 555, were completed. However, a number of students were not living with a parent during their senior year in high school (the referent period for the study) or did not complete the Conflict Tactics Scales or some other questions. Consequently, the specific number varies depending on which questions in addition to the CTS were used for the analysis. For other studies using this sample, see Hotaling, Straus, and Lincoln (1989), Straus (1973, 1974).

A limitation of the student sample is that it describes only families with a child in college. Such families and their children are far from representative. For example, since all are attending college, they may be more adequately functioning individuals and families than a representative cross section, therefore, they probably have a lower rate of social and psychological problems. Nevertheless, high rates of corporal punishment were reported, as well as a wide range of scores on measures of social and psychological problems. Moreover, the central issue is not the amount of corporal punishment, but whether corporal punishment is correlated with social and psychological problems. Since a correlation is not affected by the absolute level of the two variables, valid results are possible, even if the base rates for the two variables were low (Straus, 1969:572–73), provided there is no interaction between the reasons for the low rates and the independent or dependent variable.

Measures of Corporal Punishment. Sample 1 used the questions described in the sections on Adult Recall Measures in Chapter 3 and Appendix B.

Sample 2 used Form A of the Conflict Tactics Scales, or CTS, (see Appendix B). The data on fathers and mothers were factor-analyzed, and each resulted in a single principle component that accounted for 73 and 74 percent of the variance (Straus, 1979; 1990).

Occupational Prestige. The occupations of the respondent and the respondent's father were coded using the Standard International Occupational Prestige Scale (Treiman, 1977).

SES Index. The SES index for Sample 1 was described in the section of this appendix for Chapter 3. The SES index for Sample 2 used three items: father's education, father's income, and father's occupation, coded as 0 = manual, 1 = non-manual work. The analysis yielded a single factor that explained 68 percent of the variance of these three indicators.

Witnessing Violence Between Parents. See the section of this appendix for Chapter 5.

Violence in Marriage of the Respondent. See the section on the Conflict Tactics Scales in Appendix B.

Reasoning and Nurturance. Parental use of reasoning with the child was measured by the reasoning index of the Conflict Tactics Scales (Straus, 1979, 1990). Parental nurturance was measured by four items from the Cornell Parent Behavior Inventory (Bronfenbrenner and Devereaux, 1970; Siegelman, 1965). These asked, "During your last year in high school, how often did your parents do each of the following: Comforted me and helped me when I had trouble; I could talk with him (her) about everything; Taught me things which I wanted to learn; Helped me with schoolwork when I didn't understand something." A principle components factor analysis found that all four loaded on one factor that accounted for 64 percent of the variance.

TABLE C–14. Logistic Regression Analysis

Independent Variable	Odds Ratio	Standard Error	t	p <
A. Occupational/Economic Achievement				
(1975 National Sample of 1,337 Men)				
Corporal punishment	-.0905	.0411	-2.20	.014
Gender of respondent	-.0234	.1624	-0.14	.443
Father's occupation	.3497	.1669	2.10	.018
Marital violence	.4811	.2304	2.09	.017
Age of respondent	.0159	.0062	2.57	.005
Education of respondent	-.7209	.0459	15.72	.001
B. Alienation				
(1972 Sample of 238 College Students)				
Corporal punishment by father	.2797	.1597	1.751	.040
Gender of student	-.6310	.3556	-1.776	.039
SES of parents	-.0074	.0090	-0.797	.213
Violence between parents	.1051	.4793	0.219	.037
Nurturance of father	-.0519	.1943	-0.267	.395
Reasoning by father	.0150	.1875	0.084	.467

Alienation. This was measured by an abbreviated version of the Dean Alienation Scale (Dean, 1961; Zeller *et al.*, 1980). It consists of three items from the powerlessness sub-scale and three from the normlessness subscale. Since almost identical results were found using these sub-scales separately, we report only the data on the overall alienation scale because the larger number of items makes it a more reliable measure.

Dichotomization of Dependent Variables. The theoretical and practical issue of this chapter is whether corporal punishment interferes with high-level occupational and economic achievement. To identify high achievers, we created a dummy variable to classify those at the 80th percentile or higher as 1, and all others as zero.

For similar theoretical reasons we wanted to focus on the presence of a high level of the hypothesized intervening variables. For example, a certain level of alienation and depressive symptoms is widespread. For this reason Jacobson and Revenstorf (1988) argue that the important issue is whether there is a high or chronic level of alienation or depressive symptoms. Therefore, the alienation measure was dichotomized at the 80th percentile.

Logistic Regression. Logistic regression, or logit, was used to test the hypotheses because logit permits use of dichotomous dependent variables.

Model Specification. Each logit model included a number of independent variables in addition to corporal punishment, as listed in Table C–14.

Charts. Each chart plots the predicted probabilities based on the logistic regression coefficient for corporal punishment in the first row of each panel of Table C–14.

Notes

Chapter 1

1.   This brief discussion shows that the fact that a physical assault took place does not explain the underlying violence. Several other dimensions also need to be considered. Among them are: (1) the seriousness of the assault; (2) whether a physical injury was produced; (3) The motivation, which might range from concern for someone's safety to hostility so intense that the death of the person is desired; and (4) whether the act of violence is normatively legitimate (slapping a child) or illegitimate (slapping a spouse), and which set of norms is applicable (legal, ethnic or class, couple, and so on). It is important to measure each of these dimensions separately so that their causes, consequences, and joint effects can be investigated. See Gelles and Straus (1979) and Straus (1990b) for further analyses of these issues.

2.   There is a fine line between physical punishment and physical abuse. See Gelles and Straus (1979) and Straus (1990a) for a discussion of the concept of abuse.

3.   Among the hundreds of parental advice books currently in print, some of the few (but growing number) that do tell parents not to spank are Crary, 1993; Glenn, Lott, and Nelson, 1993; Leach, 1990, 1991; Wyckoff and Unell, 1984, 1991.

4.   Berk, 1989; Clark-Stewart and Koch (1985); Cole and Cole, 1989; Harris and Lisbert (1987); Heatherton and Parke (1986); Perry and Bussey (1989); Scarr, Weinberg, and Levine (1986); Schaffer (1989); Stroufe and Cooper (1988); and Zigler and Finn-Stevenson (1987).

5.   Fortunately, there are some exceptions that did not fall within Carson's sample, for example, the book by Ames (1979). If Carson's study were to be repeated today, the trends described in Chapter 11 suggest that there would be more exceptions, such as those described in books by Leach (1990, 1991).

Chapter 2

1.   The data for 1985 includes both single- and two-parent families, but the data for 1975 includes only two-parent households.

2.   The ages had to be kept the same because, as Graph 2–1 shows, the age of the child strongly affects whether he or she will be hit. This also may apply to whether the child is living with two parents.

Omitting children under three and children from single-parent families is necessary to determine if the corporal punishment rate changed from 1975 to 1985, but it means the rates in this chapter are different from the rates in other publications based on the 1985 National Family Violence Survey, such as Wauchope and Straus (1990). Those publications used the entire sample, not just children aged 3 to 17 and children who lived with two parents.

Chapter 3

1.   The median was 4 for both the adult recall and the contemporary samples. Frequency was computed for the adolescents who experienced one or more instances of corporal punishment.

2.   See the "By Either" columns in Table 3–1 in Appendix C. The contemporary data in the table also show high percentages of adolescents who were hit six or more times, but that data is not available for both parents. If it were, the percentages probably would be even higher.

Chapter 4

1.   As a result of excluding parents who not only spanked and slapped but also more severely attacked the child, certain statistics differ from the statistics in the previous chapter, in Wauchope and Straus (1990), and in other books and papers. The previous chapter gives rates based on all the parents. Although these differences might be confusing, they are a reasonable price to pay for being able to focus exclusively on ordinary and culturally legitimate corporal punishment. In addition to excluding parents who engaged in physical abuse, this chapter also differs from the Wauchope and Straus study by examining additional independent variables and employing logistic regression. It also uses an improved measure of family socioeconomic status.

2.   Chart 4–1 is based on the parents in the first National Family Violence Survey. A similar analysis could not be done for the second survey because questions on attitudes about corporal punishment were not included in that survey. See the section of Appendix C for Chapter 4 for information on the Corporal Punishment Approval Index, and the statistical analysis used to create Chart 4–1.

3.   Chart 4–1. shows how the "predicted probability" of hitting a child age four and age 16 increases as favorable attitudes toward corporal punishment increase. Strictly speaking, it is not appropriate to express the "predicted probabilities" on the vertical axis of Chart 4–1 as percentages. However, I believe that readers

who are not trained in advanced statistics are more likely to understand the findings when they are expressed as percentages. The predicted probabilities were estimated using logistic regression. See the section in Appendix C on logistic regression.

4. These percentages are estimates based on a logistic regression analysis. See the previous note and Appendix C for an explanation.

5. The research on physical abuse however, has found higher rates of this more extreme violence toward children among lower-class families (Gelles and Straus, 1988).

Chapter 5

1. Greven (1991) argues that Freud could not bring himself to acknowledge the legitimate experiential basis for the fantasies of being beaten because he himself was a product of corporal punishment and had internalized its values. He makes a similar argument to explain why contemporary psychiatrists and psychologists have not explored the effects of corporal punishment.

Chapter 6

1. However, the National Committee to Prevent Child Abuse (NCPCA) may be moving toward such an approach because it recently started distributing pamphlets on discipline that advise against corporal punishment. Nevertheless, no NCPCA literature mentions corporal punishment as a risk factor for physical abuse.

2. We could not test the parts of the model that deal with non-compliance by the child because the data set used for this study does not include that information. We also could not directly test the part of the model that deals with escalation from the use of corporal punishment such as spanking and slapping. Consequently, including socially acceptable forms of corporal punishment in the model would amount to regressing the dependent variable on itself.

3. The path coefficients showing the relation of the seven control variables to physical abuse are in Appendix C, Table 6–9.

Chapter 7

1. See Straus (1993) for data on the high rate of violence by wives against husbands and the implications of that violence for primary prevention of wife beating.

Chapter 8

1. These sexual interests used to be classified as sexual perversions, and much of the public continues to use that term. However, since the publication of

the *Diagnostic and Statistical Manual* by the American Psychiatric Association, the professional term has become *paraphilia*. "Paraphilias are characterized by arousal in response to sexual objects or situations that are not part of normative arousal-activity patterns, and that in varying degrees may interfere with the capacity for reciprocal, affectionate sexual activity" (American Psychiatric Association, 1991, p. 279). Masochism is part of the class of paraphilias that Money (1986) terms "sacrificial/expiatory." This class includes sadism, bondage and discipline, flagellation, and masochism. We use the term *masochistic sex* rather than just *masochism*, because in the future we plan to investigate non-sexual masochistic behavior.

2. However, although the findings on the combination of spanking and warmth in Appendix C are in the predicted direction, they are not quite strong enough to be statistically dependable. According to some statisticians, they should be dismissed. Other statisticians agree with us that dismissing them might be a serious error. The lack of statistical dependability may simply be because the measures used are not very reliable and the sample is small, rather than because the theory is incorrect. We think that with the combination of a better measure of masochism and a larger sample, the findings would support the last hypothesis.

Chapter 10

1. The average age is eight because almost no one remembers anything specific about what happened at ages two and three the actual peak years for corporal punishment, as shown in Chapter 3. Even at age eight, memory for specific details is poor. So the figure of an average of six times is almost certainly much lower than the actual number of times these students were hit when they were eight years old.

2. Charts 10–1 and 10–2 are based on data from Sears, Maccoby, and Levin (1957).

References

Agnew, Robert 1983. "Physical Punishment and Delinquency." *Youth and Society* 15:225-236.

Akers, Ronald L., Marvin D. Krohn, Lonn Lanza-Kaduce, and Marcia Radosevich. 1979. "Social Learning and Deviant Behavior: A Specific Test of a General Theory." *American Sociological Review* 44:637-47.

Aldrich, John H., and Forrest D. Nelson. 1984. *Linear Probability, Logit and Probit Models*. Newberry Park, CA: Sage Publishers.

Allport, Floyd H. 1933. *Institutionalized Behavior*. Chapel Hill NC: University of North Carolina Press.

Alvy, Kerby T. 1987. *Black Parenting: Strategies for Training*. New York, NY: Irvington Publishers, Inc.

Alvy, Kirby T. and Marilyn Marigna. 1987. *Effective Black Parenting*. Studio City, CA: Center for the Improvement of Child Caring.

American Academy of Pediatrics. 1998. "Guidance for Effective Discipline (RE9740)." *Pediatrics* 101:723-728.

American Psychiatric Association. 1991. *Diagnostic and Statistical Manual of Mental Disorders (Revised)*. American Psychiatric Association.

Ames, Louise Bates. 1979. *Child Care and Development*. Revised edition. New York: Harper/Lippincott.

Anderson, John E. [1936] 1972. *The Young Child in the Home*. New York: Arno.

Anderson, Kathryn A. and David E. Anderson. 1976. "Psychologists and Spanking." *Journal of Clinical Child Psychology* 70:46-49.

Archer, Dane and Rosemarie Gartner. 1984. *Violence and Crime in Cross-National Perspective*. New Haven, CT: Yale University Press.

Aronson, Naomi. 1984. "Science as a Claims-Making Activity: Implications for Social Problems Research." Pp. 1-30 in *Studies in the Sociology of Social Problems*, edited by J. Schneider and J. Kitsuse. Menlo Park, CA: Cummings.

Axelrod, Saul and Jack Apsche, eds. 1983. *The Effects of Punishment on Human Behavior*. New York: Academic Press.

Bachman, Jerald G. 1967. *Youth in Transition*. Ann Arbor MI: Institute for Social Research, University of Michigan.

Baher, Edwina, Clare Hyman, Carolyn Jones, Ronald Jones, Anna Kerr, and Ruth Mitchell. 1976. *At Risk: An Account of the Work of the Battered Child Research Department*, NSPCC. London: Routledge and Kegan Paul.

Bandura, Albert and Richard H. Walters. 1959. *Adolescent Aggression: A Study of the Influence of Child Training Practices and Family Interrelationships*. New York: Ronald Press.

Bandura, Albert. 1971. *Psychological Modeling*. Chicago: Aldine-Atherton.

Bandura, Albert. 1973. *Aggression: A Social Learning Analysis*. Englewood Cliffs, NJ: Prentice-Hall.

Barbach, Lonnie G. and Linda Levine. [1980] 1989. *Shared Intimacies: Women's Sexual Experiences*. New York: Bantam Books.

Baron, Larry and Murray A. Straus. 1989. *Four Theories of Rape in American Society*. New Haven, CT: Yale University Press.

Baron, Larry, Murray A. Straus, and David Jaffee. 1988. "Legitimate Violence, Violent Attitudes, and Rape: A Test of the Cultural Spillover Theory." In *Human Sexual Aggression Current Perspectives*, vol. 528, edited by R.A. Prentsky and V.L. Quinsey. Annals of the New York Academy of Sciences.

Baumrind, Diana. 1991. "Parenting Styles and Adolescent Development." Pp. 746-58 in *The Encyclopedia on Adolescence*, edited by R. Lerner, A. Petersen, and J. Brooks-Gunn. New York: Garland.

Baumrind, Diana. 1996. "Parenting: The Discipline of Controversy Revisited." *Family Relations* 45:405-414.

Bavolek, Stephen J. 1992. *The Nurturing Programs*. Park City Utah: Family Development Resources.

Becker, Wesley C. 1964. "Consequences of Different Kinds of Parent Discipline." *In Review of Child Development Research*, edited by M.L. Hoffman and L.W. Hoffman. New York: Russell Sage Foundation.

Becker, Wesley C., Donald R. Peterson, Zella Luria, Donald J. Shoemaker, and Leo A. Hellmer. 1962. "Relations of Factors Derived From Parent-Interview Ratings to Behavior Problems of Five-Year-Olds." *Child Development* 33:509-35.

Bell, Daniel. 1973. *The Coming of Post-Industrial Society: A Venture in Social Forecasting*. New York: Basic Books.

Berger, Peter L. 1973. *Invitation to Sociology: A Humanistic Perspective*. Woodstock, NY: Overlook Press.

Berk, Laura. 1989. *Child Development*. Needham Heights, MA: Allyn and Bacon.

Berkowitz, Leonard. 1962. *Aggression: A Social Psychological Analysis*. New York: McGraw-Hill.

Berkowitz, Leonard. 1993. *Aggression: Its Causes, Consequences, and Control*. Philadelphia: Temple University Press.

Berlin, Isaiah. 1998. *The Proper Study of Mankind: An Anthology of Essays: Edited by Henry Hardy and Roger Hausheer*. NY: Farrar, Straus and Giroux.

Best, Joel. 1987. "Rhetoric in Claims-Making." *Social Problems* 34: 101-21.

Blakeslee, Sandra. 1995. "In Brain's Early Growth, Timetable May Be Crucial." Pp. C1 in *The New York Times*. New York.

Blauner, Robert. 1964. *Alienation and Freedom: The Factory Worker and His Industry*. Chicago: University of Chicago Press.

Bowers, William J. 1984. *Legal Homicide*. Boston: Northeastern University Press.

Breines, Wini and Linda Gordon. 1983. "Review Essay: The New Scholarship on Family Violence." *Signs: Journal of Women in Culture and Society* 8: 490-531.

Brezina, Timothy. 1999. "Teenage Violence Toward Parents As an Adaptation to Family Strain: Evidence from a National Survey of Male Adolescents." *Youth & Society* 30:416-444.

Bronfenbrenner, Urie. 1958. "Socialization and Social Class Through Time and Space." Pp. 400-25 in *Readings in Social Psychology*, edited by E.E. Maccoby, T.M. Newcomb, and E.L. Hartley. New York: Holt, Reinhart, and Winston.

Bryan, Janice W. and Florence W. Freed. 1982. "Corporal Punishment: Normative Data and Sociological and Psychological Correlates in a Community Poplation." *Journal of Youth and Adolescence* 11: 77-87.

Burns, Nanci M. and Murray A. Straus. 1987. "Cross-National Differences in Corporal Punishment, Infant Homicide, and Socioeconomic Factors." Durham, NH: Family Research Laboratory, University of New Hampshire, unpublished manuscript.

Brush, Lisa D. 1990. "Violent Acts and Injurious outcomes in Married Couples: Methodical Issues in the national Survey of Families and Households." *Gender and Society* 4: 56-67.

Bybee, Rodger W. 1979. "Violence Toward Youth: A New Perspective." *Journal of Social Issues: Violence Toward Youth in Families* 35 :1-14.

Byer, Curtis O. and Louis W. Shainberg. 1991. *Dimensions of Human Sexuality.* Dubuque, IA: William C. Brown.

Calvert, Robert. 1974. "Criminal and Civil Liability in Husband-Wife Assaults." Chapter 9 in *Violence in the Family*, edited by S.K. Steinmetz and M.A. Straus. New York: Harper and Row.

Caplan, Gerald. 1974. *Support Systems and Community Mental Health.* New York: Behavioral Publications.

Carson, Barbara A. 1986. *Parents Who Don't Spank: Deviation in the Legitimation of Physical Force.* Durham, NH: University of New Hampshire, Ph.D. dissertation.

Carson, Barbara A. 1988. "Advice of Child-Rearing Manuals on the Use of Physical Punishment." Presented at the Third International Conference of Family Violence Researchers. Durham, NH: Family Research Laboratory, University of New Hampshire.

Cazenave, Noel A. and Murray A. Straus. 1990. "Race, Class Network Embeddedness, and Family Violence: A Search for Potent Support Systems." *Journal of Comparative Family Studies* 10:280-99. Also reprinted in Straus and Gelles, 1990.

Charney, Elizabeth and Myrna M. Weissman. 1988. "Epidemiology of Depressive and Manic Syndromes." Pp. 26-52 in *Depression and Mania*, edited by A. Georgotas and R. Cancro. New York: Elsevier Science Publishing.

Cicchetti, Dante and Vicki Carlson. 1989. *Child Maltreatment: Theory and Research on the Causes and Consequences of Child Abuse and Neglect.* Cambridge: Cambridge University Press.

Clark-Stewart, Alison Susan Friedman and Joanne Koch, 1985. *Child Development: A Topical Approach.* New York: John Wiley & Sons.

Cohen, Patricia. 1996. "Response: How Can Generative Theories of the Effects of Punishment Be Tested?" *Pediatrics. The Short- and Long-Term Consequences of Corporal Punishment* (supplement) 98:834–837.

Cole, Michael and Sheila Cole. 1989. *The Development of Children.* New York: Scientific American Books.

Connelly, Cynthia D. and Murray A. Straus. 1992. "Mother's Age and Risk for Physical Abuse." *Child Abuse and Neglect* 16:709-18.

Coverman, Shelly and Joseph F. Sheley. 1986. "Change in Men's Housework and Child-Care Time, 1965-1975." *Journal of Marriage and the Family* 48 :413-22.

Cowen, Emory. 1978. "Demystifying Primary Prevention." Chapter 2 in *Primary Prevention of Psychopathology*, edited by D.G. Forgays. Hanover, NH: University of New England Press.

Crozier, Jill and Roger C. Katz. 1979. "Social Learning Treatment of Child Abuse." *Journal of Behavioral Therapy and Psychiatry* 10:213-20.

Daley, Suzanne. 1985. "Man Tells Police He Shot Youths in Subway Train." *New York Times*, 1 January, p. 1.

Daro, Deborah. 1988. *Confronting Child Abuse: Research for Effective Program Design.* New York: The Free Press.

Daro, Deborah and Richard J. Gelles. 1992. "Public Attitudes and Behaviors With Respect to Child Abuse Prevention." *Journal of Interpersonal Violence.* 7:517-531.

Day, Dan E. and Mark W. Roberts. 1983. "An Analysis of the Physical Punishment Component of a Parent Training Program." *Journal of Abnormal Child Psychology* 11:141-52.

De Mause, Lloyd. 1984. *The History of Childhood.* New York: Psychohistory Press.

Dean, Dwight G. 1961. "Alienation: Its Meaning and Measurement." *American Sociological Review* 26:753-58.

Deley, Warren W. 1988. "Physical Punishment of Children: Sweden and the USA." *Journal of Comparative Family Studies* 19:419-31.

Devenson, Anne. 1982. "Violence in Society." Pp. 231-38 in *Child Abuse: A Community Concern,* edited by K. Oates. New York: Brunner/Mazel Pub.

Dewey, John. 1939. *Freedom and Culture.* NY: Capricorn Books.

Dinkmeyer Sr., Don and Gary D. McKay. 1989. *Systematic Training for Effective Parenting.* Circle Pines, MN: American Guidance Service.

Dobson, James C. 1970. *Dare to Discipline.* Wheaton, IL: Tyndale.

Dobson, James C. 1988. *The Strong-Willed Child.* Wheaton, IL: Tyndale.

Dobson, James C. 1992. *The New Dare to Discipline.* Wheaton, IL: Tyndale House Publishers.

Dohrenwend Barbara S., Larry Kranoff, Alexander R. Askenasy, and Bruce P. Dohrenwend. 1976. "Exemplification of a Method for Scaling Life Events: The PERI Life Events Scale." *Journal of Health and Social Behavior* 19:205-29.

Dohrenwend, Bruce P., Itzhak Levav, Patrick E. Shrout, Sharon Schwartz, Guedalia Naven, Bruce G. Link, Andrew E. Skodol, and Ann Stueve. 1992. "Socioeconomic Status and Psychiatric Disorders: The Causation-Selection Issue." *Science* 255:946-51.

DuRant, Richard H., Alan Getts, Chris Cadenhead, and S. Jean Emans. 1995. "Exposure to Violence and Victimization and Depression, Hopelessness, and Purpose in Life Among Adolescents Living in and Around Public Housing." *Journal of Deviant Behavior in Pediatrics* 16:233-237.

Durrant, Joan E. 1999. "Evaluating the Success of Sweden's Corporal Punishment Ban." *Child Abuse & Neglect* 23:435-448.

Edfeldt, Ake W. 1979. *Violence Towards Children: An International Formulative Study.* Stockholm, Sweden: Akademilitteratur.

Edgerton, Robert B. 1992. *Sick Societies: Challenging the Myth of Primitive Harmony.* New York: Free Press.

Egeland, Byron, L., Alan Sroufe, and Martha F. Erickson. 1983. "The Developmental Consequence of Different Patterns of Maltreatment." *Child Abuse and Neglect* 7:459-69.

Elder, Glen H. and Charles E. Bowerman. 1963. "Family Structure and Child Rearing Patterns: The Effect of Family Size and Sex Composition." *American Sociological Review* 28:891-905.

Ellison, Christopher G. and Darren E. Sherkat. 1993. "Conservative Protestantism and Support for Corporal Punishment." *American Sociological Review* 58:131-44

Elmer, Elizabeth. 1967. *Children in Jeopardy: A Study of Abused Minors and Their Families.* Pittsburgh: University of Pittsburgh Press.

Elmer, Elizabeth. and G. Gregg. 1967. "Developmental Characteristics of Abused Children." *Pediatrics* 69:596-602.

Embree, John F. 1950. "Thailand—A Loosely Structured Social System." *American Anthropologist* 52:181-93.

Empey, LaMar T. 1982. *American Delinquency: It's Meaning and Construction.* Homewood, IL: The Dorsey Press.

Erikson, Erik H. 1959. "Identity and the Life Cycle." *Psychological Issues* (Monograph No. 1). New York: International Universities Press.

Erikson, Erik H.1963. *Childhood and Society*. 2d ed. New York: W.W. Norton & Co.

Erlanger, Howard S. 1974. "Social Class and Corporal Punishment in Childrearing: A Reassessment." *American Sociological Review* 39:68-85. Also in *Violence in the Family*, edited by S.K. Steinmetz and M.A. Straus. New York: Harper & Row.

Eron, L.D. 1987. "The Development of Agressive Behavior from the Perspective of a Developing Behaviorism." *American Psychologist* 42:435-42.

Eron, Leonard D., Leopold O. Walder, and Monroe M. Lefkowitz. 1971. *Learning of Aggression in Children*. Boston: Little, Brown.

Escovar, Luis A. and Peggy L. Escovar. 1985. "Retrospective Perception of Parental Child-Rearing Practices in Three Culturally Different College Groups." *International Journal of Intercultural Relations* 9:31-49.

Ezzo, Gary. 1995. *On Becoming Babywise. Book Two: Parenting Your Pre-Toddler Five to Fifteen Months*. Sisters, OR: Multnomah Books.

Fagan, Jeffrey A. 1988. "Cessation of Family Violence: Deterrence and Dissuasion." In *Crime and Justice, An Annual Review of Research*, edited by M. Tonry and L. Ohlin, University of Chicago Press.

Farrell, Ronald A. and Victoria Lynn Swigert. 1988. *Social Deviance*. 3d ed. Belmont, CA: Wadsworth Publishing Company.

Federal Bureau of Investigation. 1988. *Crime in the United States*. Uniform Crime Reports. Washington, DC: U.S. Government Printing Office.

Feld, Scott L., and Murray A. Straus. 1990. "Escalation and Desistance from Wife Assault." In Murray A. Straus and Richard J. Gelles (Eds.), *Physical Violence in American Families: Risk Factors and Adaptations to Violence in 8,145 Families* (pp. 489-505). New Brunswick, NJ: Transaction Publishers.

Feshbach, Norma D. 1980. "Tomorrow is Here Today in Sweden." *Journal of Clinical Child Psychology* 9:109-12.

Finkelhor, David and Kersti Yllo. 1985. *License to Rape: Sexual Abuse of Wives*. New York: Free Press.

Flanagan, Timothy J. and Kathleen Maguire, eds. 1992. *Sourcebook of Criminal Justice Statistics 1991*. U.S. Department of Justice, Bureau of Justice Statistics. Washington DC: U.S. Government Printing Office.

Foucault, Michel. 1979. *Punishment and Discipline*. New York: Vintage.

Freud, Sigmund. 1919. "A Child is Being Beaten" In *Collected Papers*, Volume 4, Joan Riviere, translator. New York: Basic Books, 1959

Freud, Sigmund. 1961. "The Economic Problem of Masochism." *Standard Edition* 19: 157-70.

Friedman, Stanford B. and S. Kenneth Schonberg. 1996. "Consensus Statements." Pp. 853-856 in *The Short- and Long-Term Consequences of Corporal Punishment*, vol. 98, edited by S. B. Friedman and S. K. Schonberg. American Academy of Pediatrics.

Frude, Neil and Alison Goss. 1979. "Parental Anger: A General Population Survey." *Child Abuse and Neglect* 3:331-33.

Gagnon, John. 1977. *Human Sexualities*. Glenview, IL: Scott, Foresman.

Garbarino, James, Edna Guttman, and Janis W. Seeley. 1986. *The Psychologically Battered Child*. San Francisco: Jossey Bass.

Garbarino, James. 1986. "Can We Measure Success in Preventing Child Abuse? Issues in Policy, Programming, and Research." *Child Abuse and Neglect* 10:143-56.

Gelles, Richard J. 1973. "Child Abuse as Psychopathology: A Sociological Critique and Reformulation." *American Journal of Orthopsychiatry* 43:611-621.

Gelles, Richard J. 1990. "Methodological Issues in the Study of Family Violence." In *Depression and Aggression in Family Interaction*, edited by G.R. Patterson. Hillsdale, NJ: Lawrence Earlbaum Associates.

Gelles, Richard J. and Jane B. Lancaster, eds. 1987. *Child Abuse and Neglect: Biosoical Dimensions*. New York: Aldine de Gruyter.

Gelles, Richard J. and Murray A. Straus. 1979. "Determinants of Violence in the Family: Towards a Theoretical Integration." Chapter 21 *in Contemporary Theories About the Family*, vol. 1, edited by W.R. Burr, Rueben Hill, F.I. Nye, and I.L. Reiss. New York: Free Press.

Gelles, Richard J. and Murray A. Straus. 1988. *Intimate Violence*. New York: Simon & Schuster.

Gibson, Ian. 1978. *The English Vice: Beating, Sex, and Shame in Victorian England and After*. London: Duckworth.

Gil, David G. 1970. *Violence Against Children: Physical Child Abuse in the United States*. Cambridge, MA: Harvard University Press.

Giovannoni, Jeanne M. and Rosina M. Becerra. 1979. *Defining Child Abuse*. New York: The-Free Press.

Glaser, Daniel. 19S6. "Criminality Theories and Behavioral Images." *American Journal of Sociology* 61: 440-41.

Glenn, Myra C. 1984. *Campaigns Against Corporal Punishment: Prisoners, Sailors, Women, and Children in Antebellum America*. Albany, NY: State University of New York Press.

Glickauf-Hughes, Cheryl and Marolyn Wells. 1991. "Current Conceptualizations on Masochism: Genesis and Object Relations." *American Journal of Psychotherapy* 45:53-68.

Goodenough, Florence L. [1931] 1975. *Anger in Young Children*. Westport, CT: Greenwood Press.

Gordon, Thomas. 1975. *Parent Effectiveness Training*. New York: New American Library.

Graff, Thomas T. 1979. *Personality Characteristics of Battered Women*. Provo. UT: Brigham Young University, unpublished Ph.D. dissertation.

Grasmick, Harold G., Robert J. Bursik, Jr., and M'lou Kimpel. 1991. "Protestant Fundamentalism and Attitudes Toward Corporal Punishment of Children." *Violence and Victims* 6:282-98.

Graziano, Anthony M. and Karen A. Namaste. 1990. "Parental Use of Physical Force in Child Discipline: A Survey of 679 College Students." *Journal of Interpersonal Violence* 5:449-463.

Greven, Philip. 1991. *Spare the Child: The Religious Roots of Physical Punishment and the Psychological Impact of Physical Abuse*. New York: Knopf.

Groves, Robert M. and Robert L. Kahn. 1979. *Surveys by Telephone: A National Comparison with Personal Interviews*. New York: Academic Press.

Guarendi, Ray and David Paul Eich. 1990. *Back to the Family: How to Encourage Traditional Values in Complicated Times*. New York: Villard Books.

Gunnoe, Marjorie Linder and Carrie Lea Mariner. 1997a. "Toward a Developmental-Contextual Model of the Effects of Parental Spanking on Children's Aggression." *Archives in Pediatric Adolescent Medicine* 151:768-775.

Gusfield, Joseph R. 1963. *Symbolic Crusade: Status Politics and the American Temperance Movement*. Urbana, IL: University of Illinois Press.

Gusfield, Joseph R. 1981. *The Culture of Public Problems: Drinking, Drivin$ and the Symbolic Order*. Chicago: University of Chicago Press.

Gusfield, Joseph R. 1989. "Constructing the Ownership of Social Problems: Fun and Profit in the Welfare State." *Social Problems* 36:431-41.

Haeuser, Adrienne A. 1988. *Reducing Violence Towards U.S. Children: Transferring Positive Innovations from Sweden*. Milwaukee WI: Department of Social Welfare, University of Wisconsin, Milwaukee.

Haeuser, Adrienne A. 1990. "Banning Parental Use of Physical Punishment: Success in Sweden." Presented at the Eighth International Congress on Child Abuse and Neglect, Hamburg, Germany, 2-6 September.

Hall, G. Stanley. [1926] 1972. *Youth: Its Education, Regimen, and Hygiene.* New York: Arno.

Hamilton, Lawrence C. 1993. *Statistics with Stata 3.* Pacific Grove, CA: Brooks/Cole.

Hamilton, Lawrence C. 1992. *Regression with Graphics.* Pacific Grove, CA: Brooks/Cole.

Harris, Judith Rich and Robert Liebert, 1987. *The Child: Development through Birth to Adolescence.* 2d ed. New York: Prentice Hall.

Harris, Marvin. 1977. *Cannibals and Kings: The Origins of Cultures.* New York: Random House.

Hawkins, Richard. 1989. "Cultural Spillover Theory: Some Directions for Development." Durham, NH: Family Research Laboratory, University of New Hampshire.

Hazelwood, Robert R. 1983. Autoerotic Fatalities. New York: Lexington Books.

Henry, Jules. [1963] 1974. "Making Pete Tough." Pp. 238–10 in *Violence in the Family*, edited by S.K. Steinmetz and M.A. Straus. New York: Harper and Row.

Hetherington, E. Marvis and Ross D. Parke. 1999. *Child Psychology: A Contemporary Viewpoint.* New York: McGraw-Hill.

Higgins, E. Tory and John A. Bargh. 1987. "Social Cognitions and Social Perception. " *Annual Review of Psychology* 38:369025.

Hirschi, Travis. 1969. *The Causes of Delinquency.* Berkeley and Los Angeles: University of California Press.

Hochschild, Arlie. 1989. *The Second Shift: Working Parents and the Revolution at Home.* New York: Viking.

Holden, Constance. 1991. "Depression: The News Isn't Depressing." *Science* 254: 1450–52.

Holden, George W. 1989. "Parental Selection of Responses to Misbehavior: The Case of Physical Punishment." In *Beyond Belief: Information Processing Approaches to Parents.* Symposium conducted at the biennial meeting of the Society for Research in Child Development, Kansas City, April.

Holloway, Susan D. 1996. "Beating the Devil Out of the Reader: Review of Murray A. Straus, Beating the Devil Out of Them: Corporal Punishment in American Families." *Contemporary Psychology* 41:604

Hotaling, Gerald T. and Murray A. Straus with Alan J. Lincoln. 1989. "Intrafamily Violence and Violence and Other Crime Outside the Family." Pp. 315–75 in *Family Violence*, edited by L. Ohlin and M. Tonry. Chicago: University of Chicago Press. Also reprinted in *Physical Violence in American Families: Risk Factors and Adaptations to Violence in 8,145 Families*, edited by M.A. Straus and R.J. Gelles. New Brunswick, NJ: Transaction Publishers.

Huggins, Martha D. and Murray A. Straus. 1980. "Violence and the Social Structure as Reflected in Children's Books from 1850 to 1970." Chapter 4 in *The Social Causes of Husband-Wife Violence*, edited by M. A. Straus and G. T. Hotaling. Minneapolis, MN: University of Minnesota Press.

Hyland, Diane T. and Adele M. Ackerman. 1988. "Reminiscence and Autobiographical Memory in the Study of Personal Past." *Journal of Gerontology* 43:35-39

Hyman, Batya. 1993. *The Economic Consequences of Child Sexual Abuse in Women.* Waltham, MA: Brandeis University, Ph.D. dissertation.

Hyman, Irwin A. 1987. "Psychological Correlates of Corporal Punishment." In *Psychological Maltreatment of Children and Youth*, edited by M.R. Brassard, R.B. Germain, and S.N. Hart. New York: Pergamon Press.

Hyman, Irwin A. and James H. Wise. 1979. *Corporal Punishment in American Education.* Philadelphia: Temple University Press.

Hyman, Irwin A. 1990. *Reading, Writing, and the Hickory Stick.* Lexington, MA: D.C. Heath, Lexington Books.

Jacobson, Neil S. and Dirk Revenstorf. 1988. "Statistics for Assessing the Clinical Significance of Psychotherapy Techniques: Issues, Problems, and New Developments." *Behavioral Assessment* 10: 133-45.

Jaffe, Peter G., David A. Wolfe, and Susan Kaye Wilson. 1990. *Children of Bat- tered Women.* Newbury Park, CA: Sage Publications.

Jaffe, P. G., M. Suderman, and Reitzel. 1992. Child Witness of Marital Violence." Pp. 313-331 in *Assessment of Family Violence: A Clinical and Legal Sourcebook,* edited by R. T. Ammerman and M. Hersen. NY: Wiley.

Janowitz, Morris. 1978. *The Last Half Century.* Chicago: University of Chicago Press.

Johnson, Mark H. 1999. "Into the Minds of Babes." *Science,* 8 October, pp. 247.

Jouriles, E. N., W. D. Norwood, R. McDonald, J. P. Vincent, and A. Mahoney. 1996. "Physical Violence and Other Forms of Marital Agression: Links with Children's Behavior Problems." *Journal of Family Psychology* 10:223-234

Kadushin, Alfred and Judith A. Martin. 1981. *Child Abuse: An Interactional Event.* New York: Columbia University Press.

Kandel, Elizabeth. 1991. "Physical Punishment and the Development of Aggressive and Violent Behavior: A Review." Durham, NH: Family Research Laboratory University of New Hampshire, unpublished manuscript.

Kaplan, Abraham. 1964. The Conduct of Inquiry: Methodology for Behavioral Science. San Francisco: Chandler Publication Co.

Katz, Jack 1988. *Seductions of Crime.* New York: Basic Books.

Kaufman Kantor, Glenda and Murray A. Straus. 1990. "Response of Victims and the Police to Assaults on Wives." In *Physical Violence in American Families: Risk Factors and Adaptations to Violence in 8,145 Families,* edited by M.A. Straus and R.J. Gelles. New Brunswick, NJ: Transaction Publishers.

Kaufman Kantor, Glenda. 1990. "Parental Drinking, Violence, and Child Aggression: A Multigenerational Model of Family Violence." Paper presented at American Psychological Association Annual Meetings: Conference on Substance Abuse and Violence, Aug., Boston.

Kempe, Ruth S. and C. Henry Kempe. 1978. *Child Abuse.* London: Fontana/Open Books.

Kinsey, Alfred C., Wardell B. Pomeroy, and Clyde E. Martin. 1948. *Sexual Behavior in the Human Male.* Philadelphia: W.B. Saunders.

Kinsey, Alfred C., Wardell B. Pomeroy, Clyde E. Martin, and Paul H. Gebhard. 1953. *Sexual Behavior in the Human Female.* Philadelphia: W.B. Saunders.

Kohlberg, Lawrence. 1969. "Stage and Sequence: The Cognitive Development Approach to Socialization." In *Handbook of Socialization Theory and Research,* edited by D. Goslin. Chicago: Rand-McNally.

Kohn, Melvin L. 1977. *Class and Conformity: A Study in Values.* 2d ed. Chicago: University of Chicago Press.

Kohn, Melvin L. and Carmi Schooler. 1983. *Work and Personality: An Inquiry into the Impact of Social Stratification.* Norwood, NJ: Ablex Publishing Corp.

Korsch, Barbara M., Jewell B. Christian, Ethel K. Gozzi, and Paul V. Carlson. 1965. "Infant Care and Punishment: A Pilot Study." *American Journal of Public Health* 55:1880-88.

von Krafft-Ebing, Richard. 1895. *Psychopathia Sexualis.* London: F.A. Davis.

Lambert, William W., Leigh Minturn Triandis, and Margery Wolf. 1959. "Some Correlates of Beliefs in the Malevolence and Benevolence of Supernatural Beings: A Cross-Societal Study." *Journal of Abnormal and Social Psychology* 58: 162-69.

Larzelere, Robert E. 1986. "Moderate Spanking: Model or Deterrent of Children's Aggression in the Family?" *Journal of Family Violence* 1:27-36.

Larzelere, Robert A. 1994. "Should the Use of Corporal Punishment by Parents Be Considered Child Abuse?—Response." Pp. 217-218 in *Debating Children's Lives: Current Controversies on Children and Adolescents*, edited by M. Mason and E. Gambrill. Thousand Oaks, California: Sage Publications.

Larzelere, Robert E.1994. "Empirically Justified Uses of Spanking: Toward a Discriminating View of Corporal Punishment." *Journal of Psychology and Theology*.

Larzelere, Robert E. 1996. "A Review of the Outcomes of Parental Use of Nonabusive or Customary Physical Punishment." *Pediatrics* 98:824-831.

Larzelere, Robert E., Diana Baumrind, and Kenneth Polite. 1998. "The Pediatric Forum: Two Emerging Perspectives of Parental Spanking from Two 1996 Conferences." *Archives of Pediatrics and Adolescent Medicine* 152:303.

Larzelere, Robert E., Paul R. Sather, William N. Schneider, David B. Larson, and Patricia L. Pike. 1998. "Punishment Enhances Reasoning's Effectiveness As a Disciplinary Response to Toddlers." *Journal of Marriage and the Family* 60:388-403.

Larzelere, Robert E., William N. Schneider, David B. Larson, and Patricia L. Pike. 1996. "The Effects of Discipline Responses in Delaying Toddler Misbehavior Recurrences." *Child and Family Therapy* 18:35-37.

LaVoie, Joseph C. 1974. "Type of Punishment as a Determination of Resistance to Deviation." *Developmental Psychology.* 10:181-189.

Lefkowitz, Monroe M., Leonard D. Eron, Leopold O. Walder, and L. Rowell Huesmann, 1977. *Growing Up to Be Violent: A Longitudinal Study of the Development of Aggression*. New York: Pergamon.

Lehman, Betsy A. 1989. "Spanking Teaches the Wrong Lesson." *Boston Globe*, 13 March, p. 27.

Lemonick, Michael D. and Alice Park 1997. "Spare the Rod? Maybe." *Time*, August 25, 1997, pp. 65.

Levinson, David. 1989. *Family Violence in Cross-Cultural Perspective*. Newbury Park, CA: Sage Publications.

Libby, Roger and Murray A. Straus. 1979. "Make Love Not War? Sex, Sexual Meanings, and Violence in a Sample of College Students." *Archives of Sexual Behavior* 9: 133-48.

Lincoln, Alan J. and Murray A. Straus. 1985. *Crime and the Family. Springfield*, IL: C.C. Thomas.

Lipset, Seymour Martin. 1963. *The First New Nation*. New York: Doubleday.

Lynch. Margaret A. and Jacqueline Roberts. 1982. *Consequences of Child Abuse*. New York: Academic Press.

Lytton, Hugh. 1979. "Disciplinary Encounters Between Young Boys and Their Mothers and Fathers: Is There a Contingency System?" *Developmental Psychology* 153:256-68.

Maccoby, Eleanor E. and Carol N. Jacklin. 1974. *The Psychology of Sex Differences*. Stanford, CA: Stanford University Press.

Maccoby, Eleanor E. and J. Martin. 1983. "Parent-Child Interaction" Pp 1–102 in E. M. Hetherington (Ed), *Handbook of Child Psychology*. Vol 4. New York: Wiley.

MacDonald, A.P. 1971. "Internal-External Locus of Control: Parental Antecedents." *Journal of Consulting & Clinical Psychology* 37:141-47.

MacMillan, Harriet L., Michael H. Boyle, Maria Y-Y. Wong, Eric K. Duku, Jan E. Fleming, and Christine A. Walsh. 1999. "Slapping, Spanking and Lifetime Psychiatric Disorder in a Community Sample of Ontario Residents." *Canadian Medical Association Journal* 7:805-809.

Marcus, Alfred C. and Lori A. Crane. 1986. "Telephone Surveys in Public Health Research." *Medical Care* 24:97-112.

Marion, Marian. 1982. "Primary Prevention of Child Abuse: The Role of the Family Life Educator." *Family Relations* 31 :575-82.

Marks, Gary. 1984. "Thinking One's Abilities Are Unique and One's Opinions Are Common." *Personality and Social Psychology Bulletin* 10:203-08.

Martin, Douglas. 1993. "For Many Fathers, Roles Are Shifting." *New York Times*, 20 June, p. 20.

Maslow, A.H. 1970. *Motivation and Personality.* 2d ed. New York: Harper.

Mattson, Margaret E., Earl S. Pollack, and Joseph W. Cullen. 1987. "What Are the Odds that Smoking Will Kill You?" *American Journal of Public Health* 77:425-31.

Maurer, Adah. 1974. "Corporal Punishment." *American Psychologist* 29:614-26.

Maurer, Adah. 1976. "Institutional Assault on Children." *Clinical Psychologist* 29:23-25.

McCord, Joan. 1988. "Parental Aggressiveness and Physical Punishment in Long-Term Perspective." In *Family Abuse and its Consequences*, edited by G.T. Hotaling, D. Finkelhor, J.T. Kirkpatrick, and M.A. Straus. Newbury Park, CA: Sage Publications.

McCord, Joan. 1991. "Questionning the value of punishment." *Social Problems.* 38: 167-197

McCormick, Kenelm F. 1992. "Attitudes of Primary Care Physicians Toward Corporal Punishment." *JAMA* 267:3161-3164.

Mednick, Martha T. 1989. "Single Mothers: A Review and Critique of Current Research." In *Family in Transition*, edited by A. Skolnick and J. Skolnick. Glenview, IL: Scott, Foresman.

Merton, Robert K. 1938. *Science, Technology, and Society in Seventeenth-Century England.* Chapter XI. Bruges: Osiris History of Science Monographs.

Merton, Robert K. 1949. *Social Theory and Social Structure: Toward the Codification of Theory and Research.* Glencoe, Illinois: The Free Press.

Miller, Alice. 1983. *For Your Own Good: Hidden Cruelty in Child-Rearing and the Roots of Violence.* New York: Farrar, Straus, and Giroux.

Miller, Daniel R. and Guy E. Swanson. 1958. *The Changing American Parent.* New York: Wiley.

Miller, Daniel R. and Guy E. Swanson. 1960. *Inner Conflict and Defense.* "Expressive Styles II: Directness with Which Anger is Expressed." Pp. 315-36. New York: Henry Holt.

Money, John. 1986. *Lovemaps: Clinical Concepts of Sexual/Erotic Health and Pathology, Paraphilia, and Gender Transposition in Childhood*, Adolescence and Maturity. New York: Irvington Publishers.

Money, John. 1987. "Masochism: On the Childhood Origin of Paraphilia, Opponent-Process Theory, and Antiandrogen Therapy." *The Journal of Sex Research* 23:273-75.

Money, John. 1989. "Paleodigms and Paleodigmatics: A New Theoretical Construct Applicable to Munchausen's Syndrome by Proxy, Child-Abuse Dwarfism, Paraphilias, Anorexia Nervosa, and Other Syndromes." *American Journal of Psychotherapy* 43:15-24.

Montague, Ashley, ea., 1978. *Learning Non-Aggression: The Experience of Non-Literate Societies.* New York: Oxford University Press.

Moore, David W. and Murray A. Straus. 1987. "Violence of Parents Toward Their Children." Report submitted to the New Hampshire Task Force on Child Abuse and Neglect. Durham, NH: Family Research Laboratory, University of New Hampshire.

Nagaraja, Jaya. 1984. "Non-Compliance—A Behaviour Disorder." *Child Psychiatry Quarterly* 17:127-32.

National Center on Child Abuse and Neglect. 1992. *Caregivers of Young Children: Preventing and Responding to Child Maltreatment.* Washington, DC: U.S. Department of Health and Human Services.

National Institute of Education. 1978. *Violent Schools - Safe Schools: The Safe School Study Report to the Congress.* Vol. 1. U.S. Dept of Health, Education, and Welfare.

Washington, D.C. New Hampshire Criminal Code 627.6:1. 1985. Oxford, NH: Equity Publishing.

Neisser, Ulric. 1997. "Rising Scores on Intelligence Tests: Test Scores Are Certainly Gong up All Over the World, but Whether Intelligence Itself Has Risen Remains Controversial." *American Scientist* 85:440-447.

Newell, Peter. 1989. *Children Are People Too: The Case Against Physical Punishment*. London: Bedford Square Press.

Newmann, Joy P. 1984. "Sex Differences in Symptoms of Depression: Clinical Disorder or Normal Distress." *Journal of Health and Social Behavior* 25:136-59.

Newson, John and Elizabeth Newson. 1963. *Patterns of Infant Care in an Urban Community*. Baltimore: Penguin Books.

Norusis, Marija J. 1992. *SPSS/PC+ Version 5 Base Manual*. Chicago: SPSS Inc.

Oates, R. Kim, A.A. Davis, M.G. Ryan, and L.F. Stewart. 1979. "Risk Factors Associated with Child Abuse." *Child Abuse and Neglect*.3: 542-45.

Owens, David J. and Murray A. Straus. 1975. "The Social Structure of Violence in Childhood and Approval of Violence as an Adult." *Aggressive Behavior* 1:193-211.

Pagelow, Mildred Daley. 1984. *Family Violence*. New York: Prager.

Papalia, Diane E. and Sally Wendkos Olds. 1993. *A Child's World: Infancy Through Adolescence*. New York: McGraw-Hill.

Parke, Ross D. 1977. "Punishment in Children: Effects, Side Effects and Alternative Strategies." In *Psychological Processes in Early Education*, vol. 71-97, edited by H. Hom and P. Robinson. New York: Academic Press.

Parke, Ross D. 1982. "Theoretical Models of Child Abuse: Their Implications for Prediction, Prevention, and Modification." Pp. 31-66 in *Child Abuse Prediction: Policy Implication*, edited by R.H. Starr, Jr. Cambridge, MA: Ballinger Publishing Co.

Patterson, Gerald R. 1982. "A Social Learning Approach to Family Intervention: III." *Coercive Family Process*. Eugene, OR: Castalia.

Patterson, Gerald R., Lew Bank, and John B. Reid. 1987. "Delinquency Prevention Through Training Parents in Family Management." *Behavior-Analyst* 10:75-82.

Pearlin, Leonard I. 1971. *Class Context and Family Relations: A Cross-National Study*. Boston: Little, Brown.

Peltoniemi, Teuvo. 1983. "Child Abuse and Physical Punishment of Children in Finland." *Child Abuse and Neglect* 7:33-36.

Pelz, Donald C. 1978. "Some Expanded Perspectives on the Use of Social Science in Public Policy." Pp. 346-57 in *Major Social Issues: A Multidisciplinary View*. New York: Free Press.

Perry, David G. and Kay Bussey. 1989. Social Development. New York: Prentice-Hall.

Petersen, L.R., G.R. Lee, and G.J. Ellis. 1982. "Social Structure, Socialization Values, and Disciplinary Techniques: A Cross-Cultural Analysis." *Journal of Marriage and the Family* 44:131-42.

Piaget, Jean. 1965. *The Moral Judgement of the Child*. New York: Free Press.

Pleck, Joseph H. 1986. *Working Wives/Working Husbands*. Beverly Hills, CA: Sage Publications.

Radbill, Samuel X. 1987. "Children in a World of Violence: A History of Child Abuse and Infanticide." Pp. 3–24 in *The Battered Child*. 4th ed., edited by R.E. Helfer and C.H. Kempe. Chicago: University of Chicago Press.

Redd, William H., Edward K. Morris and Jerry A. Martin. 1975. "Effects of Positive and Negative Adult-Child Interactions on Children's Social Preference." *Journal of Experimental Child Psychology* 19:153-164.

Ritchie, Jane and James Ritchie. 1981. *Spare the Rod*. Sydney: George Allen and Unwin.

Roberts, Mark W. 1988. "Enforcing Timeouts with Room Timeouts." *Behavior Modifications* 4:353-370.

Roberts, Mark W. and Scott W. Powers. 1990. "Adjusting Chair Timeout Enforcement Procedures for Oppositional Children." *Behavior Therapy* 21:257-271.

Rose, Geoffrey. 1985. "Sick Individuals and Sick Populations." *International Journal of Epidemiology* 14:32-38.

Rosellini, Lynn 1998. "When to Spank." *U.S. News & World Report*, April 13, pp. 52-58.

Rosemond, John K. 1981. *Parent Power, A Common Sense Approach to Raising Your Children in the '80s*. Charlotte, NC: East Woods Press.

Rosemond, John K. 1994. *To Spank or Not to Spank: A Parents' Handbook*. Kansas City: Andrews & McMeel, A Universal Press Syndicate Company.

Rosenthal, R. 1984. *Meta-analytic Procedures for Social Research*. Newbury Park, CA: Sage.

Rousseau, Jean-Jacques. 1928. *The Confessions of Jean-Jacques Rousseau. Translated by W.C. Mallory*. Montreal: Louis Carrier.

Ryan, Bryce F. and Murray A. Straus. 1954. *The Integration of Sinhalese Society*. Pullman, WA: Research Studies of the State College of Washington, 22(4).

Salkin, Paul. 1990. "Vandalized Lovemaps—Book Review." *Journal of Sex and Marital Therapy* 16:189-9i.

Scarr, Sandra, Richard Weinberg and Ann Levine, 1986. *Understanding Development*. New York: Harcourt Brace Jovanovich.

Schaffer, David R. 1989. *Developmental Psychology: Childhood and Adolescence*. Pacific Grove, CA: Brooks/Cole (Wadsworth).

Scheff, Thomas. 1984. *Being Mentally Ill: A Sociological Theory*. 2d ed. Hawthorne, NY: Aldine de Gruyter.

Schenck, Eliza R., Robert D. Lyman, and S. Douglas Bodin. 2000. "Ethical Beliefs, Attitudes, and Professional Practices of Psychologists Regarding Parental Use of Corporal Punishment: A Survey." *Children's Services: Social Policy*, Research, and Practice 3:23-38.

Seligman, M. E. P. and G. Garber. 1982. *Human Helplessness*. New York: Academic Press.

Sears, Robert R., Eleanor C. Maccoby, and Harry Levin. 1957. *Patterns of Child Rearing*. Evanston, IL: Row, Peterson, and Company.

Shapiro, Deborah. 1979. *Parents and Protectors: A Study in Child Abuse and Neglect*. New York: Child Welfare League of America.

Simons, Ronald L., Kuei-Hsiu Lin, and Leslie C. Gordon. 1998. "Socialization in the Family of Origin and Male Dating Violence: A Protective Study." *Journal of Marriage and the Family* 60:467-478.

Shwed, John A. and Murray A. Straus. 1979. "The Military Environment and Child Abuse." Durham, NH: Family Research Laboratory, University of New Hampshire.

Siegelman, Marvin. 1965. "Evaluation of Bronfenbrenner's Questionnaire for Children Concerning Parental Behavior." *Child Development* 36:163-74.

Smith, Michael D. 1986. "Effects of Question Format on the Reporting of Woman Abuse: A Telephone Survey Experiment." *Victimology*.

Smith, Selwyn M. 1975. *The Battered Child Syndrome*. London: Butterworth.

Solheim, Joan S. 1982. "A Cross-Cultural Examination of the Use of Corporal Punishment on Children: A Focus on Sweden and the United States." *Child Abuse and Neglect* 6: 147–54.

Spector, Malcolm and John I. Kitsuse. 1977. *Constructing Social Problems*. Menlo Park, CA: Cummings.

Spock, Benjamin. 1988. *Dr. Spock on Parenting: Sensible Advice from America's Most Trusted Child-Care Expert*. New York: Simon and Schuster.

Stark, Rodney and James McEvoy III. 1970. "Middle Class Violence." *Psychology Today* 4:52-65.

Steinmetz, Suzanne K. 1971. "Occupation and Physical Punishment: A Response to Straus." *Journal of Marriage and the Family* 33:664-66.

Steinmetz, Suzanne K. and Murray A. Straus. 1973. "The Family as a Cradle of Violence." *Society* 10(Sept.–Oct.):50-56. Also Chapter 1 in Steinmetz and Straus, 1994.

Steinmetz, Suzanne K. 1974. "Occupational Environment in Relation to Physical Punishment and Dogmatism." In *Violence in the Family*, edited by S.K. Steinmetz and M.A. Straus. New York: Harper and Row.

Steinmetz, Suzanne K. and Murray A. Straus. 1974. *Violence in the Family*. New York: Harper and Row. (Originally published by Dodd, Mead, and Company)

Steinmetz, Suzanne K. 1979. "Disciplinary Techniques and Their Relationship to Aggressiveness, Dependency, and Conscience." Chapter 16 in *Contemporary Theories About the Family*, vol. 1, edited by W.R. Burr, R. Hill, F.I. Nye, and I.L. Reiss. New York: Free Press.

Stern, Daniel. 1977. *The First Relationship: Mother and Infant*. Cambridge, MA: Harvard University Press.

Stets, Jan E. and Murray A. Straus. 1990a. "Gender Differences in Reporting Marital Violence and its Medical and Psychological Consequences." In *Physical Violence in American Families: Risk Factors and Adaptations to Violence in 8,145 Families*, edited by M.A. Straus and R.J. Gelles. New Brunswick, NJ: Transaction Publishers.

Stets, Jan E. and Murray A. Straus. 1990b. "The Marriage License as a Hitting License: A Comparison of Assaults in Dating, Cohabiting, and Married Couples." Chapter 13 in Murray A. Straus and Richard J. Gelles (Eds.), *Physical Violence in American Families: Risk Factors and Adaptations to Violence in 8,145 Families*. New Brunswick, NJ: Transaction Publishers.

Strassberg, Zvi, Kenneth A. Dodge, Gregory S. Pettit, and John E. Bates. 1994. "Spanking in the Home and Children's Subsequent Aggression Toward Kindergarten Peers." *Development and Psychopathology* 6:445-461.

Straus, Jacqueline H. and Murray A. Straus. 1953. "Suicide, Homicide, and Social Structure in Ceylon." *American Journal of Sociology* 63: 461-469.

Straus, Murray A. 1971a. "Social Class and Sex Differences in Socialization for Problem Solving in Bombay, San Juan, and Minneapolis." Pp. 282-301 in *Family Problem Solving*, edited by J. Aldous, T. Condon, R. Hill, M. Straus, and I. Tallman. Hinsdale, IL: Dryden Press.

Straus, Murray A. 1971b. "Some Social Antecedents of Physical Punishment: A Linkage Theory Interpretation." *Journal of Marriage and the Family* 33:658-63.

Straus, Murray A. 1973. "A General Systems Theory Approach to a Theory of Violence Between Family Members." *Social Science Information* 12:105-25.

Straus, Murray A. 1977. "Societal Morphogenesis and Intrafamily Violence in Cross-Cultural Perspective." *Annals of the New York Academy of Sciences*, 285:718-30.

Straus, Murray A. 1978. "Wife Beating: How Common and Why?" *Victimology* 2: 443-458.

Straus, Murray A. 1979 "Family Patterns and Child Abuse in a Nationally Representative American Sample." *Child Abuse and Neglect* 3:213-25. Also reprinted in C. Henry Kempe, A.W. Franklin, and C. Coope, eds. 1980. *The Abused Child in the Family and in the Community*, vol. I, pp. 213-25. London: Pergamon Press.

Straus, Murray A. 1979 "Measuring Intrafamily Conflict and Violence: The Conflict Tactics (CT) Scales." *Journal of Marriage and the Family* 41:75-88. Revised version in *Physical Violence in American Families: Risk Factors and Adaptations to Violence in 8,145 Families*, edited by M.A. Straus and R.J. Gelles. New Brunswick, NJ: Transaction Publishers.

Straus, Murray A. 1980. "The ZP scale: A percentaged Z score." Durham, NH: Family Research Laboratory, University of New Hampshire.

Straus, Murray A. 1983. "Corporal Punishment, Child Abuse, and Wife Beating: What Do They Have in Common?" Pp. 213-34 in *The Dark Side of Families: Current Family Violence Research*, edited by D. Finkelhor, R.J. Gelles, G.T.

Hotaling, and M.A. Straus. Newbury Park, CA: Sage Publishers. (Former title "Ordinary Violence, Child Abuse, and Wife Beating: What Do They Have in Common?")

Straus, Murray A. 1985. "Family Training in Crime and Violence." In *Crime and the Family*, edited by A.J. Lincoln and M.A. Straus. Springfield, IL: C.C. Thomas.

Straus, Murray A. 1986. "Domestic Violence and Homicide Antecedents." *Bulletin of the New York Academy of Medicine*." 62:446-65.

Straus, Murray A. 1990a. "The Conflict Tactics Scales and its Critics: An Evaluation and New Data On Validity and Reliability." In *Physical Violence in American Families: Risk Factors and Adaptations to Violence in 8,145 Families*, edited by M.A. Straus and R.J. Gelles. New Brunswick, NJ: Transaction Publishers.

Straus, Murray A. 1990b "Injury and Frequency of Assault and the "Representative Sample Fallacy." In *Physical Violence in American Families: Risk Factors and Adaptations to Violence in 8,145 Families*, edited by M.A. Straus and R.J. Gelles. New Brunswick, NJ: Transaction Publishers.

Straus, Murray A. 1990c. *Manual For the Conflict Tactics Scales*. Durham, New Hampshire, Family Research Laboratory, University of New Hampmshire.

Straus, Murray A. 1991. "Discipline and Deviance: Physical Punishment of Children and Violence and Other Crime in Adulthood." *Social Problems* 38:101-23.

Straus, Murray A. 1992a. "Sociological Research and Social Policy: The Case of Family Violence." *Sociological Forum* 7:211-37.

Straus, Murray A. 1992b. "Children as Witness to Marital Violence: A Risk Factor for Life-Long Problems among a Nationally Representative Sample of American Men and Women." Pp. 98-109 in *Children and Violence: Report of the Twenty-Third Ross Roundtable on Critical Approaches to Common Pediatric Problems*, edited by D.F. Schwartz. Columbus, OH: Ross Laboratories.

Straus, Murray A. 1993a. "Physical Assaults By Wives: A Major Social Problem" In Richard J. Gelles and Donileen Loseke (eds.) *Current Controversies In Family Violence*. Thousand Oaks, CA: Sage.

Straus, Murray A. 1994b. "State-to-State Differences in Social Inequality and Social Bonds in Relation to Assaults on Wives in the United States." *Journal of Comparative Family Studies* 25: 7-24.

Straus, Murray A. 1997. "Beating Up the Bearer of the Bad News about Corporal Punishment." *Contemporary Psychology* 42:759-761.

Straus, Murray A. and Denise Donnelly. 1993. "Corporal Punishment of Teen Age Children in the United States." *Youth and Society* 24:419-42.

Straus, Murray A., and Richard J. Gelles, eds. 1990. *Physical Violence in American Families: Risk Factors and Adaptations to Violence in 8,145 Families*. New Brunswick, NJ: Transaction Publishers.

Straus, Murray A. and Richard J. Gelles. 1986. "Societal Change and Change in Family Violence from 1975 to 1985 as Revealed by Two National Surveys." *Journal of Marriage and the Family* 48:465-80.

Straus, Murray A., Richard J. Gelles, and Suzanne K. Steinmetz. 1980. *Behind Closed Doors: Violence in the American Family*. NY, New York: Doubleday/Anchor.

Straus, Murray A., Sherry L. Hamby, Susan Boney-McCoy, and David B. Sugarman. 1996. "The Revised Conflict Tactics Scales (CTS2): Development and Preliminary Psychometric Data." *Journal of Family Issues* 17:283-316.

Straus, Murray A., Sherry L. Hamby, David. Finkelhor, David W. Moore, and Desmond Runyan. 1998. "Identification of Child Maltreatment with the Parent-Child Conflict Tactics Scales: Development and Psychometric Data for a National Sample of American Parents." *Child Abuse and Neglect* 22:249-270.

Straus, Murray A. and Glenda Kaufman Kantor. 1987. "Stress and Child Abuse." Pp. 42-59 in *The Battered Child*. 4th ed., edited by R.E. Helfer and R.S. Kempe. Chicago: University of Chicago Press.

Straus, Murray A. and Glenda Kaufman Kantor. 1994. "Corporal Punishment of Adolescents by Parents: A Risk Factor in the Epidemiology of Depression, Suicide, Alcohol Abuse, Child Abuse and Wife Beating." *Adolescence* 29:543-561.

Strauss, Murray A. and Sean Lauer. 1993. "Corporal Punishment and Crime in Ethnic Group Context." Revised version of a paper presented at the 1992 meeting of the American Society of Criminology. Durham, NH: Family Research Laboratory, University of New Hampshire.

Straus, Murray A. and Anita K. Mathur. 1995. "Corporal Punishment of Adolescents and Academic Attainment." paper presented at the annual meeting of the Pacific Sociological Association. San Francisco. Durham, NH: Family Research Laboratory, University of New Hampshire.

Straus, Murray A. and Anitia K. Mathur. 1996. "Social Change and Change in Approval of Corporal Punishment by Parents from 1968 to 1994." Pp. 91-105 in *Family Violence Against Children: A Challenge for Society*, edited by D. Frehsee, W. Horn, and K. D. Bussmann. New York: Walter deGruyter.

Straus, Murray A. and David W. Moore. 1990. "Differences Among States in Child Abuse Rates and Programs." In Douglas Besharov, editor, *Family Violence: Research and Public Policy Issues*. Washington, DC: American Enterprise Institute for Public Policy Research.

Straus, Murray A. and Vera E. Mouradian. 1998. "Impulsive Corporal Punishment by Mothers and Antisocial Behavior and Impulsiveness of Children." *Behavioral Sciences and the Law* 16:353-374.

Straus, Murray A. and Mallie J. Paschall. 1999. "Corporal Punishment by Mothers and Children's Cognitive Development: A Longitudinal Study of Two Age Cohorts." paper presented at the Sixth International Family Violence Research Conference. Durham, NH: Family Research Laboratory, University of New Hampshire.

Straus, Murray A. and Christine Smith. 1990. "Family Patterns and Child Abuse." In *Physical Violence in American Families: Risk Factors and Adaptations to Violence in 8,145 Families*, edited by M.A. Straus and R.J. Gelles. New Brunswick NJ: Transaction Publishers.

Straus, Murray A. and Julie H. Stewart. 1999. "Corporal Punishment by American Parents: National Data on Prevalence, Chronicity, Severity, and Duration, in Relation to Child, and Family Characteristics." *Clinical Child and Family Psychology Review* 2:55-70.

Straus, Murray A., David B. Sugarman, and Jean Giles-Sims. 1997. "Spanking by Parents and Subsequent Antisocial Behavior of Children." *Archives of Pediatric and Adolescent Medicine* 151:761-767.

Straus, Murray A. and Carrie L. Yodanis. 1996. "Corporal Punishment in Adolescence and Physical Assaults on Spouses Later in Life: What Accounts for the Link?" *Journal of Marriage and the Family* 58:825-841.

Stroufe, L. Alan and Robert H. Cooper, 1988. *Child Development: Its Nature and Course*. New York: Knopf.

Sugarman, David B. and Murray A. Straus. 1988. "Indicators of Gender Equality for American States and Regions." *Social Indicators Research* 20:229-70.

Suitor, J. Jill, Karl A. Pillemer, and Murray A. Straus. 1990. "Marital Violence in A Life Course Perspective." In *Physical Violence in American Families: Risk Factors and Adaptations to Violence in 8,145 Families*, edited by M.A. Straus and R.J. Gelles. New Brunswick, NJ: Transaction Publications.

Sutherland, Edwin, H. 1947. *Principles of Criminology*. Philadelphia: J.B. Lippincott

Tannatt, Lupita Montoya and Kirby T. Alvy. 1989. *Los Ninos Bien Educados Program*. Studio City, CA: Center for the Improvement of Child Caring.

Tappan, Paul W. 1960. *Crime, Justice, and Correction*. New York: McGraw-Hill.

Teske, Raymond H. C., and M. L. Parker. 1983. *Spouse Abuse in Texas: A Study of Women's Attitudes and Experiences*. Huntsville, TX: Criminal Justice Center, Sam Houston State University.

Texas Penal Code 9.61 1983. St. Paul, MN: West Publishing Co.

Thompson, Elizabeth E. In press. "The Short- and Long- Term Effects of Corporal Punishment on Children: A Meta-analytic Review." *Psychological Bulletin*.

Touliatos, John, Barry F. Perlmutter, and Murray A. Straus, eds. 1990. *Handbook of Family Measurement Techniques*. Newbury Park, CA: Sage Publications.

Treiman, Donald J. 1977. *Occupational Prestige in Comparative Perspective*. New York: Academic Press.

Trickett, Penelope K. and Leon Kuczynski. 1986. "Children's Misbehaviors and Parental Discipline Strategies in Abusive and Nonabusive Families." *Development Psychology* 22:115-23."

Turner, Heather and David Finkelhor. 1996. "Corporal Punishment as a Stressor Among Youth." *Journal of Marriage and the Family* 58:155-166.

U.S. Advisory Board on Child Abuse and Neglect. 1993. *The Continuing Child Protection Emergency: A Challenge to the Nation*. Washington, D.C. Department of Health and Human Services. Publication Stock Number 017-092-00104-5.

U.S. Department of Health, Education, and Welfare. 1978. *National Safe School Study*. Washington, DC: U.S. Government Printing Office.

Vissing, Yvonne M., Murray A. Straus, Richard J. Gelles, and John W. Harrop. 1991. "Verbal Aggression by Parents and Psychosocial Problems of Children." *Child Abuse and Neglect* 15:223-38.

Wauchope, Barbara and Murray A. Straus. 1990. "Physical Punishment and Physical Abuse of American Children: Incidence Rates by Age, Gender, and Occupational Class." In *Physical Violence in American Families: Risk Factors and Adaptations to Violence in 8,145 Families*, edited by M.A. Straus and R.J. Gelles. New Brunswick, NJ: Transaction Publishers.

Webb, Eugene J., Donald T. Campbell, Richard D. Schwartz, Lee Sechrest, and Janet Belew Grove. 1981. *Nonreactive Measures in the Social Sciences*. 2d ed. Boston: Houghton-Mifflin Company.

Webster-Stratton, Carolyn, Mary Kolpacoff, and Terri Hollinsworth. 1988. "Self-Administered Videotape Therapy for Families with Conduct-Problem Children: Comparison with Two Cost-Effective Treatments and a Control Group." *Journal of Consulting and Clinical Psychology* 56:558–66.

Webster-Stratton, Carolyn. 1990. "Enhancing the Effectiveness of Self-Administered Videotape Parent Training for Families with Conduct-Problem Children. " *Journal of Abnormal Child Psychology* 18: 479-92.

Weisbrod, Susan A. 1976. *Physical Violence in American Families: A Methodological Report*. Princeton NJ: Response Analysis Corp.

Weiss, Carol H. and Michael J. Bucuvalas. 1980. "Research Notes: Truth Tests and Utility Tests: Decision Makers' Frames of Reference for Social Science Research." *American Sociological Review* 45:302-13.

White, Burton L. 1985. *The First Three Years of Life*. Revised edition. New York: Prentice Hall.

White, Kristin 1993. "Where Pediatricians Stand on Spanking." *Pediatric Management*, pp. 11-15.

Widom, Cathy Spatz. 1989. "The Cycle of Violence." *Science* 244:160-66.

Williams, Gertrude J. 1983. "Child Abuse Reconsidered: The Urgency of Authentic Prevention." *Journal of Clinical Psychology* 12:312-19.

Wolfe, David A. 1987. *Child Abuse: Implications for Child Development and Psychopathology*. Newbury Park, CA: Sage Publications.

Wolfe, David A., Keith Kaufman, John Aragona, and Jack Sandier. 1981. The Child Management Program for Abusive Parents. Winter Park, FL: U.S. Government Printing Office.

Yodanis, Carrie L. 1992. *Corporal Punishment and the Fusion of Love and Violence.* Durham, NH: University of New Hampshire, unpublished masters thesis.

Ziegert, Klaus A. 1983. "The Swedish Prohibition of Corporal Punishment: A Preliminary Report." *Journal of Marriage and the Family* 45:917-26.

Zigler, Edward and Matia Finn-Stevenson, 1987. *Children: Development and Social Issues.* Lexington, MA: D.C. Heath & Co.

Zigler, Edward and Nancy W. Hall. 1989. "Physical Child Abuse in America: Past, Present, and Future." Pp. 38-75 in *Child Maltreatment: Theory and Research on the Causes and Consequences of Child Abuse and Neglect*, edited by D. Cicchetti and V. Carlson. New York: Cambridge University Press.

Index